Understanding Money Mechanics

Understanding Money Mechanics

By Robert P. Murphy

MISES INSTITUTE
AUBURN, ALABAMA

Published 2021 by the Mises Institute.

Mises Institute
518 West Magnolia Avenue
Auburn, Ala. 36832

ISBN: 978-1-61016-745-1

Contents

PART IV: CHALLENGES

Acknowledgements

I would like to thank Bill McKivor (of The Copper Corner) for his permission to reproduce photos of privately-minted coins and tokens, as well as his generous time in advising me on the topic. George Selgin introduced me to Mr. McKivor and provided guidance on the mechanics of the US gold standard. Joe Salerno also provided numerous recommendations of readings on the gold standard's theory and history. Finally, I would like to thank Scott Sumner for helpful feedback on an initial draft of my critique of Market Monetarism.

Introduction

The purpose of this short book is to provide the intelligent layperson a concise yet comprehensive overview of the theory, history, and practice of money and banking, with a focus on the United States. Although the author (Murphy) considers himself an Austrian school economist, most of the material in this book is a neutral presentation of historical facts and an objective description of the mechanics of money creation in today's world.

The book is intended to be a reference for all readers, whether "Austrian" or not. (For this reason, when possible, material coming from Federal Reserve–affiliated sources is cited.) To be sure, those readers interested in a more detailed treatment of the theory and history of central banking from an Austrian perspective should pursue the topic, starting with the seminal works of Murray Rothbard.[1] The Chicago Federal Reserve's book "Modern Money Mechanics" is also a useful guide.[2] The present book is not intended as a substitute for the more detailed treatment of Rothbard and others.

Yet despite the existence of several "classic" treatments of money and banking, their drawback is that they can be difficult reading, especially in our day of

1. For example, see Murray N. Rothbard's *The Case Against the Fed* (1994; repr. Auburn, AL: Ludwig von Mises Institute, 2007); *The Mystery of Banking*, 2d ed. (Auburn, AL: Ludwig von Mises Institute, 2008); and *The Origins of the Federal Reserve* (Auburn, AL: Ludwig von Mises Institute, 2009). The latter is an excerpt from his treatment of the subject in *A History of Money and Banking in the United States: The Colonial Era to World War II* (Auburn, AL: Ludwig von Mises Institute, 2002). All items available for free in PDF form at www.mises.org.

2. Dorothy M. Nichols, *Modern Money Mechanics: A Workbook on Bank Reserves and Deposit Expansion*, rev. Anne Marie L. Gonczy, rev. ed. (1961; Chicago: Federal Reserve Bank of Chicago, 1994). Available at https://upload.wikimedia.org/wikipedia/commons/4/4a/Modern_Money_Mechanics.pdf.

social media and short attention spans. At the same time, the "extraordinary" measures of quantitative easing (QE) implemented by central banks around the world following the 2008 crisis have made these issues incredibly relevant. Discussions of QE vs. TARP (Troubled Asset Relief Program) are difficult if half of the commentators don't really know the difference between granting a loan and recapitalization. And it's difficult to evaluate the wisdom of the Fed's operations in the repo market, when most people don't really know what "the repo market" *is*. The present book seeks to bridge the gap by providing a crash course in the necessary theory and history while keeping the discussion tethered to current events.

Finally, the present book addresses some of the challenges to the textbook treatment that have arisen over the years. For example, is it true that commercial banks must wait for new deposits before they can advance new loans—or does it work the other way around in the real world? Why didn't consumer prices go through the roof after the start of QE programs, as many economists (including the present author!) were worried might occur? And how does the standard economist story about the emergence of money out of a state of barter apply—if at all—to cryptocurrencies like bitcoin?

Although the present book with its necessarily brief treatment will not provide definitive resolutions to these controversies, it will seek to at least clarify the disputes so that readers can advance their own understanding of the issues.

Introduction

Lays out the scope and purpose of the book.

PART I: THEORY AND HISTORY

Chapter 1: The Theory and Brief History of Money and Banking

Covers Menger's theory of the origin of money, and briefly mentions the anthropological critique (David Graeber). Gives a standard history of the origin and development of modern banking, including some important court rulings. Mentions the history of private mints.

Chapter 2: A Brief History of the Gold Standard, with a Focus on the United States

Explains why gold is the market's money of choice—and stresses the difference between the definition of money ("commonly accepted medium of exchange") and the attributes that make something a convenient money (durability, homogeneity, etc.). Draws a connection with Menger's theory, presented in the previous chapter, and shows why gold (and silver) were chosen, rather than (say) diamonds or platinum. Explains the operation of the classical gold standard and how it evolved during the World Wars, Bretton Woods, and, finally, the Nixon Shock. Also includes a discussion of Civil War inflation.

Chapter 3: The History and Structure of the Federal Reserve System

Explains the unusual circumstances of the Fed's origin, and mentions "conspiracy theory" treatments. Explains how power was consolidated in DC and away from Reserve Banks under FDR, and how the Fed's mandate was again altered in 1977. Concludes with an overview of the modern organization of the Fed, including the number of member banks, how the Federal Open Market Committee (FOMC) is selected (length of terms, etc.), how the chairman is picked, etc.

PART II: THE MECHANICS

Chapter 4: Standard Open Market Operations: How the Fed and Commercial Banks "Create Money"

Explains the "textbook" mechanics of the Fed buying assets to create new reserves, and then how commercial banks create new loans on top. Defines the various monetary aggregates (base, M1, M2, "Austrian true money supply," etc.).

Chapter 5: Beyond the Fed: "Shadow Banking" and the Global Market for Dollars

Defines the concept of shadow banking and gives a brief history, plus some stats for context. Defines things like "eurodollar," LIBOR, etc. Explains the Bank of International Settlements (BIS) and the Basel Accords. Explain the basics of the repo market and the difference between capital requirements and reserve requirements.

Chapter 6: Central Banking Since the 2008 Financial Crisis

Explains the "emergency" measures that the Fed adopted (Term Auction Facility, QE rounds, interest on reserves). Explains how Maiden Lane programs are arguably illegal.

Chapter 7: The Fed's Policies Since the 2020 Coronavirus Panic

Explains some of the major changes implemented in the wake of the pandemic, such as the abolition of reserve requirements, unprecedented asset purchases, and a redefinition of M1.

PART III: APPLICATIONS

Chapter 8: Ludwig von Mises's "Circulation Credit Theory of the Trade Cycle"

Lays out the basics of Austrian boom-bust theory. Explains that Mises developed it in *The Theory of Money and Credit*, in which he also said that fiat money was a theoretical possibility (!); this means that Mises clearly didn't think that boom-bust was restricted to fiat money regimes. Using Mises's analogy of a master builder running out of bricks, illustrates the difference between "overinvestment" and "malinvestment" theories, and also why continued pump-priming a bad idea.

Chapter 9: Monetary Inflation and Price Inflation

Starts with Friedman's measures of money stock and (consumer price) inflation, and summarizes cases of hyperinflation (Civil War, Weimar Republic, Zimbabwe, Venezuela). Documents change in how the word "inflation" is used. Explains the famous equation of exchange (MV=PQ) and why Mises and Rothbard didn't like it.

Chapter 10: The Inverted Yield Curve and Recession

Documents this surprisingly good forecasting tool, and then shows that it fits quite nicely within Austrian framework.

Chapter 11: The Fed and the Housing Bubble/Bust

Shows that the textbook Austrian story fits the empirical facts of the housing boom/bust.

PART IV: CHALLENGES

Chapter 12: Does Textbook Explanation Get Money and Banking Backward?

Is the "textbook" description (covered in chapter 4 above) actually wrong? Deals with the (relatively) recent claims—coming not just from internet critics but also a major UK institution—that bank lending is not reserve constrained. Also addresses that the idea that "lending creates deposits" rather than vice-versa, as the orthodox economists claim.

Chapter 13: Crying Wolf on (Hyper)Inflation?

Explains that some (including the present author) made erroneous warnings about (consumer price) inflation when QE was first implemented, and asks whether this invalidates the textbook treatment. Is it true that QE was "just an asset swap" and "wasn't money printing"?

Chapter 14: The Keynesians on the Cause of, and Cure for, Depression

Explains the Keynesian perspective. Contrasts Austrians and Keynesians on the Great Depression. Explains the "liquidity trap" and why Keynesians think Say's law works in the special case of "full employment" but that we need a general theory of employment, etc.

Chapter 15: The "Market Monetarists" and NGDP Targeting

Gives a brief history of the historical battles between original monetarists and Keynesians (Friedman/Phelps on the Phillips curve, the Robert Lucas critique, and rational expectations framework). Then explains how people like Scott Sumner updated Friedman's monetarism and now offer the goal of "level targeting" of stable NGDP growth, which some Austrians argue is similar to Hayek's approach.

Chapter 16: Bitcoin and the Theory of Money

Applies the earlier theoretical framework to bitcoin to answer questions such as "Is it money?" Addresses the challenge that bitcoin violates Mises's regression theorem.

Chapter 17: An Austrian Reaction to Modern Monetary Theory (MMT)

The review of Stephanie Kelton's popular book explaining MMT, *The Deficit Myth: Modern Monetary Theory and the Birth of the People's Economy*, by Dr. Murphy, which appeared in the *Quarterly Journal of Austrian Economics* in 2020.

Part I
Theory and History

Chapter 1

The Theory and Brief History of Money and Banking

The ultimate purpose of this book is to give the reader a solid grasp of how money works in today's world. Yet before diving into the particulars of central banks, repo markets, and LIBOR—all topics that will be covered in future chapters—we should first provide a general framework giving the basic theory or "economic logic" of money and banking.

In short: Why do we have money in the first place? Where does it come from, and what determines its form (livestock, metal ingots, coins, paper notes, electronic ledger entries, etc.)? What qualities make for a good money? What role do banks play—is it something *other* than what money itself does for us?

In this chapter, we'll answer these elementary yet essential questions. To be clear, we are not here offering an actual history lesson, though we *do* mention some important historical episodes and illustrative examples. Rather we are providing a mental framework for understanding everything else that follows in the book.

The Limits of Direct Exchange

To understand the importance of money, let's first imagine a society without money. In a world limited to barter, or what economists more precisely call direct exchange, there would still be private property and people would still benefit from voluntary trade. Because economic value is subjective—the "utility" of a good is in the eye (or mind) of the beholder—we can have win-win exchanges, in which both parties walk away correctly believing that they got the better end of the deal.

However, if society were limited to *direct* exchange—in which individuals only accept items in trade that they plan on using personally—then people would miss out on many advantageous transactions. Let's consider a simplistic example. Suppose there are three individuals: a farmer, a butcher, and a cobbler. The farmer starts out with some eggs that he's just taken from his hens. He would like to trade his eggs in order to get his tattered shoes repaired. The problem, though, is that the cobbler doesn't want any eggs—but he *would* be willing to repair the shoes for bacon.

Unfortunately, the farmer doesn't currently have bacon. However, his neighbor the butcher *does* have bacon. Yet the butcher doesn't want to trade with the cobbler, because the butcher's shoes are just fine. What the butcher would really like are some eggs. Yet, the farmer himself doesn't like the taste of bacon, and would rather eat his own eggs.

In a world limited to direct exchange, these men are at an impasse, because no single transaction would benefit any pair of them. Yet all of them could improve their situation with a rearrangement of the goods.

The solution is to introduce *indirect* exchange, in which at least one person accepts an item in trade that he doesn't plan on using himself but holds merely to trade away again in the future. In our example, suppose that the farmer has an epiphany: Even though he personally dislikes its taste, he trades his eggs to the butcher to obtain the bacon. Then he takes the bacon to the cobbler, who accepts it as payment for fixing his tattered shoes.

After these two trades, all three individuals are better off than they were originally. Remember, though, that the solution relied on the farmer accepting an item in trade—in this case the bacon—that he didn't plan on using himself. Economists call such a good a *medium of exchange*. Just as air is a "medium" through which sound waves travel, the bacon served as a *medium* through which the farmer's ultimate exchange was effected—namely giving up his eggs in order to receive shoe-repair services.

Media of Exchange and the Origin of Money

As our fable illustrated, individuals can often improve their position by trading away goods that are less marketable and accepting goods that are more marketable, even if they don't personally plan on using the items. As the founder of the Austrian school, Carl Menger, demonstrated in an 1892 essay[1] (though earlier economists had anticipated some of the explanation), this principle is all we need to explain the emergence of money.

---

1. Carl Menger, "On the Origins of Money," *Economic Journal* 2 (1892): 239–55, https://cdn.mises.org/On%20the%20Origins%20of%20Money_5.pdf.

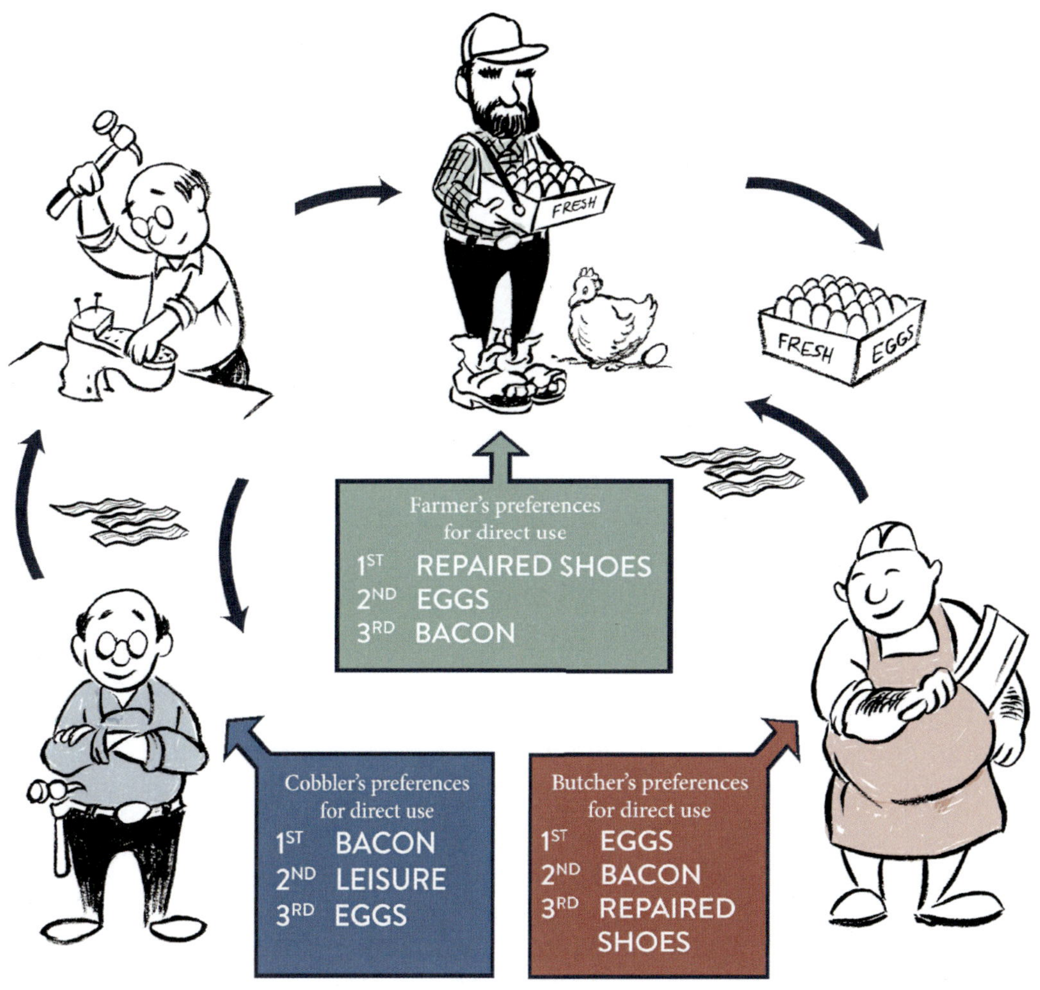

As individuals in the community seek to trade away their less marketable (or less *liquid*) goods in exchange for more marketable (or more liquid) goods, a snowball process is set in motion: those goods that started out with a wide appeal based on their intrinsic qualities see a boost in their popularity *simply because* they are so popular. (For a more modern example, the prisoners in a World War II POW camp would gladly trade away their rations in exchange for cigarettes even if they were nonsmokers, because enough of the other prisoners *were* smokers.[2]) Eventually, one or two commodities become so popular that just about everyone in the community would be willing to accept them in trade. At that point, *money* has been born.

2. The classic article from a trained economist captured by the enemy in World War II is: R. A. Radford, "The Economic Organization of a P.O.W. Camp," *Economica* 12, no. 48 (November 1945): 189–201, http://icm.clsbe.lisboa.ucp.pt/docentes/url/jcn/ie2/0POWCamp.pdf.

A formal definition for money is that it's a *universally accepted medium of exchange*. Menger's explanation showed how such a commodity could emerge from its peers merely through voluntary transactions and without any individual seeing the big picture or trying to "invent" money.[3]

The Qualities of a Good (Commodity) Money

Money that emerged in the process we've described would necessarily be *commodity money*, in which the monetary good itself is also a regular commodity. (In chapter 2 we will discuss *fiat money*, in which the monetary good serves no other function than to be the money.) Historically, many types of commodities have served as money in various regions, including livestock, shells, tobacco, and of course the precious metals gold and silver.

What would make a community gravitate toward some commodities but not others? Besides having a wide marketability, an individual would want a medium of exchange to possess the following qualities: ease of transport, durability, divisibility, homogeneity, and convenient size and weight for the intended transactions.

In our fable above, although bacon served as the medium of exchange, it would be ill-suited to serve this purpose generally, as bacon is perishable. Likewise, a shotgun might be very valuable in certain communities, but it's not divisible; you can't cut it in half to "make change." Diamonds might seem like a great candidate for a medium of exchange, but they aren't homogeneous: one giant diamond is more valuable than five smaller diamonds that (combined) weigh the same amount.

These types of considerations help explain why eventually gold and silver emerged as the market's commodity monies of choice. These precious metals satisfied all of the criteria of what makes a convenient medium of exchange, and once the community generally agreed, they were money.

Monetary Calculation

The emergence of money meant that a single commodity was on one side of every transaction. This greatly reduced the calculations required to navigate the marketplace. For example, consider a merchant whose business required him to closely follow twenty different goods. In a world of pure barter—where each good traded directly against every other good—in principle he would

3. The most prominent modern critic of the standard "economistic" explanation for money is David Graeber, in his *Debt: The First Five Thousand Years* (Brooklyn, NY: Melville House Publishing, 2011). For a review of Graeber's critique and a defense of the Mengerian approach, see Robert Murphy, "Origin of the Specie," *American Conservative*, Apr. 11, 2012, https://www.theamericanconservative.com/articles/origin-of-the-specie/.

have to keep track of 190 separate barter "prices"[4] (meaning the ratios at which one good traded for another). But if one of those twenty goods also serves as the *monetary* good—maybe it's silver—then the merchant only needs to keep track of nineteen different prices (all quoted in silver), because each of the other goods is always being bought and sold against silver.

Moving from a state of barter to a monetary economy allows for economic decisions to be appraised in terms of a standard unit. With the use of money, business owners can engage in *accounting*, where they can easily calculate whether they had a profitable year. Trying to compare revenues to expenses would be much more difficult in a pure barter system. A factory owner could know that her operation used up certain quantities of hundreds of input commodities (including labor hours), in order to produce certain quantities of dozens of outputs, but without being able to reckon these physically distinct commodities in terms of money prices, she would face the same type of problem plaguing socialist central planners.[5]

The Function of Monetary Coins (and Tokens)

We have seen how a commodity money can emerge spontaneously from a prior state of barter, facilitating exchanges and profit/loss calculations. However, even though a community benefits tremendously from the existence of money, there would still be limitations if the money remained in its "raw" form. It would hamper trade if shopkeepers had to perform metallurgical tests on hunks of metal that customers presented for payment to verify that the hunks were indeed silver (or gold, etc.) of the claimed weight.

The solution to this problem is to *coin* the raw hunks of metal into recognizable disks of a uniform size and purity (or "fineness"). We should emphasize that a full-bodied coin was not money *because* of the stamping process; the markings on the coin merely indicated to the community that the hunk of metal in question did indeed contain the specified weight in the underlying commodity that served as money.

In addition to striking full-bodied coins (meaning they contain the legally defined amount of gold or silver), another possible solution is for reputable outlets to issue *token* coins, which represent *redemption claims* on the issuer for a specified amount of the actual money commodity. Note that to perform their

---

4. For n goods, there are $n*(n-1)/2$ unique barter price ratios.

5. Ludwig von Mises is the economist whose 1920 essay launched what has become known as the "socialist calculation debate." He stressed the crucial function of economic calculation in guiding entrepreneurs in a market economy, so that they could assess whether their operations were using scarce resources for socially beneficial purposes. For an accessible discussion see Murray Rothbard, "The End of Socialism and the Calculation Debate Revisited," *Review of Austrian Economics* 5, no. 2 (1991): 51–76, https://cdn.mises.org/rae5_2_3_2.pdf.

function well, even token coins would need to be recognizable in the community and difficult to counterfeit. For a modern example, consider the plastic chips issued by casinos: A Las Vegas casino needs to have chips that are distinctive and "authentic"-looking, and which can't be easy for outsiders to replicate. Because such chips will be instantly redeemed by the casino, within its walls (and even perhaps in the surrounding neighborhood) they are "as good as money." But a gambler who travels back home wouldn't be able to buy groceries with chips issued from a Las Vegas casino.

Just as the money itself can arise without the intervention of political authorities, so too can the private sector handle the operations of turning the commodity money into coins. Indeed, numismatists agree that some of the highest-quality coins (and tokens) ever produced originated in eighteenth-century Britain from *private* mints.

The full story is too long to tell here,[6] but the quick version is that the British Royal Mint had utterly failed to provide the common people with coins that could serve their needs for everyday commerce, and regulations prohibited banks from issuing notes in small denominations. As a result, employers resorted to various inconvenient remedies, including paying their workers in waves (so that, say, the first third of the employees would spend their new wages in town, after which the employers could then collect the coins in order to pay the second third of their workers, etc.) and making arrangements with the local tavern owners so that the workers' beer tabs would effectively reduce the wages they were owed. The shortage of government-produced coinage was so severe that even obviously counterfeit coins were tolerated because bad money was better than no money at all.

In this intolerable situation, Thomas Williams, the principal owner of the giant Parys copper mine, hit upon the bright idea of installing a commercial-scale mint on the premises. He then struck (token) coins out of the copper with instructions on where they could be redeemed for money, and paid his workers—the ones actually mining the copper—with these token coins. Soon afterward Matthew Boulton, famous for his collaboration with James Watt in the refinement of the modern steam engine, followed suit with the privately owned Soho Mint, where he was the first to implement a process of using steam power to mass-produce exquisite coinage. The following photos exhibit the remarkable craftmanship of the privately struck coins and tokens from this era.[7]

6. The details of Britain's coin shortage and the private-mint response are taken from George Selgin, *Good Money* (Oakland, CA: Independent Institute, 2008), chapters 1 and 2.

7. The photos are gratefully used with permission from Bill McKivor, whose website (featuring these and other photos) is http://www.thecoppercorner.com/.

A Penny from a Soho Mint 1797 pattern striking

A 1791 token promising a half-penny to the bearer.

The Function and Origin of Banks

Even in a community with a commodity money stamped into high-quality coins, there would still be limitations on commerce. For example, wealthy individuals would be nervous about holding vast sums of gold or silver in their homes where they would be vulnerable to theft, and it would be inconvenient to transport large amounts of coin or bullion for every transaction involving a significant purchase price.

A *bank* solves these problems by providing a secure location where members of the community can store their excess supplies of money. (The other main function of banks is to serve as *credit intermediaries*, which act as a conduit between borrowers and savers.) The goldsmith was a logical person to also act as banker, because his business already involved storing stockpiles of gold. It was easy enough for members of the community to deposit coins with the goldsmith in exchange for an official receipt indicating how much of the money commodity they (the depositors) had stored with him.

The reason a book on the mechanics of money must also cover banking is that—to put it bluntly—banks enjoy the legal ability to create money. In

chapter 4 we will explain this process in much greater detail, but for now let us quote the Chicago Federal Reserve on the historical origins (at least in England) of this practice:

> [B]anks can build up deposits by increasing loans and investments so long as they keep enough currency on hand to redeem whatever amounts the holders of deposits want to convert into currency. This unique attribute of the banking business was discovered many centuries ago.
>
> It started with goldsmiths. As early bankers, they initially provided safekeeping services, making a profit from vault storage fees for gold and coins deposited with them. People would redeem their "deposit receipts" whenever they needed gold or coins to purchase something, and physically take the gold or coins to the seller who, in turn, would deposit them for safekeeping, often with the same banker. Everyone soon found that it was a lot easier simply to use the deposit receipts directly as a means of payment. These receipts, which became known as notes, were acceptable as money since whoever held them could go to the banker and exchange them for metallic money.
>
> Then, **bankers discovered that they could make loans merely by giving their promises to pay, or bank notes, to borrowers.** In this way, banks began to create money. More notes could be issued than the gold and coin on hand because only a portion of the notes outstanding would be presented for payment at any one time. Enough metallic money had to be kept on hand, of course, to redeem whatever volume of notes was presented for payment [emphasis added].[8]

---

8. Dorothy M. Nichols, *Modern Money Mechanics: A Workbook on Bank Reserves and Deposit*

Once the banker (such as the goldsmith) realized that his deposit receipts ("notes") were treated by at least some members of the community as being "as good as money," he could lend out some of the coins that his customers had deposited with him, even though the customers still held paper receipts entitling them to immediate redemption. The whole operation was viable so long as the banker always had enough coins on hand to satisfy whoever might show up to demand their deposits back.

This book will focus on the mechanics and economic implications of the fact that banks have the legal ability to create money, but we'll wrap up our historical sketch here with a note on the judicial treatment. If someone hands over an item for safekeeping in which the specific article is important—such as a college student placing her furniture in a storage unit for the summer, or a diner checking his coat when entering a restaurant—this is handled under *bailment law*. In such a situation, the person acting as a warehouser obtains physical possession but not legal ownership of the items in question, and is obligated to act as their custodian until the actual owner wishes to retrieve them. It would be a breach of contract for the manager of a storage facility to rent out the student's couch, even if he had it safely back in her storage unit when she returned from summer break.

However, when the deposited items are *fungible* goods, such as wheat or oil, then the relationship is more nuanced. With such an "irregular deposit," the

---

Expansion, rev. Anne Marie L. Gonczy, rev. ed. (1961; Chicago: Federal Reserve Bank of Chicago, 1994), p. 3, available at: https://upload.wikimedia.org/wikipedia/commons/4/4a/Modern_Money_Mechanics.pdf.

depositor isn't entitled to the specific physical items that were handed over for safekeeping, but instead merely expects to receive *comparable* items back. In the typical scenario, this is the type of deposit applicable to money; the people handing over coins to the goldsmith didn't care about receiving back *those particular* coins, they merely wanted to be assured of obtaining the same number of comparable coins when they redeemed their deposit receipts (i.e., banknotes).

As a result of various court rulings, it is now standard to treat the deposit of money with a bank as a *loan*, so that the depositor becomes a *creditor* of the bank and the actual ownership of the money transfers to the banker, even for "demand deposits," which are payable upon notice. Rightly or wrongly,[9] it is this legal treatment that allowed the proverbial goldsmith to lend out some of the coins that his depositors had placed with him for safekeeping, and which allows modern banks to engage in "fractional reserve banking." To reiterate, it is this practice by which banks can create (and destroy) money—a process that we will fully explain in chapter 4.

We will close this chapter with an excerpt from an opinion issued by Lord Cottenham in the 1848 case *Foley v. Hill and Others*:

> The money placed in the custody of a banker is, to all intents and purposes, the money of the banker, to do with as he pleases; he is guilty of no breach of trust in employing it; he is not answerable to the principal if he puts it into jeopardy, if he engages in a hazardous speculation; he is not bound to keep it or deal with it as the property of his principal; but he is, of course, answerable for the amount, because he has contracted.[10]

9. For an elaborate case arguing against the practice of fractional reserve banking on both (traditional) legal and economic grounds, see Jesús Huerta de Soto, *Money, Bank Credit, and Economic Cycles*, trans. Melinda A. Stroup (1998; Auburn, AL: Ludwig von Mises Institute, 2006), available at https://cdn.mises.org/Money_Bank_Credit_and_Economic_Cycles_De%20Soto.pdf. For a defense of the development of the legal treatment of fractional reserve banking, see George Selgin, "Those Dishonest Goldsmiths" (paper presented at "Money, Power & Print: Interdisciplinary Studies of the Financial Revolution in the British Isles, 1688–1776," University of Aberdeen, Aberdeen, Scotland, June 17–19, 2010, rev. Jan. 20, 2011), available at https://papers.ssrn.com/sol3/papers.cfm?abstract_id=1589709.

10. *Foley v. Hill and Others*, 2 H.L.C. 28, 9 E.R. 1002 (1848), quoted in Murray N. Rothbard, *The Case Against the Fed* (1994; repr. Auburn, AL: Ludwig von Mises Institute, 2007), pp. 42–43, available at: https://cdn.mises.org/The%20Case%20Against%20the%20Fed_3.pdf.

Chapter 2

A Brief History of the Gold Standard, with a Focus on the United States

To fully understand our current global monetary system, in which all of the major powers issue unbacked fiat money, it is helpful to learn how today's system emerged from its earlier form. Before fiat money, all major currencies were tied (often with interruptions due to war or financial crises) to one or both of the precious metals, gold and silver. This international system of commodity-based money reached its zenith under the so-called classical gold standard, which characterized the global economy from the 1870s through the start of World War I in 1914.

Under a genuine gold standard, a nation's monetary unit is defined as a specific weight of gold. There is "free" coinage of gold, meaning that anyone can present gold bullion to the government to be minted into gold coins of the appropriate denomination in unlimited quantities (perhaps with a small charge for the service). Going the other way, to the extent that there are paper notes or token coins issued by the government as official money, these can be presented by anyone for immediate redemption in full-bodied gold coins. Finally, under a genuine gold standard, there are no restrictions on the flow of gold into and out of the country, so that foreigners too can avail themselves of the options described above.[1]

To this day, arguments over the gold standard are not *merely* technical disagreements concerning economic analysis. Rather, the gold standard often serves

1. Our description of what constitutes a "genuine" gold standard is conventional in this literature; see for example T.E. Gregory, *The Gold Standard and Its Future*, 3d ed. (New York: E.P. Dutton and Co. Inc., 1935), pp. 7–8.

as a proxy for "sound money," which was a central element in the classical liberal tradition of limiting government's ability to wreak havoc on society. As Ludwig von Mises explains:

> **It is impossible to grasp the meaning of the idea of sound money if one does not realize that it was devised as an instrument for the protection of civil liberties against despotic inroads on the part of governments. Ideologically it belongs in the same class with political constitutions and bills of rights.** The demand for constitutional guarantees and for bills of rights was a reaction against arbitrary rule and the nonobservance of old customs by kings. The postulate of sound money was first brought up as a response to the princely practice of debasing the coinage. It was later carefully elaborated and perfected in the age which—through the experience of the American continental currency, the paper money of the French Revolution and the British restriction period—had learned what a government can do to a nation's currency system. (bold added)[2]

It should go without saying that in the present chapter, we are not offering a comprehensive history of the gold standard, even from the limited perspective of the United States. Rather, we merely attempt to explain its basic mechanics, and to highlight some of the major events in the world's evolution from a global monetary system based on market-produced commodity money to our current framework, which rests on government-issued fiat monies.

The Precious Metals: The Market's Money

In the previous chapter, we explained that money wasn't planned or invented by a wise king, but rather emerged spontaneously from the actions of individuals. We also explained why historically people settled on the precious metals, gold and silver, as the preeminent examples of commodity money.

In more recent times—specifically after 1971, as we will document later in this chapter—most people on Earth use unbacked fiat money, issued by various governments (or central banks acting on their behalf), which is not redeemable in any other commodity.

Yet between these two extremes there was a long period when governments issued sovereign currencies *that were defined* as weights of gold and/or silver. In the US, coins stamped with certain numbers of dollars would actually contain the appropriate gold or silver content, such as a $20 Double Eagle gold coin containing 0.9675 troy ounces of gold. Furthermore, after

2. Ludwig von Mises, *The Theory of Money and Credit*, trans. J.E. Batson (1953; repr., Auburn, AL: Ludwig von Mises Institute, 2009), p. 414, https://cdn.mises.org/Theory%20of%20Money%20and%20Credit.pdf.

the US government began the practice of issuing paper notes of various dollar denominations, anyone could present the paper for redemption in the corresponding full-bodied coins. Even during periods when specie redemption was suspended—as often happened during wars—the public generally assumed (correctly) that the government paper currencies would *eventually* be linked back to the precious metals, and this expectation helped anchor the value of the paper money.

Explainer: "Fixed" Exchange Rate vs. Government Price-Fixing

When multiple countries participate in a gold standard, it is typical to say their governments have adopted a regime of "fixed exchange rates," where the various sovereign currencies trade against each other in constant ratios.

In contrast, economists such as Milton Friedman have written persuasive essays[3] making the case for flexible or "floating" exchange rates, in which governments don't intervene in currency markets but rather let supply and demand determine how many pesos trade for a dollar. Part of Friedman's argument is that when governments *do* try to "fix" the value of their currency—usually propping it above the market-clearing level—it leads to a glut of the domestic (overvalued) currency and shortages of (undervalued) foreign exchange. So if economists are opposed to price-fixing when it comes to the minimum wage and rent control, shouldn't they also oppose it in the currency markets?

Milton Friedman

Although Friedman himself obviously understood the nuances, this type of reasoning might mislead the average reader. Under a gold standard, governments don't use coercion to "fix" exchange rates between different currencies. So the policy here is nothing at all like governments setting minimum wages or maximum apartment rents, where the "fixing" *is* accomplished through fines and/or prison time levied on individuals who transact outside of the officially approved range of prices.

---

3. See, for example, Milton Friedman, "Free Floating Anxiety," *National Review*, Sept. 12, 1994, pp. 32–36, https://miltonfriedman.hoover.org/friedman_images/Collections/2016c21/NR_09_12_1994.pdf. Two other quotations where Friedman gives an intuitive defense of floating exchange rates are available at: https://www.interfluidity.com/files/friedman-flexible-exchange.html. For an essay arguing that Friedman's actual views were more nuanced, and that he wasn't opposed to "fixed" exchange rates in certain contexts, see Steve H. Hanke, "Milton Friedman: Float or Fix?," Cato Institute commentary, Sept. 2, 2008, https://www.cato.org/publications/commentary/milton-friedman-float-or-fix.

Instead, under a gold standard, each government *makes the standing offer to the world* to redeem its own paper currency in a specified weight of gold. This offer is completely voluntary. No one in the community *has* to exchange currency notes for gold; people merely have the *option* of doing so.

However, given that two different governments pledge to redeem their respective currencies in definite weights of gold, it is a simple calculation to determine the "fixed" exchange rate between those two currencies. For example, in the year 1913—near the end of the era of the classical gold standard—the British government stood ready to redeem its currency at the rate of £4.25 per ounce of gold, while the US government would redeem *its* currency at the rate of (approximately) $20.67 per ounce of gold. These respective policies implied—using simple arithmetic—that the exchange rate between the currencies was "fixed" at about $4.86 per British pound. Yet this ratio wasn't maintained by coercion, and the *actual* market exchange rate of dollars for pounds did in fact deviate from the anchor point of $4.86. It's just that if the market exchange rate moved too far in either direction, it would eventually become profitable for currency speculators to ship gold from one country to the other, in a series of trades that would push the market exchange rate back toward the "fixed" anchor point.

To see how this works, suppose that the US government (back in 1913) began printing new dollars very rapidly. Other things equal, this would reduce the value of the dollar against the British pound. Suppose that when all of the new dollars flooded into the economy, rather than the usual $4.86 to "buy" a British pound, the price had been bid up to $10.

At this price, there would be an enormous arbitrage opportunity: specifically, a speculator could start out with $2,067 and present it to the US government, which would be obligated to hand over 100 ounces of gold. Then the speculator could ship the 100 ounces of gold across the ocean to London, where the gold could be exchanged with the British authorities for £425. Finally, the speculator could take his £425 to the foreign exchange market, where he could trade them for $4,250 (because in this example we supposed that the dollar price of a British pound had been bid up to $10 in the forex market). Thus, in this simple tale, our speculator started out with $2,067 and transformed it into $4,250, less the fees involved in shipping.

Besides reaping a large profit, the speculator's actions in our tale would also have the following effects: (a) they would drain gold out of US government vaults, providing the American authorities with a motivation to stop with their reckless dollar printing, (b) they would add gold reserves to British government vaults, providing the British authorities with the ability to safely print more British pounds, and (c) they would tend to push the dollar price of British pounds down, moving it from $10 back toward the anchor price of $4.86.

To be sure, I've exaggerated the numbers in this simple example to keep the arithmetic easier. In reality, as the dollar weakened against the British pound, it would hit the "gold export point" well before reaching $10. Through the arbitrage process we explained above, whenever the actual market exchange rate strayed too far above the $4.86 anchor, automatic forces would set in causing gold to flow out of US vaults and push the market exchange rate back toward the "fixed" rate. (This process would happen in reverse if the exchange rate fell too far *below* the $4.86 anchor and crossed the "gold import point": gold would flow out of the United Kingdom and into American vaults, and set in motion processes that would push the exchange rate back up toward the anchor point.)

We have spent considerable time on this mechanism to be sure the reader understands exactly what it means to say there were "fixed exchange rates" under the classical gold standard. To repeat, these were *not* based on government coercion, and did not constitute "price-fixing" by the government. No shortages of foreign exchange occur under a genuine gold standard, because exchange rates are always freely floating, market-clearing rates.

It is difficult for us, growing up in a world of fiat money, to appreciate the fact, but historically people viewed gold (and silver) as the *actual* money, with sovereign currencies being *defined* as weights of the precious metals. As Rothbard explains:

> We might say that the "exchange rates" between the various countries [under the classical gold standard] were thereby fixed. But these were

> not so much exchange rates as they were various units of weight of gold, fixed ineluctably as soon as the respective definitions of weight were established. To say that the governments "arbitrarily fixed" the exchange rates of the various currencies is to say also that governments "arbitrarily" define 1 pound weight as equal to 16 ounces or 1 foot as equal to 12 inches, or "arbitrarily" define the dollar as composed of 10 dimes and 100 cents. Like all weights and measures, such definitions do not have to be imposed by government. They could, at least in theory, have been set by groups of scientists or by custom and commonly accepted by the general public.[4]

In concluding this section, we can agree with Milton Friedman that *in a world of governments issuing their respective fiat monies*, coercive government ceilings or floors in the foreign exchange market—enforced through fines and/or prison sentences—will lead to the familiar problems characteristic of all price controls. As Rothbard conceded, "the only thing worse than fluctuating exchange rates is fixed exchange rates based on fiat money and international coordination."[5]

Murray Rothbard

However, the advocates of a genuine international gold standard stress that its underlying regime of (implied) *fixed* exchange rates would be even better, because it would effectively allow individuals around the world to benefit from the use of a common money. That is to say, for all the reasons that domestic commerce *within* the United States is fostered through the common use of dollars, commerce and especially long-term investment *between* countries will be enhanced when no one has to worry about fluctuating exchange rates on top of the other variables.

Colonial Era through 1872: Gold and Silver "Bimetallism"

Because the original thirteen American colonies were part of the British Empire, their official money was naturally that of Great Britain—pounds, shillings, and pence—which at the time was officially on a silver standard. (Indeed, the very term "pound sterling" harkens back to a weight of silver.) Yet the

4. Murray N. Rothbard, "Gold vs. Fluctuating Fiat Exchange Rates," *Gold Is Money*, ed. Hans F. Sennholz (Westport, CT: Greenwood Press, 1975), pp. 24–40, essay text available at https://mises.org/wire/gold-vs-fluctuating-fiat-exchange-rates.

5. Murray N. Rothbard, "Back to Fixed Exchange Rates," in *Making Economic Sense*, 2d ed. (Auburn, AL: Ludwig von Mises Institute, 2006), pp. 306–10, quote on p. 310, https://mises-media.s3.amazonaws.com/Making%20Economic%20Sense_3.pdf.

colonists imported and used coins from around the world, while those in rural areas even used tobacco and other commodities as money.[6]

During the Revolutionary War, the Continental Congress issued unbacked paper money called Continental currency. The predictable price inflation gave rise to the expression "not worth a Continental." (We will cover this episode in greater detail in chapter 9.)

Among the foreign coins circulating among the American colonists, the most popular was the Spanish silver dollar. This made the term "dollar" common in the colonies, explaining why the Continental currency was denominated in "dollars" and why the US federal government—newly established under the US Constitution—would choose "dollar" as the country's official unit of currency.[7]

It is crucial for today's readers to understand that from the inception of the modern (i.e., post-Constitution) United States in the late 1780s through the eve of the Civil War in 1861, the federal government issued currency *only* in the form of gold and silver coins. (The one borderline exception were the limited issues of Treasury Notes first used in the War of 1812, which were short-term debt instruments that earned interest and did not enjoy legal tender status, but of which the small denominations of the 1815 issues did serve as a form of paper quasi money among some Americans.[8])

In this early period, *banks* were allowed to issue their own paper notes that were redeemable in hard money and, to the extent that they were trusted, might circulate in the community along with full-bodied coins, but these banknotes were not the same thing, economically or legally, as gold or silver dollars. In summary, for the first seventy-odd years after the modern federal government's creation, official US dollars consisted in actual gold and silver coins that regular people carried in their pockets and spent at the store. Indeed, so bad was the constitutional framers' experience with the Continental currency, that they included in the Contract Clause the prohibition that "No State shall … make any Thing but gold and silver Coin a Tender in Payment of Debts."

In the Coinage Act of 1792, the US dollar was defined as either 371.25 grains of pure silver or 24.75 grains of pure gold, which officially established a gold-silver ratio of exactly 15 to 1. Part of the rationale for this policy of

6. See Murray N. Rothbard, *A History of Money and Banking in the United States: The Colonial Era to World War II* (Auburn, AL: Ludwig von Mises Institute, 2002), p. 47, https://cdn.mises.org/History%20of%20Money%20and%20Banking%20in%20the%20United%20States%20The%20Colonial%20Era%20to%20World%20War%20II_2.pdf.

7. Rothbard, *History of Money and Banking in the United States*, p. 65.

8. For a scholarly case that the 1815 Treasury Note issues constituted the first federally issued paper money, see Donald H. Kagin, "Monetary Aspects of the Treasury Notes of the War of 1812," *Journal of Economic History* 44, no. 1 (March 1984): 69–88.

"bimetallism"—in which new coins (of various denominations of dollars) could be minted from either of the precious metals—was that silver coins were convenient for small denominations (including fractions such as a half dollar, quarter dollar, dime, etc.), while gold coins were preferable for larger denominations (such as $10 and $20 pieces). By providing "dollars" consisting of both small-value silver coins and high-value gold coins, the idea was that bimetallism would allow Americans to conduct all of their transactions in full-bodied coins (without resort to paper notes or token coinage).

However, the problem with bimetallism is the phenomenon known as Gresham's law, summarized in the aphorism "Bad money drives out good." Specifically, when a government defines a currency in terms of both silver and gold, unless the implied value ratio of the two metals is close to the *actual* market exchange rate, one of the metals will necessarily be overvalued, while the other is undervalued. People then only spend the overvalued metal, while hoarding (or melting, or sending abroad) the undervalued metal.

In the case of the United States, when it established the 15-to-1 ratio in 1792, this was actually close to the actual market exchange rate between gold and silver. However, increased silver production led to a gradual erosion of the world price of silver, moving the actual market ratio closer to 15½ to 1. (This familiar ratio was partly held in place by France's *own* bimetallic policy following the French Revolution, maintained by the French government's large reserves of both metals.[9])

As the world price of silver slipped relative to gold, the gap between market values and the US dollar's definition eventually became so large that only silver was presented to the Mint for new coinage, while existing gold coins disappeared from commerce. As Rothbard reports: "From 1810 until 1834, only silver coin ... circulated in the United States."[10] For a modern example of Gresham's law in action, the reader can reflect that one would be a fool today to spend a pre-1964 quarter in a standard commercial transaction, since its silver content is worth far more than twenty-five cents.

The Coinage Acts of 1834 and 1837 revised the (implied[11]) content of the gold dollar down to 23.22 grains of pure gold, while leaving the silver dollar at 371.25 grains. Because there are 480 grains in a troy ounce, these definitions

9. See Leland Yeager, *International Monetary Relations: Theory, History, and Policy*, 2d ed. (New York: Harper and Row, 1976), p. 296.

10. Rothbard, *History of Money and Banking in the United States*, p. 67.

11. We say "implied" content of the gold dollar because the Coinage Act of 1834 combined with the adjustment in the 1837 act actually specified that a *ten-dollar* gold eagle coin would contain 232.2 grains of pure gold. Individual dollar gold coins weren't issued until 1849. (The language in the 1837 act specifies 258 grains of standard weight, with nine-tenths fineness, working out

of the metallic content of the dollar implied a gold price of (approximately) $20.67 per ounce, and an unchanged silver price of (approximately) $1.29.

Thus the revised gold content of the dollar moved the gold/silver ratio to just under 16 to 1. This was now *higher* than the global price ratio of (roughly) 15½ to 1, meaning that the new definition favored gold and undervalued silver. Consequently, little silver was brought to the US Mint to be turned into new coinage—since the market value of the metal in a "silver dollar" coin was higher than $1—and the US, though still officially committed to a bimetallic standard, after 1834 flipped from a *de facto* silver standard to a *de facto* gold standard.

When the United States fell into Civil War in 1861, both sides resorted to the printing press and suspended specie payment. The North famously issued inconvertible paper notes called "greenbacks," which led to large-scale price inflation. (We will cover this and other famous episodes of inflation in greater detail in chapter 9.)

US Participation in the Classical Gold Standard, 1873/1879–1914

The classical gold standard refers to the period beginning in the late nineteenth century when a growing number of countries tied their currencies to gold. Because the process was gradual, it is difficult to state precisely *when* the period began: "In 1873 there were some nine countries on the gold standard; in 1890, 22 countries; in 1900, 29 countries; and in 1912, 49 countries."[12]

Recall from the previous section that going into the Civil War, the US dollar was defined in grains of the precious metals that implied a mint price of *either* $20.67 per troy ounce of gold, or of $1.29 per troy ounce of silver, for a gold-silver ratio of about 16 to 1. Because world prices of gold and silver were closer to 15½ to 1, there was little incentive to bring silver to the US Mint for conversion into coins.

Consequently, there was little opposition in 1873 when Congress discontinued the "free coinage" of the standard silver dollar (free coinage of fractional dollar silver coins having ended in 1853),[13] as there had been little demand for

---

to 232.2 grains of pure gold.) See Lawrence H. Officer, "Coinage Acts," Encyclopedia.com, Aug. 11, 2020, last modified Aug. 25, 2020, https://www.encyclopedia.com/social-sciences-and-law/law/law-divisions-and-codes/coinage-acts. For the legislative text of the Coinage Act of 1837, see: "CoinWeek IQ: Coinage Act of January 9, 1837," *CoinWeek*, Sept. 14, 2018, https://coinweek.com/us-coins/coinweek-iq-coinage-act-of-january-9-1837/.

12. D.L. Kemmerer, "The Gold Standard in Historical Perspective," *Commercial and Financial Chronicle* (New York), August 5, 1954, qtd. in Melchior Palyi, *The Twilight of Gold, 1914–1936: Myths and Realities* (Chicago: Henry Regnery Company, 1972), p. 8.

13. Strictly speaking, the free coinage of all silver coins *except* the silver dollar had ended as a

the option. However, later in the decade, when world silver prices dropped—partly as a result of silver discoveries and partly as a result of other countries demonetizing silver, particularly the German Empire—the change of policy would be viewed in a different light. Indeed, pro-silver interests eventually referred to the momentous event as "the Crime of '73."[14]

The 1873 policy change, along with the growing limitations on the legal tender status of existing silver coins completed by 1874, officially ended the era of bimetallism in the United States:[15] silver had been demonetized, rendering America a gold standard country. However, because the US remained in the "greenback" period left over from the Civil War, it actually was on *neither* metallic standard at the time, as it had suspended specie payment. Consequently, it can be argued that the US was not truly a participant in the classical gold standard until 1879, when the government resumed specie payment in gold (as required in the 1875 Specie Payment Resumption Act).

There was much drama in the battle between silver and gold interests, most notably William Jennings Bryan's famous "Cross of Gold" speech—which called for a return to bimetallism and the free coinage of silver as a method of helping indebted farmers at the expense of the Wall Street elites—delivered at the 1896 Democratic National Convention, where he was nominated for president. Yet Bryan lost the general election to the pro-gold Republican William McKinley, who signed the Gold Standard Act of 1900 into law. This legislation codified the definition of the gold dollar that had been established back in 1837, which (we recall) implied a dollar/gold price of about $20.67 per ounce. This was the dollar's gold

William Jennings Bryan delivering his Cross of Gold speech at the Democratic National Convention in Chicago, July 9, 1896 (https://en.wikipedia.org/wiki/Cross_of_Gold_speech#/media/File:Bryan_after_speech.jpg).

result of legislation in 1853, while the 1873 legislation took away this last source of new silver money, except for a silver "trade dollar" intended for use in foreign transactions. (Even coinage of the silver trade dollar was discontinued in 1887.) See Officer, "Coinage Acts," for a comprehensive history of legislation concerning US coinage.

14. Leland Yeager, *International Monetary Relations: Theory, History, and Policy*, 2d ed. (New York: Harper and Row, 1976), pp. 296–97.

15. For an excellent summary of the nuances of free coinage and legal tender status of gold and silver coins of various denominations, see Officer, "Coinage Acts."

content throughout the classical gold standard period, and would prevail until FDR's devaluation in 1933/1934, described later in this chapter.

Although many modern economists scoff at the gold standard, in its "classical" heyday it was a quite remarkable achievement. Economic historian Carl Wiegand writes: "The decades preceding the First World War were characterized by a degree of economic and personal freedom rarely, if ever, experienced in the history of mankind." He goes on to explain, "An essential part of this system was the gold standard."[16]

To give a flavor of this unrivalled degree of freedom before the Great War, consider this description from the famous economist Oskar Morgenstern:

> [T]here was freedom of travel without passports, freedom of migration, and freedom from exchange control and other monetary restrictions. Citizenship was freely granted to immigrants...capital would move unsupervised in any direction....There were hardly any quantitative restrictions on international trade...[I]t was a world of which recently many...would have been inclined to assert that it could not be created because it could never work.[17]

Alas, among the casualties of the world war would be the classical gold standard and its associated freedoms.

World War I and Its Aftermath

If the beginning of the classical gold standard is up for scholarly dispute, everyone agrees that it *ended* with World War I. Indeed, the Great War was only possible because the major governments abandoned their commitment to gold. As Melchior Palyi explains:

> "This war cannot last longer than a few months" was a widely held conviction at the outset of World War I. All involved would go "bankrupt" shortly and be forced to come to terms, perhaps without a decision on the battle fields. The belligerents would simply cease to be credit-worthy. **Such was the frame of the European mind in 1914; the idea that credit and the printing press might be substituted for**

16. Palyi, *The Twilight of Gold*, p. 2. As explained in the book's preface, Palyi died before finishing his manuscript, and Professor Carl Wiegand of Southern Illinois University therefore wrote the introductions to each chapter of the book; the quotation in the text is drawn from one such introduction.

17. Oskar Morgenstern, *International Financial Transactions and Business Cycles* (New York: National Bureau of Economic Research, 1957), pp. 17–19, qtd. in Palyi, *The Twilight of Gold*, pp. 6–7.

> **genuine savings was "unthinkable."** "Sound money" ruled supreme, supported by the logic of the free market. (bold added)[18]

Many commentators use war or other emergencies as examples of the *problem* with a strict gold standard—it allegedly ties the hands of government to respond in a crisis. However, that is an odd way of framing the matter. After all, printing unbacked fiat money doesn't actually give the government access to extra tanks, bombers, and artillery; those all come from real resources, the availability of which is not directly affected by the quantity of paper money.

American troops in France, July 1918. Getty Images: DEA Picture Library / Contributor. De Agostini Collection. No. 164077352.

To say that World War I would have been "unaffordable" on the classical gold standard really just means that the citizens of the countries involved wouldn't have tolerated the huge increases in explicit taxation and/or regular debt issue to pay for the conflict. Instead, to finance such unprecedented expenditures, their governments had to resort to the hidden tax of inflation, where the transfer of purchasing power from their peoples would be cloaked in rising prices that could be blamed on speculators, trade unions, profiteers, and other villains, rather than the government's profligacy. This is why Ludwig von Mises said that inflationary finance of a war was "essentially antidemocratic."[19]

In light of these realities, when joining the war the major belligerents all broke from the gold standard, although the United States's deviation consisted only in President Wilson embargoing the export of gold bullion and coin in 1917.[20] After the war, the major powers made halfhearted attempts to restore some semblance of the international gold standard, but these were counterfeit versions (as we will detail below). The First World War thus dealt a mortal blow to the gold standard from which it never recovered.

18. Palyi, *The Twilight of Gold*, p. 2.

19. Ludwig von Mises, *Omnipotent Government: The Rise of the Total State and Total War* (1944; repr., Auburn, AL: Ludwig von Mises Institute, 2010), p. 252, https://cdn.mises.org/Omnipotent%20Government%20The%20Rise%20of%20the%20Total%20State%20and%20Total%20War_3.pdf.

20. George Selgin, *The Rise and Fall of the Gold Standard in the United States*, Policy Analysis, no. 729, Cato Institute, June 20, 2013, p. 12, https://www.cato.org/sites/cato.org/files/pubs/pdf/pa729_web.pdf.

We should take a moment in our discussion to explain the role of central banks, which also saw a major break with the start of the war. Although central banks were not necessary for the administration of the classical gold standard—the Federal Reserve didn't even exist until late 1913—those countries that had central banks expected them to be independent from narrow political matters. Although the central banks engaged in discretion in influencing interest rates and providing credit with the aim of—in our modern terminology—smoothing out the business cycle, they were ultimately bound by the "rules of the game" of the international gold standard and had to protect their gold reserves.

Once war broke out, however, not only was the link to gold severed, but the role of the central bank changed as well. The central banks of the belligerent powers all became subservient to the fiscal needs of their respective governments. As American economist Benjamin Anderson described the wartime operations of the British and American central banks (and note that in later chapters we will elaborate on the mechanisms Anderson mentions):

> The [British] Government first borrowed from the Bank of England on Ways and Means Bills, and the Bank bought short term Treasury Bills also. This had the double purpose of giving the Government the cash it immediately needed, and of putting additional deposit balances with the Bank of England into the hands of the Joint Stock Banks.... **This increased the volume of reserve money for the banking community and made money easy**, permitting an expansion of general bank credit which enabled the banks to buy Treasury Bills and Government bonds.... [T]he exigencies of war justified everything...
>
> Speedily, too, the British financial authorities learned the process of regulating outside money markets in which they wished to borrow ... especially, the New York money market. **If an issue of bonds of the Allies...was to be placed in our [US] market, it was preceded by the export of a large volume of gold, accurately timed, to increase surplus reserves in the New York banks** and to facilitate an expansion of credit in the United States which would make it easy for us to absorb the foreign loan. (bold added)[21]

After the wartime experience, the "traditional gold standard had ceased to be 'sacrosanct,'" in the words of Palyi. "Events proved, supposedly, that mankind could prosper without it."[22] After all, if the gold standard could be violated and central banks could use their discretionary powers to help with the war effort, why not do the same for *other* important social goals, like promoting economic growth and reducing inequality?

---

21. Benjamin M. Anderson Jr., *Chase Economic Bulletin* (New York Chase National Bank), Sept. 29, 1930, qtd. in Palyi, *The Twilight of Gold*, pp. 31–32.

22. Palyi, *The Twilight of Gold*, p. 52.

Because of the severe wartime price inflation, after the 1918 armistice the major powers desired a return to gold. However, resuming specie payment at the prewar parities would have proven very painful, since their currencies had been inflated so much during the war. The United States, for its part, ended the embargo on gold export in 1919, but in order to staunch the resulting outflow of gold and maintain the prewar dollar-gold ratio, the Federal Reserve was forced to raise interest rates and massively contract credit, resulting in the Depression of 1920–21.

At the 1922 Genoa Conference, a plan was hatched for a "gold exchange standard," in which central banks around the world could hold financial claims on the Bank of England and the Federal Reserve as their reserves, rather than physical gold. However, so long as the Bank of England and the Fed themselves stood ready to redeem sterling and dollar assets in gold, there was still *some* discipline imposed on the system.

Yet even here, the redemption policy was only effective for large amounts and hence only relevant for large institutions, as opposed to the universal policy under the classical gold standard. As Selgin explains:

> A genuine gold standard must ... provide for *some* actual gold coins if paper currency is to be readily converted into metal even by persons possessing relatively small quantities of the former. A genuine gold standard is therefore distinct from a gold "bullion" standard of the sort that several nations, including the United States, adopted between the World Wars. **The Bank of England, for example, was then obliged to convert its notes into 400 fine ounce gold bars only, making the minimum conversion amount, in ca. 1929 units, £1,699, or $8,269.** (bold added)[23]

The interwar gold exchange standard sought to "economize" on gold holdings: rather than storing physical gold in central bank vaults around the world, only the United States and Great Britain needed to redeem their currencies in the yellow metal, while the rest of the world could stockpile paper claims against the financial titans. Yet this system was very fragile, relying on cooperation among the central banks so as not to threaten the smaller gold reserves that were doing much more "work" than they had under the classical standard.

As an example of the necessary coordination, when then chancellor of the Exchequer Winston Churchill in 1925 sought to resume specie payments at the prewar parity and restore the pound to its traditional value of $4.86, in order to avoid a massive deflation in British prices, the Federal Reserve (under the leadership of Benjamin Strong) agreed to an easy-credit policy, thus weakening the

23. Selgin, "The Rise and Fall of the Gold Standard in the United States," p. 3.

dollar in order to close some of the gap between the currencies.[24] Economists of the Austrian school argue that the Fed's loose policies of the 1920s helped fuel an unsustainable boom that led to the 1929 stock market crash.[25]

The Great Depression and Bretton Woods

In the depths of the Great Depression, the newly inaugurated president Franklin D. Roosevelt euphemistically declared a "national bank holiday" on March 6, 1933, in response to a run on the gold reserves of the New York Fed. During the week-long closure, FDR ordered the banks to exchange their gold holdings for Federal Reserve notes, to cease fulfilling transactions in gold, and to provide lists of their customers who had withdrawn gold (or "gold certificates," which were legal claims to gold for the bearer) since February of that year.[26]

President Franklin Delano Roosevelt, 1939. Getty Images. Underwood Archives: 143128630.

FDR would issue an even more draconian executive order on April 5, 1933, which required all citizens to turn in virtually all holdings of gold coin, bullion, and certificates in exchange for Federal Reserve notes, under penalty of a $10,000 fine and up to ten years in prison. Although US citizens couldn't buy gold, foreigners still traded in the world market, and there the US dollar now fluctuated against the metal, the $20.67 anchor having been severed. The Roosevelt administration in 1934 officially devalued the currency some 41 percent by locking in a new definition of the dollar that implied a gold price of $35 per troy ounce. However, this redemption privilege was only offered to foreign central banks; American citizens were still barred from holding gold, and even from writing contracts using the international price of gold as a benchmark.

24. For an interesting narrative of the events surrounding the British and American experience with the interwar gold exchange standard, see Ryan Brown, "The Burden of Statesmanship: Churchill as Chancellor 1924–1929," *Finest Hour* 153 (Winter 2011–12): 12–19, https://winstonchurchill.org/publications/finest-hour/finest-hour-153/the-burden-of-statesmanship-churchill-as-chancellor-1924-1929/.

25. See, for example, Murray N. Rothbard, *America's Great Depression*, 5th ed. (Auburn, AL: Ludwig von Mises Institute, 2000).

26. See Selgin, "The Rise and Fall of the Gold Standard in the United States," p. 15.

Mount Washington Hotel, Bretton Woods, New Hampshire

As the Allied victory in World War II became more certain, the Western powers hammered out the postwar monetary arrangements in the famous Bretton Woods Conference, a nineteen-day affair held at a New Hampshire hotel which led to the creation of the International Monetary Fund (IMF) and the World Bank. Following the war, the global financial system would rest on a refined gold exchange standard in which the US dollar—rather than physical gold—displaced sterling and became the sole reserve asset held by central banks around the world.

Under the Bretton Woods system, other countries could still hold gold reserves, but they typically defined their currencies with respect to the US dollar and dealt with trade imbalances by accumulating dollar assets, rather than draining gold from countries with overvalued currencies. In theory the Federal Reserve kept the whole system tied to gold by pledging to redeem *for central banks* dollars for gold at the new $35/ounce rate, but in practice even central banks were discouraged from invoking this option. Furthermore, governments only gradually lifted restrictions on international transactions following the war, so that the Bretton Woods gold exchange framework—tepid as it was—was really only fully operational by the late 1950s.[27]

The Nixon Shock and Fiat Money

The US government relied on Federal Reserve monetary inflation to help finance the Vietnam War and the so-called War on Poverty. For a while other central banks were content to let their dollar reserves pile up, but French authorities eventually blinked in 1967, when they began to request the transfer of gold from New York and London to Paris. By 1968 the Americans had capitulated and let the unofficial market price of the dollar deviate from the official Bretton Woods

27. Craig K. Elwell, *Brief History of the Gold Standard in the United States*, Congressional Research Service, June 23, 2011, pp. 11–12,

value, relying on diplomatic pressure to dissuade other governments from exploiting the discrepancy and "running" on the Fed's increasingly inadequate gold reserves.[28]

Eventually the weight became too much to bear, and President Richard Nixon formally suspended the dollar's convertibility on August 15, 1971. Along with other interventions in the economy (such as wage and price controls), this official closing of the gold window has been dubbed the "Nixon shock."

Although Nixon assured the public that the gold suspension would be temporary, and that his policy would stabilize the dollar, neither promise would be fulfilled. From this point forward, the US—and hence the rest of the world—would operate on a purely fiat monetary system.

28. Elwell, *Brief History of the Gold Standard in the United States*, p. 13.

Chapter 3

The History and Structure of the Federal Reserve System

This chapter will provide a brief sketch of the historical context in which the Federal Reserve was founded, summarize some of the major changes to the Fed's institutional structure and mandate over the years, and end with a snapshot of the Fed's current governing structure. (Chapters 1 and 2 of this book cover more of the historical context, while chapters 4 and 6 explain the mechanics of Federal Reserve operations in much greater detail.)

Historical Context

After a bitter power struggle,[1] President Andrew Jackson achieved his goal of "killing" the Second Bank of the United States when its charter expired in 1836. The year 1837 is considered the beginning of the so-called Free Banking era in the United States, because the federal government conferred no special privileges on individual banks, while some states—most notably New York—allowed relatively free entry into the banking industry.[2] (It's important to note

1. For a fascinating account of Andrew Jackson's battle against Nicholas Biddle, head of the Second Bank of the United States, from an Austrian perspective, see Dan Sanchez, "The 19th-Century Bernanke," *Mises Wire*, Sept. 1, 2009, https://mises.org/library/19th-century-bernanke-0. For a conventional historical discussion, see "Andrew Jackson Shuts Down Second Bank of the U.S.," History, updated Sept. 6, 2019, https://www.history.com/this-day-in-history/andrew-jackson-shuts-down-second-bank-of-the-u-s.

2. For two essays on the so-called Free Banking era in the United States written by Federal Reserve-affiliated economists, see Daniel Sanches, "The Free-Banking Era: A Lesson for Today?," Federal Reserve Bank of Philadelphia Research Department, *Economic Insights* (Third

that "free banking" in this context merely means that no special charter was required to open a new bank; the label does *not* mean that banks were unregulated or even that they were treated the same way as other businesses.[3]) The Free Banking era ended during the Civil War, after the National Bank Act of 1863 gave the federal government authority to charter national banks.

However, even the various rounds of National Bank Act legislation during the 1860s did not establish a single, central bank of the kind seen in Europe, the most obvious example being the Bank of England (established in 1694). Indeed, in January 1907, investment banker Paul Warburg—widely considered one of the intellectual architects of the Federal Reserve System—wrote:

> It is a strange fact that, while in the development of all other commercial phenomena the United States has been foremost, the country should have progressed to so slight an extent in the form of its commercial paper. **The United States is in fact at about the same point that had been reached by Europe at the time of the Medicis, and by Asia, in all likelihood, at the time of Hammurabi.** Most of the paper taken by the American banks still consists of simple promissory notes, which rest only on the credit of the merchant who makes the notes, and which are kept until maturity by the bank or corporation that discounts them....
>
> **In Europe ... there are scores of banks ... which give their three-months' acceptance for the commercial requirements of trade,** or which make it their specific business to indorse [*sic*] commercial bills.... This banker's acceptance, or this indorsed paper, can be readily negotiated by the buyer at any time.... **The holder will always be able to dispose of it, either through private discounting or, in case of need, by selling ... to the Bank of England, the Banque de France, or the German Reichsbank.** (emphasis added)[4]

As Warburg's discussion indicates, the original justification for the creation of another central bank—one with more power than the Second Bank of the United States had had—did *not* allude to the modern goals of "full employment"

Quarter 2016): 9–14, https://www.philadelphiafed.org/-/media/research-and-data/publications/economic-insights/2016/q3/eiq316_free_banking_era.pdf; and Gerald P. Dwyer, Jr., "Wildcat Banking, Banking Panics, and Free Banking in the United States," Federal Reserve Bank of Atlanta, *Economic Review* (December 1996): 1–20, https://www.frbatlanta.org/-/media/documents/research/publications/economic-review/1996/vol81nos3-6_dwyer.pdf. These two essays in turn cite several works by the two most prominent members of the Austrian "free banker" camp, namely George Selgin and Lawrence White.

3. On this point, see Sanches, "Free-Banking Era," p. 9.

4. Paul Warburg, "Defects and Needs of Our Banking System," *New York Times*, January 6, 1907, available (with subscription) at https://www.nytimes.com/1907/01/06/archives/defects-and-needs-of-our-banking-system-paul-warburg-of-kuhn-loeb.html.

and "price stability." Rather, the pleas of the time called for an "elastic currency" that would expand or contract according to the "needs of trade."

Some nine months after Warburg's essay appeared, a failed bid by speculators triggered a run on depository institutions and eventually swelled into the Panic of 1907. Insolvent banks collapsed, while solvent yet illiquid banks had to go hat in hand to private lenders such as J.P. Morgan. The experience bolstered calls for the creation of a publicly run "lender of last resort," and conventional histories cite this episode as pivotal in building support for the creation of a new central bank.[5] However, dissenting scholars argue that a group of powerful financial interests had been agitating for a US central bank for years—and Warburg's essay indirectly confirms this.[6]

Much of the structure of what would become the Federal Reserve Act was laid out during secret meetings held at Jekyll Island (off the coast of Georgia) in November 1910. Present at the meetings were Senator Nelson Aldrich (and his secretary Arthur Shelton), Henry P. Davison (a J. P. Morgan partner), President[7] Frank A. Vanderlip of the National City Bank of New York (now Citibank), Assistant Secretary of the Treasury A. Piatt Andrew, and Paul Warburg himself.[8]

These prominent figures from government and banking knew that they should keep a low profile, going so far as to book their travel to Jekyll Island under assumed names (so that the press wouldn't begin wondering why such powerful men were meeting clandestinely). Such intrigue has understandably fueled an entire genre of commentary on the Fed. As journalist Roger Lowenstein put it during his *Marketplace* interview:

---

5. For an example of the conventional treatment of the Panic of 1907 and its relation to the Federal Reserve, see Jon R. Moen and Ellis W. Tallman's "The Panic of 1907," Federal Reserve History, Dec. 4, 2015, https://www.federalreservehistory.org/essays/panic_of_1907. The essay was written for the Federal Reserve, and Tallman works at the Federal Reserve Bank of Cleveland.

6. See, for example, the work of Murray N. Rothbard, *The Origins of the Federal Reserve* (Auburn, AL: Ludwig von Mises Institute, 2009), https://cdn.mises.org/The%20Origins%20of%20the%20Federal%20Reserve_2.pdf (excerpted from Rothbard's *A History of Money and Banking in the United States: the Colonial Era to World War II*).

7. Some libertarian authors state that Vanderlip was *vice* president of the National City Bank. It's true that when he originally joined the bank, Vanderlip held the position of vice president, but by the time of the Jekyll Island meeting, he had been elected president. See C. E. Booth, "Biography of Frank A. Vanderlip: A Brief Biography of Rockefeller protege [*sic*] Frank Vanderlip," 1914, Modern History Project, accessed Jan. 1, 2020, https://modernhistoryproject.org/mhp?Article=VanderlipBio.

8. Gary Richardson and Jessie Romero, Federal Reserve Bank of Richmond, "The Meeting at Jekyll Island," Federal Reserve History, Dec. 4, 2015, https://www.federalreservehistory.org/essays/jekyll_island_conference.

> You gotta hand it to the conspiracy theorists, because, in fact, there was a conspiracy.... I call it a patriotic conspiracy, but there was a senator from Rhode Island, a guy named Nelson Aldrich.... [L]ate in his career, he decided we needed a central bank. So he organized—now I'm not making this up, it doesn't come from Warner Bros. studio or anything—he organized a faux hunting trip to an island off the coast of Georgia [Jekyll Island] where there was an exclusive resort where J.P. Morgan was a member. [Morgan] made sure there was no one else in the club. And the senator, three bankers, the assistant secretary of the treasury—who, by the way, didn't tell his boss—went down there for a week. They were plied with wild turkey, quail, stuffed oyster. They wrote what became the first draft of the Federal Reserve Act.[9]

The Federal Reserve Act of 1913

On the Federal Reserve's website, in its About section, the Fed describes its enabling legislation as follows: "The Federal Reserve Act of 1913 established the Federal Reserve System as the central bank of the United States to provide the nation with a safer, more flexible, and more stable monetary and financial system."[10]

The original Federal Reserve Act was signed into law by President Woodrow Wilson on at 6:02 PM on December 23, 1913. (The fact that such a significant piece of legislation was enacted the night before Christmas Eve helps fuel the suspicion surrounding the Fed that we mentioned.) The previous day, the House had approved the final bill by a vote of 298–60, with the Senate approving it on December 23 by a vote of 43–25.[11]

PRESIDENT'S SIGNATURE ENACTS CURRENCY LAW

Wilson Declares It the First of Series of Constructive Acts to Aid Business.

Makes Speech to Group of Democratic Leaders.

Conference Report Adopted in Senate by Vote of 43 to 25.

Banks All Over the Country Hasten to Enter Federal Reserve System.

Gov-Elect Walsh Calls Passage of Bill A Fine Christmas Present.

WILSON SEES DAWN OF NEW ERA IN BUSINESS

HOME VIEWS OF CURRENCY ACT

FOUR PENS USED BY PRESIDENT

Source: Wikimedia Public Domain

As is typical, the enabling legislation didn't specify all the operational details of the new American central bank. As Sandra Kollen Ghizoni of the Federal Reserve Bank of Atlanta explains:

9. Roger Lowenstein, quoted in Kai Ryssdal and Bridget Bodnar, "How a Secret Meeting on Jekyll Island Led to the Fed," Marketplace, Oct. 20, 2015, https://www.marketplace.org/2015/10/20/how-secret-meeting-jekyll-island-led-fed/.

10. "Federal Reserve Act," Board of Governors of the Federal Reserve System, accessed Jan. 8, 2020, https://www.federalreserve.gov/aboutthefed/fract.htm.

11. Voting record for Federal Reserve Act taken from "The Federal Reserve Act of 1913 – A Legislative History," Law Librarians' Society of Washington, D.C., last modified August 2009, https://web.archive.org/web/20100324115751/http://www.llsdc.org/FRA-LH/.

Wilbur G. Kurtz Sr., Signing the Federal Reserve Act, 1923. *Photo of painting courtesy of Woodrow Wilson Presidential Library and Museum, Staunton, Virginia*

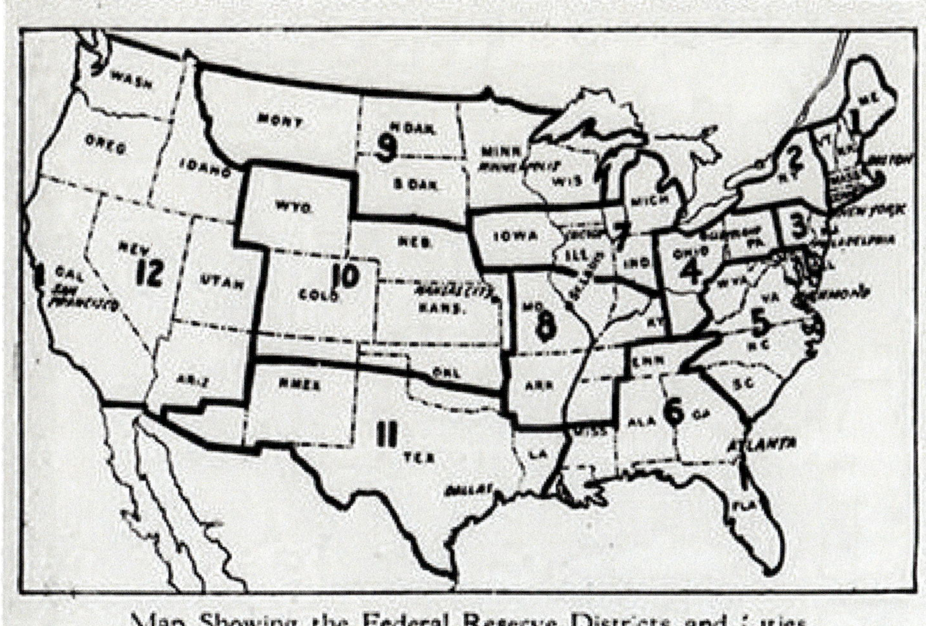

New U.S. Banking System Announced
The Sun [New York], April 1914

The [Federal Reserve] Act established a Reserve Bank Organization Committee (RBOC) to select locations for Reserve Banks and draw district boundaries.

The RBOC comprised Secretary of the Treasury William G. McAdoo, Secretary of Agriculture David F. Houston, and Comptroller of the Currency John Skelton Williams. The RBOC was charged with designating between eight and twelve cities as Federal Reserve cities and apportioning the country into districts, each of which would contain one Reserve Bank city. Furthermore, the boundaries of each district had to take into account that region's "convenience and customary course of business."...

RBOC members spent six weeks traveling 10,000 miles to allow business leaders, bankers, chambers of commerce, clearing house associations, and other representatives to make a case for why a Federal Reserve Bank should be located in their city. Public hearings were held in eighteen cities.... The hearings generated more than 5,000 pages of testimony and covered a wide range of topics....

Some cities were obvious choices, such as New York, Chicago, and St. Louis, which were designated central reserve cities under the National Banking Act of 1863 and subsequent legislation. **Despite the RBOC's efforts to clarify the criteria used to draw district lines and select Reserve Bank cities, several cities nevertheless sparked controversies over the eventual decisions....**

Federal Reserve Bank Districts

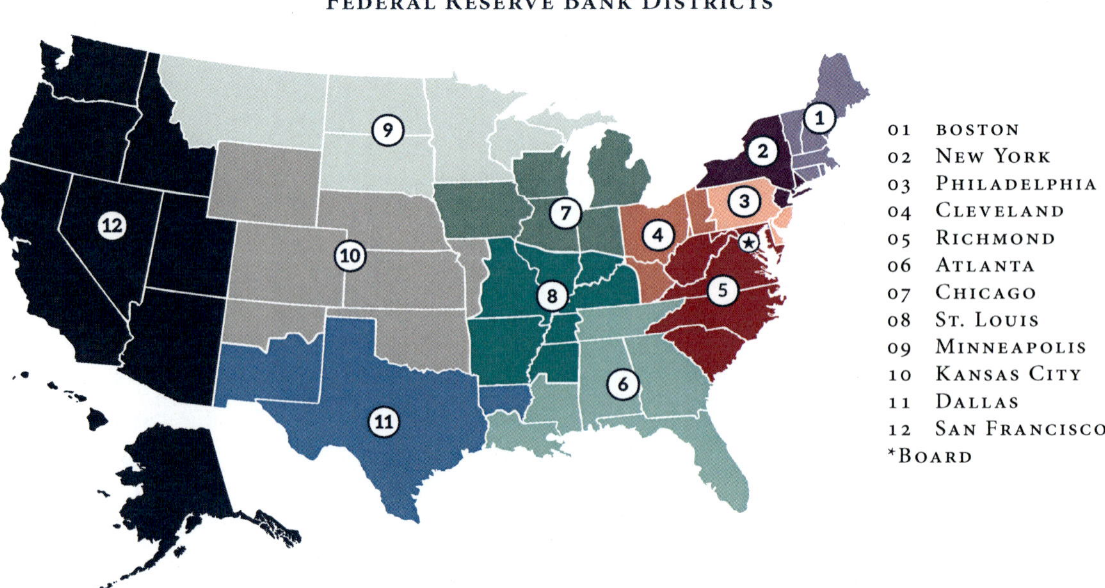

NOTE: the district boundaries do not necessary line up with state boundaries.

> Of the thirty-seven cities that applied to have Reserve Banks, these twelve were selected: Boston (District 1), New York (District 2), Philadelphia (District 3), Cleveland (District 4), Richmond [VA] (District 5), Atlanta (District 6), Chicago (District 7), St. Louis (District 8), Minneapolis (District 9), Kansas City (District 10), Dallas (District 11), and San Francisco (District 12). (emphasis added)[12]

It is important to understand that originally each of the twelve Reserve Banks exercised considerable autonomy: each Reserve Bank, under the leadership of its respective governor, set its own policies. In contrast to our day, there was no such thing as "the Fed's" discount rate but instead the discount rate charged by, say, the Reserve Bank of St. Louis or of Dallas.[13] This would all change in 1935, as we will explain in the next section.

Major Amendments to the Federal Reserve Act

Congress has amended the Federal Reserve Act several times since its inception. In this section we will describe two of the most significant episodes.

The Banking Act of 1935

Although sweeping legislation affecting the American banking system was passed in 1932 and 1933—including the famous Banking Act of 1933 (commonly known as Glass-Steagall)—the most significant changes to the structure of the Federal Reserve System itself came in the Banking Act of 1935.

This new legislation strengthened the overall power of the Federal Reserve System and consolidated it in Washington, DC, *away* from the Fed's own Reserve Banks. However, the Banking Act of 1935 *also* served to make the Fed more autonomous from the federal government. As Gary Richardson, the Fed's official historian at the Reserve Bank of Richmond, explains in a coauthored essay,

---

12. Sandra Kollen Ghizoni, Federal Reserve Bank of Atlanta, "Reserve Bank Organization Committee Announces Selection of Reserve Bank Cities and District Boundaries," Federal Reserve History, Nov. 22, 2013, https://www.federalreservehistory.org/essays/reserve_bank_organization_committee.

13. The author (Murphy) encountered this dichotomy when writing his book on the Great Depression. In order to rebut the (now standard) allegation that the Fed's "tight money" policy caused the economic calamity of the 1930s, Murphy wanted to contrast "the Fed's" interest rate targets back in the early 1920s with those of the early 1930s. But in fact there was no such target, as the Federal Reserve Banks didn't *have* a unified policy until the 1935 legislation was enacted. (Incidentally, Murphy made his point using the New York Fed's discount rates, which were at then record highs in 1920–21, and what were then record lows from 1929–31, making it difficult to reconcile the history of the Roaring '20s and the Great Depression with standard claims of "tight money" after the stock market crash of 1929.) See Robert P. Murphy, *The Politically Incorrect Guide to the Great Depression and the New Deal* (Washington, DC: Regnery 2009), pp. 76–80.

The reorganization included cosmetic and consequential changes.... **The leader of the Board of Governors (previously called the governor of the Federal Reserve Board) became the chairman [while] ... [a]ll members of the Board (formerly just called members) received the title of governor.**

The Board of Governors became increasingly independent from the executive branch of the federal government. **The secretary of treasury, who had served as the chairman of the Federal Reserve Board, and the comptroller of the currency, who had served as a member of the Federal Reserve Board, ceased to serve with the Federal Reserve after 1936. The Federal Reserve moved its meetings from the Treasury Department to a new building** constructed on Constitution Avenue and consolidated its staff at that location....

In each Federal Reserve district, the chief executive officer, who had been labeled the governor, received the title of president....

Changing the titles of the Federal Reserve's leaders had symbolic and legal significance. **Around the world, the final decision-maker in a central bank held the title of governor....** The Federal Reserve Act of 1913 labeled the chief executive officers at reserve banks as governors because the Fed's founders viewed the system as a confederation of autonomous reserve banks, each operating independently under general oversight of the Federal Reserve Board in Washington, DC. Governors were active executive officers who directed the day-to-day operations of their organization.

The Banking Act of 1935 changed the titles of the System's leaders to signify the centralization of authority at the Board of Governors and the reduction in the independence and stature of the twelve Federal Reserve District Banks....

In this rewriting of the [Federal Reserve Act], the reserve banks lost certain legal powers and much policy independence. Originally, each bank directed open-market operations in its own district. Banks decided what securities to purchase at what price for their own accounts....

The Banking Act of 1935 superseded [the previous interim] arrangement by creating the [Federal Open Market Committee's] FOMC's modern structure....**The FOMC directed open market operations for the system as a whole[,] implemented through the trading facilities at the Federal Reserve Bank of New York. Within this structure, the district banks participated in the creation of a coordinated, national monetary policy, rather than pursuing independent policies in their own districts.**

> **Control of the most important tool of monetary policy, open market operations, was vested in the FOMC, where voting rules favored the Board of Governors.** The Banking Act of 1935 [also] gave the Board of Governors control over other tools of monetary policy. The act authorized the Board to set reserve requirements and interest rates for deposits at member banks. (endnotes removed; emphasis added)[14]

And thus, through the 1935 legislation, the United States created a truly "modern" central bank patterned after the European model. Setting aside the question of the merits of this consolidation of power in Washington, it is safe to say that *this* version of the Federal Reserve would not have been approved politically back in late 1913. Indeed, the very term *federal* had been picked in order to assure Americans that this would be a relatively decentralized network of autonomous banks.

The Federal Reserve Reform Act of 1977

The other major reform we will discuss is the aptly titled Federal Reserve Reform Act of 1977. If the legislation of 1935 gave the Fed more autonomy from the federal government, the 1977 act arguably tightened the leash.

The biggest takeaway from the 1977 legislation is its explicit assignment of what is commonly referred to as the Fed's "dual mandate." As Joy Zhu of the Federal Reserve Bank of Philadelphia explains:

> When the Federal Reserve was first established in 1913, Congress directed it only to "furnish an elastic currency, to afford means of rediscounting commercial paper" and "to establish a more effective supervision of banking in the United States." **In effect, the Federal Reserve's central founding purpose was to provide a more flexible supply of currency and bank reserves in order to stem banking panics.** The original act assumed continued adherence to the gold standard regime, which tended to keep inflation under control automatically over the long run....
>
> By the 1970s, the gold standard had been abandoned and the worsening inflation and unemployment experience called into question the conduct of monetary policy. **The 1977 Reform Act amended the original act by explicitly directing the Federal Reserve to "maintain long run growth of the monetary and credit aggregates commensurate with the economy's long run potential to increase production, so as to promote the goals of maximum employment, stable prices, and moderate long-term interest rates."**

---

14. Gary Richardson, Alejandro Komai, and Michael Gou, "Banking Act of 1935," Federal Reserve History, Nov. 22, 2013, https://www.federalreservehistory.org/essays/banking_act_of_1935.

> Although the Reform Act directs the Federal Reserve to pursue three policy goals, the Federal Reserve focuses on employment and prices. (emphasis added)[15]

Thus, Congress's so-called dual mandate to the Fed is to promote maximum employment and stable prices. The debates over monetary policy among professional economists tend to focus on which policy tools and/or institutional frameworks are most conducive to achieving these two goals, which—according to those economists who subscribe to the "Phillips curve"[16]—are in tension, at least in the short run.

The Current Organization of the Federal Reserve System

There are twelve Federal Reserve Banks, one for each district, each located in its respective city. The Board of Governors is located in Washington, DC.

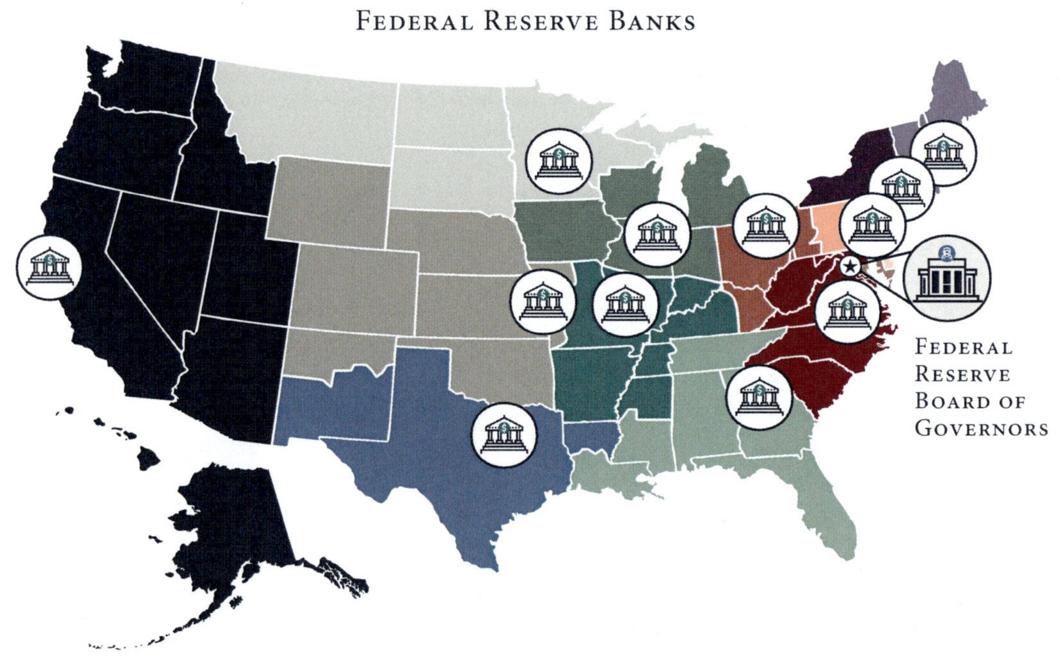

15. Joy Zhu, Federal Reserve Bank of Philadelphia, "Federal Reserve Reform Act of 1977," Nov. 22, 2013, https://www.federalreservehistory.org/essays/fed_reform_act_of_1977.

16. The Phillips curve describes an alleged tradeoff between the rate of unemployment and price inflation. See Kevin D. Hoover, "Phillips Curve," Library of Economics and Liberty (Econlib), Liberty Fund, Inc., accessed Jan. 8, 2020, https://www.econlib.org/library/Enc/PhillipsCurve.html.

In terms of personnel, the Board of Governors consists of seven members, each of whom has the title of governor (hence the *Board* of Governors). Each governor on the Board is appointed for a fourteen-year term, after being nominated by the president of the United States and confirmed by the Senate. The president must also nominate, and the Senate confirm, two members of the Board of Governors to be the chairman and vice chairman. These are only four-year-term positions, however.[17]

As the name suggests, the seven-member Board of Governors is the overarching authority over Federal Reserve actions. However, the specific component of monetary policy known as "open market operations" (analyzed in detail in chapter 4) is handled by the twelve-member Federal Open Market Committee (FOMC).

The seven members of the Board of Governors are always on the FOMC, and the remaining five members are presidents of the Reserve Banks: one is *always* the president of the New York bank, while the remaining four are drawn from the other eleven districts, serving one-year terms on a rotating basis.[18]

To conclude, the following diagram should help illustrate the relationships:

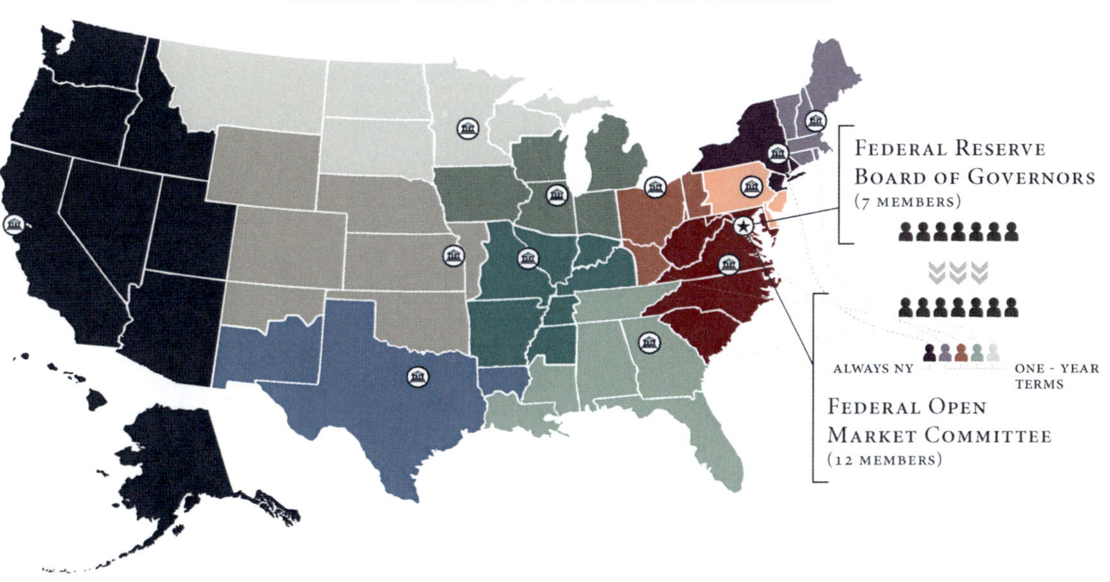

17. See "About the Federal Reserve System," and "Federal Reserve Board," Structure of the Federal Reserve System, Board of Governors of the Federal Reserve System, accessed Jan. 8, 2020, https://www.federalreserve.gov/aboutthefed/structure-federal-reserve-system.htm and https://www.federalreserve.gov/aboutthefed/structure-federal-reserve-board.htm.

18. See "About the FOMC," Federal Open Market Committee, Board of Governors of the Federal Reserve System, accessed Jan. 8, 2020, https://www.federalreserve.gov/monetarypolicy/fomc.htm.

Part II
The Mechanics

Chapter 4

Standard Open Market Operations: How the Fed and Commercial Banks "Create Money"

In this chapter we will define some of the conventional "monetary aggregates," such as M1 and M2. Then we will summarize the textbook description of how the Federal Reserve and commercial banking system "create money" when the Fed buys assets and the commercial banks extend new loans.

Although the operations we describe in this chapter are somewhat simplistic, this type of baseline description is necessary for anyone who wants to understand how money is created (and destroyed) in modern economies. In chapter 6 we will discuss the new techniques that central banks have been using since the 2008 financial crisis, while in chapter 12 we will address critics who argue that the textbook approach given in this chapter doesn't accurately reflect the causal relationship between bank reserves and new deposits.

Various Measures of "How Much Money" Is in the Economy

As we explained in chapter 1, a standard definition of *money* is that it's a medium of exchange that is (nearly) universally accepted in trade among a given community of people. However, in practice there are different ways of applying this definition, because of the special economic nature of *claims* on money.

Think back to our discussion of the historical goldsmiths. In a town where everyone agrees that gold is money, how should we treat a paper note issued by a reputable goldsmith that is an *airtight and immediate redemption ticket* entitling the bearer to a gold coin? If all of the merchants in town are just as willing to sell merchandise in exchange for these paper notes as they are for actual gold, then doesn't that render the notes issued by the goldsmith a "universally accepted medium of exchange"? So if we're trying to count up "how much money" is held by the townsfolk, shouldn't we count the physical gold *and* the total number of paper notes issued by the reputable goldsmiths?

These are the complications that give rise to different *monetary aggregates*. The following list defines some of the most popular ones, with an application to the United States today.[1]

M0: The narrowest definition of money, M0 refers to the actual physical items, such as $20 bills and coins. (Note that some classifications consider M0 equivalent to the monetary base.)

Monetary Base: The monetary base includes paper currency and coins, as well as commercial banks' (electronic) deposits at the Federal Reserve. Up until the change in regulations made in 2020, commercial banks in the US were required to keep some money "in reserve" in order to satisfy the demands of their customers who might show up to pull some cash out of their checking accounts. These "reserve requirements" could be satisfied by *either* literal paper currency in the banks' vaults, or by commercial banks' deposit balances with the Federal Reserve.

For example, suppose a particular bank had customers with total checking account balances of $1 billion. If the reserve requirement were 10 percent, then the bank would need to hold $100 million in reserves. It could satisfy this legal requirement if it held (say) $30 million in physical US currency in its own vaults on location and the Fed's own computer system said that the bank had $70 million in its own account with the Fed.

M1: When going from the monetary base to M1, we need to be careful, because we don't merely add another component, but also subtract two. Specifically, M1 consists of official US paper currency and coins held by the general public (but not in bank vaults, to avoid double counting), plus demand deposits and other checkable deposits (e.g., negotiable order of withdrawal (NOW) accounts), plus traveler's checks issued by nonbank institutions. That means M1 does not include commercial bank reserves, whether they consist in notes and coins in the vault or electronic entries on the Fed's books.

The intuition behind this classification is that M1 measures the amount of money and "very close money substitutes" held by the general public. A money

1. The description of various monetary aggregates is a condensed version of the following article by the same author: Robert P. Murphy, "The Definition of Various Monetary Aggregates," *Mises Wire*, Sept. 1, 2016, https://mises.org/library/definition-various-monetary-aggregates.

substitute, as the name suggests, is an immediately redeemable claim on actual money that everyone in the market expects to be honored at par.

M2: Everything in M1, plus most savings account balances, so-called money market account balances, the balances on retail money market mutual funds, and small denomination time deposits (including bank certificates of deposit—CDs—of less than $100,000).

There are other popular aggregates, such as MZM (money of zero maturity) and M3, which of course is M2 *plus* some additional items that are claims on actual money that are not as "economically equivalent" to money as the components in the previous categories. (For example, the implied dollar value of certain repurchase agreements, or "repos," is included in M3 but not in M1 or M2.) Fans of the Austrian school will be interested in the "true money supply" (TMS) aggregate developed by Murray Rothbard and Joseph Salerno, which corresponds to the Austrian theoretical definition of money.[2]

To avoid confusion, we should stress that *moneyness is not the same thing as liquidity.* If someone owns a $200,000 house and also has $200,000 in stocks, we would typically say that the stocks are more liquid than the house. What we mean is that the person can fairly quickly *convert* the stocks into $200,000 in actual currency (if so desired), whereas several months would be required to convert a house that's "worth $200,000."

Yet even though shares of corporate stock (especially those listed on major exchanges) are very liquid, we don't include them in the definition of money. This is because a share of stock is a claim on ownership of the corporation, not a claim on a certain amount of dollars. The price of a share of stock—quoted in dollars—can fluctuate rapidly, meaning that your "$200,000 in stocks" could fall to zero depending on the news. In contrast, if you have traveler's checks, those are claims denominated in dollars. They are not literally the same thing as money—if you're trying to pay a cab driver, it's better to have a $50 bill than a traveler's check entitling you to a $50 bill—but traveler's checks are nonetheless much better money-substitutes than shares of stock.

Figure 1 on the next page from the St. Louis Fed's website displays the monetary base, M1, and M2 for the United States since 1984. The rapid expansion of the base and M1 following the financial crisis in 2008 is evident.

---

2. Joe Salerno explains the "true money supply" aggregate, and compares it with other popular measures, in this 1987 article: Joseph T. Salerno, "The 'True' Money Supply: A Measure of the Supply of the Medium of Exchange in the U.S. Economy," *Austrian Economics Newsletter*, Spring 1987, pp. 1–6, https://cdn.mises.org/aen6_4_1_0.pdf.

Figure 1: Various US Monetary Aggregates

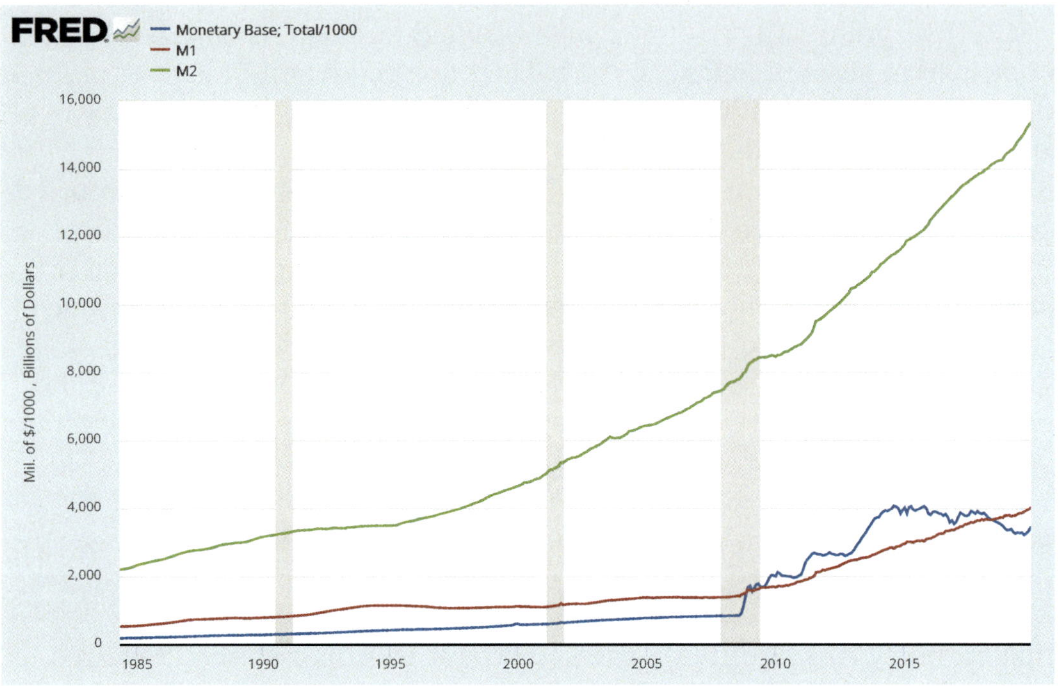

Source: St. Louis Federal Reserve (US). (Monthly data not seasonally adjusted, May 1984–December 2019)

How Commercial Banks "Create Money" under Fractional Reserves

As explained in chapter 2, our current monetary system is based on *fiat* money; there is nothing "backing up" the US dollar. The ability of the federal government/Federal Reserve to create new money simply by printing up green pieces of paper—or nowadays just through electronic activities that don't even involve physical currency—might lead some people to believe that it is *only* in a fiat money system that this type of money creation "out of thin air" is possible. However, *if they maintain less than 100 percent reserves on their checking accounts* (demand deposits), commercial banks also have the ability to create money through their lending decisions.

To see how this works, let's first imagine a town where the banks keep 100 percent reserves. Suppose there are 100,000 gold coins held by the townsfolk. Out of concerns for safety and convenience, the people deposit (say) 80,000 of the gold coins with the bankers, for which they receive paper notes entitling them to their 80,000 coins.

Now suppose the banks do *not* practice fractional reserve banking, but instead maintain 100 percent reserves. That is to say, for every paper banknote held by someone in the town, there is an actual gold coin in a bank vault to "back it."

In this arrangement, notice that the public's decision to hold some of their money in the form of banknotes rather than physical gold coins does *not* affect the total amount of money in the town. The townsfolk still hold 20,000 of the gold coins in their direct physical possession, and they also have 80,000 banknotes entitling them to gold coins. So, if each person reports how many gold coins he or she effectively has, their answers will sum up to 100,000 gold coins, which is the same amount they would have reported before using the banks.

Incidentally, we should point out that 100 percent reserve banking is *possible*, whether or not one thinks that it is desirable. Banks can charge a fee for the warehousing of their customers' money, just as the owners of storage units manage to stay in business even though they don't rent out their clients' furniture. Furthermore, remember that we are here talking about *demand deposits* (think checking accounts), where the depositors believe they are entitled to obtain their money upon demand. If instead a customer buys (say) a one-year bank certificate of deposit (CD), the bank can lend that money out to a borrower even while practicing 100 percent reserve banking, because the CD is not a promise for immediate redemption.

But now suppose that the bankers in our hypothetical town don't maintain 100 percent reserves but instead practice fractional reserve banking. The bankers realize that the public has come to trust the redeemability of the banknotes, and that *most* of the 80,000 in gold coins in their vaults will just sit there. Perhaps the bankers look at the history of transactions and conclude that so long as they always have enough gold coins in the vault to satisfy just 10 percent (say) of their total outstanding banknotes, they should be safe. In other words, the bankers reason that it would be very unlikely that the public would show up at the same time to demand more than 10 percent of the total paper notes that they'd issued.

In this case, the bankers see a great new way to earn income. Rather than "uselessly" keeping so many gold coins in their vaults, they *lend* some of the coins out to new borrowers. The borrowers then spend the money in the town, and the recipients in turn deposit the coins back into their own checking accounts at the banks. The process plays out until each gold coin sitting in a bank vault "backs up" *ten* paper banknotes held by people in the town. (See footnote 3 for links to methodical explanations of this process.[3])

In this new scenario, in which the banks only keep 10 percent reserves, what happens to the "total amount of money" in our town? If we calculate M0, the answer is still the same: there are 100,000 gold coins in the town, period. Issuing paper notes and making loans doesn't alter that fact.

3. For a more methodical explanation (including balance sheet analysis) of fractional reserve banking and central bank open market operations, see Murray N. Rothbard, *The Mystery of Banking*, 2d ed. (Auburn, AL: Ludwig von Mises Institute, 2008), chaps. 7, 9, 10, and 11, https://cdn.mises.org/Mystery%20of%20Banking_2.pdf. (Note that Rothbard is hostile toward fractional reserve banking and central banking, but his explanation of how these processes actually work is still very helpful even to readers who do not share his attitude.) For a video presentation of similar material, see Robert P. Murphy, "The Theory of Central Banking," Mises Academy, lecture presented on Jan. 16, 2011, YouTube video, https://youtu.be/6HAEPSt_12U.

However, if we use a broader aggregate such as M1, then the banks' actions *do* affect the total. Specifically, there are 20,000 gold coins still held by the public, plus *800,000* banknotes held by the public, each entitling the holder to a gold coin. In other words, the public's decision to keep 80,000 gold coins in the banks' vaults, combined with the bankers' decision to issue additional loans until the point at which they only held 10 percent reserves, caused M1 to grow from 100,000 gold coins to 820,000 gold coins. (Note that the actual unit of money would be something like a gold ounce rather than "gold coin.")

We have deliberately worked with an example of *commodity* money—in our example, gold—in order to isolate the role played by fractional reserve banking. Because the broader monetary aggregates (M1, M2, etc.) include not just the base money but also *very reliable and quick claims* on it, the actions of banks can expand or contract the total amount of money when measured in the broader sense of these aggregates. In the modern United States, the base money is actual US dollars. But if someone has $100 in a checking account at Citibank, she really thinks she *has* $100, even though Citibank might only be holding (say) $10 in its vault (proportionate to each customer) to back her checking account balance.

How the Central Bank Can Affect the Total Quantity of Bank Reserves

For a community whose base money is hunks of gold, the reserves held in bank vaults would of course be determined by how much of the yellow metal had been mined (and fashioned into bars or coins). Yet today in the United States, because the underlying base money is the US dollar itself—meaning that it currently has no redemption option but is simply fiat money—the reserves held in bank vaults are green pieces of paper featuring US presidents. In addition, a commercial bank in the US could also satisfy its reserve requirements by having (electronic) balances on deposit with the Federal Reserve. Legally speaking, a commercial bank can itself hold a "checking account" with the Fed, and its deposit balance is "as good as" currency that the commercial bank holds in its own vaults.

Because of this situation, the Federal Reserve is able to affect the monetary base through its actions. Suppose that Fed officials want to adopt an "easier" policy that increases the quantity of money in the system and also (other things equal) tends to push down short-term interest rates. To accomplish these goals, the Fed can simply buy assets, writing checks on itself.

To give a specific example, suppose the Fed buys $10 million worth of Treasury bonds originally held by a dealer in the private sector. The Fed obtains the $10 million in bonds, adding them to its balance sheet. The seller of the bonds, in turn, receives payment in the form of a check written on the Federal Reserve. Legally, the Fed can't "bounce a check"—there are no limits operationally on how much it can spend. When the dealer that sold the bonds deposits the check into its *own* bank account (at Citibank, say), the dealer's checking account balance goes up, of course, by $10 million.

Now here is the important part of the story: Citibank passes along its customer's deposited check to the Fed, which then credits *Citibank's account with the Fed* by $10 million as well. At this initial stage, Citibank itself is just treading water; its liabilities have gone up by $10 million (because the bond dealer now thinks it has an extra $10 million in its checking account with Citibank), but its assets have also gone up by $10 million—represented by Citibank's higher account balance with the Fed.

Yet look at what has happened. From Citibank's perspective, a customer effectively just deposited $10 million in new base money that entered the financial system at the moment the Fed wrote the initial check. It is as if new gold coins had suddenly entered our hypothetical town from the earlier discussion and customers had deposited the new coins with the bankers. As we saw earlier, an influx of newly deposited base money sitting in the vaults of the commercial banks allows for new lending by the banks.

The same process happens here. Because Citibank's reserves have gone up by $10 million, while its total outstanding customer deposit balances have also gone up by $10 million, it is now holding more than it needs to. Citibank can effectively lend out some of the newly deposited money, because it doesn't need to hold the entire $10 million in new reserves to back up the $10 million in extra checking account funds now held by its customers.

If the commercial banks follow a 10 percent reserve rule and the system becomes "fully loaned up" after the Fed's injection of $10 million, then the *total* increase in M1 will ultimately be $100 million. To sum up: the Fed's decision to buy $10 million in bonds created $10 million in new (base) money, but then the banking system itself effectively creates $90 million in new (broader) money on top of it.

As before, we point interested readers to the footnotes for further reading that spells out this process more exhaustively. For our purposes here, there are two crucial takeaway messages:

1. In our current fiat money system, the Federal Reserve creates new base money when it buys assets by writing checks on itself. Going the other way, the Federal Reserve *destroys* base money by selling assets (or by letting its assets mature and refraining from rolling over the proceeds). These actions do not require a literal printing press, as they can be achieved through electronic operations.

2. When the Fed injects new base money into the system, it will often be deposited into commercial banks, where it will add to reserves. Under fractional reserve banking, the new reserves give the commercial banks the ability to pyramid *new* money (as measured by M1, M2, etc.) on the system through the process of granting new loans. Going the other way, when the commercial banks restrict their loan portfolios or the public withdraws base money from the banks, it causes the broader aggregates (M1, M2, etc.) to shrink.

Chapter 5

Beyond the Fed: "Shadow Banking" and the Global Market for Dollars

Although it conjures up scary imagery, *shadow banking* is simply a term for banking operations that occur through financial intermediaries that are not traditional commercial banks. The term was coined in 2007 by economist Paul McCulley and is related to the fact that standard banking regulations often do not apply to nonbank institutions (such as hedge funds and private equity lenders), which are hence operating "in the shadows." According to estimates of nonbank credit intermediation made by the Financial Stability Board, "the global

shadow system peaked at $62 trillion in 2007, declined to $59 trillion during the crisis, and rebounded to $92 trillion by the end of 2015."[1]

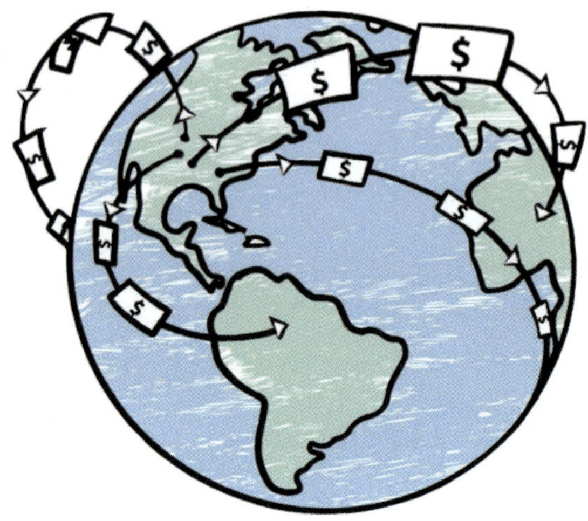

The existence of a shadow banking system thus limits the ability of governments to regulate the credit markets if they merely restrict attention to traditional banks. To understand the mechanics of today's monetary system, it is therefore important to recognize that the nexus between savers and borrowers doesn't necessarily flow through a commercial bank, the way economics textbooks often imply.

Similarly, American textbook treatments often provide a USA-specific viewpoint, even though in reality there is a global market for US dollars. In this chapter we will provide an overview of these complications to give a more accurate description of money and banking practices.

Mises and Hayek on Regulation versus Economic Reality

Although they didn't use the term "shadow banking," the Austrian economists Ludwig von Mises and Friedrich von Hayek made observations consistent with the theme of this chapter. Mises argued that Peel's Act of 1844 in England failed in its attempt to mitigate the business cycle because it limited the ability of banks to issue paper banknotes unbacked by gold but *didn't* limit banks' ability to issue customer checkbook deposits. This inconsistent regulation—which ignored the economic equivalence between banknotes and "checkbook money"—ended up discrediting the Currency school, which (in Mises's view) correctly perceived unbacked bank credit as the source of business instability.[2] See chapter 8 for more on Mises's theory of the boom-bust

1. See Laura E. Kodres, "Shadow Banks: Out of the Eyes of Regulators," Finance and Development, May 31, 2018, https://www.imf.org/external/pubs/ft/fandd/basics/52-shadow-banking.htm.

2. See Joseph T. Salerno, "Ludwig von Mises as Currency School Free Banker," in Jörg Guido Hülsmann, ed., *The Theory of Money and Fiduciary Media: Essays in Celebration of the Centennial* (Auburn, Ala.: Mises Institute, 2012), chap. 5. https://cdn.mises.org/Theory%20of%20Money%20and%20Fiduciary%20Media.pdf.

cycle, and see this chapter's footnotes for an academic paper extending Misesian business cycle theory in light of shadow banking.[3]

For his part, Hayek in a 1931 lecture gave a very modern statement of the issues involved with shadow banking, though he did not use the term:

> **[I]t is necessary to take account of certain forms of credit not connected with banks which help, as is commonly said, to economize money, or to do the work for which, if they did not exist, money in the narrower sense of the word would be required.** The criterion by which we may distinguish these circulating credits from other forms of credit which do not act as substitutes for money is that they give to somebody the means of purchasing goods without at the same time diminishing the money spending power of somebody else. This is most obviously the case when the creditor receives a bill of exchange which he may pass on in payment for other goods. It applies also to a number of other forms of commercial credit, as, for example, when book credit is simultaneously introduced in a number of successive stages of production in the place of cash payments, and so on. **The characteristic peculiarity of these forms of credit is that they spring up without being subject to any central control, but once they have come into existence their convertibility into other forms of money must be possible if a collapse of credit is to be avoided**. (bold added)[4]

These brief references illustrate that economists have been aware of the issues surrounding shadow banking for a century. The specific market structures may be new, but the issue is not.

Shadow Banking during the Housing Boom

The nature and potential problems with the shadow banking system became apparent during the housing boom of the 2000s. To illustrate, we can consider a typical example: suppose in 2006, during the height of the boom, a couple in Phoenix applies for a traditional mortgage at their local bank. The bank approves the application and lends the money to the couple, who then buy the house, which serves as the collateral on the loan. However, rather than holding the mortgage for thirty years as an asset on its own books, the com-

---

3. See Arkadiusz Sieroń, "The Role of Shadow Banking in the Business Cycle," *Quarterly Journal of Austrian Economics* 19, no. 4 (2016), available at: https://mises.org/wire/role-shadow-banking-business-cycle

4. F.A. Hayek, "Lecture IV: The Case for and Against an 'Elastic Currency,'" in Joseph T. Salerno, ed., *Prices and Production and Other Works: F.A. Hayek on Money, the Business Cycle, and the Gold Standard* (1931; repr., Auburn, Ala.: Ludwig von Mises Institute, 2008), pp. 283–300, https://mises.org/library/prices-and-production-and-other-works.

mercial bank in Phoenix turns around and sells it to a major investment bank in New York.

The Wall Street–based investment bank then takes the mortgage tied to the home in Phoenix and packages it with hundreds of other mortgages tied to houses across the United States, in order to create a "mortgage-backed security" (MBS). Every month, the incoming mortgage payments from the homebuyers across the country flow into the bucket represented by the MBS. The investment bank then sells "tranches" of the MBS to other investors, and these tranches have different risk characteristics. For example, the safest claims represent the lowest "slice" of the bucket being filled each month, whereas the riskiest claims point to the highest "slice" of the bucket. If, in a given month, some of the homebuyers fall behind on their mortgage payments, then the top slices of the bucket do not get filled, and the investors holding those particular tranches don't get paid. This relative risk was reflected in the original (lower) price for these tranches, however; there was a chance to make a higher rate of return if things went well, but it came with a higher risk of loss.[5]

In contrast, those investors who purchased the safest tranches of the MBS thought they were being quite prudent—and indeed, the credit ratings agencies (such as Moody's, Fitch, and S&P) agreed with them, giving these complex derivative assets triple-A ratings. Because the pool of mortgages was spread across the country, and because people believed "real estate was local," it seemed very unlikely that homebuyers would fall behind in their mortgages *for the whole bucket.* Even though the credit agencies' computer models recognized that, say, the Phoenix real estate market could suddenly crash 20%, that same outcome happening in Miami or San Francisco was treated as an independent statistical event. In retrospect, what *actually* happened—namely, all of the major US real estate markets crashed simultaneously—had been modeled as a once-in-a-thousand-years scenario.

Because the major ratings agencies gave their highest seal of approval to (certain types of) derivative assets tied to mortgages, pension funds and other institutional investors—including foreign ones—were allowed to gain exposure to the "hot" real estate market but apparently without taking on the usual risk. Because the commercial bank in Phoenix was not intending to hold the original mortgage, it had less incentive to vet the application provided by the couple, to make sure they had steady incomes and could afford the house. The entire process helps to explain why the usual credit safeguards were abandoned, and how buyers could continue to push up home prices as the bubble grew.

---

5. For a primer on investing in tranches derived from mortgage-based assets, see: James Chen, "Tranches," Investopedia, last modified Nov. 27, 2020, https://www.investopedia.com/terms/t/tranches.asp.

Depending on their world views and political orientations, analysts had vastly different reactions to the housing boom and bust. Some blamed "deregulation" and pointed to the shadow banking system as proof that more government oversight was needed to plug the holes. Others argued that government would never be able to keep up with evolving markets, and that it was government housing subsidies and central banks with their easy-credit policies that were to blame.[6] Either way, it is important to understand the role of shadow banking to make sense of the financial crisis that erupted in the fall of 2008.

LIBOR and the Eurodollar

LIBOR stands for London inter-bank offered rate, and is a survey average of the interest rate that leading banks in London estimate they would be charged for loans from other banks. Thomson Reuters had traditionally calculated LIBOR for five different currencies (US dollar, euro, pound sterling, yen, and Swiss franc), and seven borrowing periods (ranging from an overnight loan to a maturity length of one year). For decades, the relevant measure of LIBOR served as a benchmark against which other interest rates and derivative assets were calibrated. However, in the wake of criminal settlements due to allegations of "price-fixing" by major banks and other evolving factors in global finance, LIBOR is scheduled to be discontinued by the end of 2021.

The term *Eurodollar* actually refers to any US dollar-denominated deposit held at a financial institution outside of the United States, *or* even a USD deposit held by a foreign bank within the US. It thus has nothing to do with the euro currency, and is not restricted to dollars held in Europe; they are dollar deposits that are not subject to the same regulations as US dollars held by American banks, nor are they guaranteed by FDIC (Federal Deposit Insurance Corporation) protection (and hence they tend to earn a higher rate of return). As the CME Group explains on its website:

> After World War II when recovering economies gradually began to accumulate U.S. dollars, some countries preferred not to repatriate U.S. dollars through U.S. banks, but instead held them "off-shore", primarily in London-based banks out of the reach of the United States government.
>
> Over time, a bank lending market grew up around this pool of funds.

6. Chapter 11 makes the case that the Federal Reserve contributed to the US housing bubble. For a more elaborate treatment, including the role of federal government programs and regulations that encouraged mortgage lending to high-risk borrowers, see Thomas E. Woods, Jr., *Meltdown: A Free-Market Look at Why the Stock Market Collapsed, the Economy Tanked, and Government Bailouts Will Make Things Worse* (Washington, D.C.: Regnery Publishing, 2009).

> British bankers began referring to the lending rates in this market as the London Inter-Bank Offer Rate, also known as ICE LIBOR.[7]

By its nature, the Eurodollar market is harder to quantify than the more conventional US-based market. However, one study estimated that at its peak before the 2008 financial crisis, the size of the Eurodollar market was 87 percent of the US banking system.[8]

The Repo Market and the Fed

A *repurchase agreement* (or "repo") is a convenient method for market participants to trade short-term collateralized loans. If a firm holds liquid assets, such as US Treasury securities, but needs a quick infusion of cash, it can sell its Treasurys along with a contractual obligation to repurchase them in the near future, at a slightly higher price. Conceptually, this arrangement is equivalent to borrowing money and agreeing to repay the principal plus interest, while pledging the Treasurys as collateral in case of default. (A *reverse repo* is the same operation, seen from the point of view of the counterparty that is effectively lending its excess cash balances.) As the market has gravitated toward repos as a popular method of short-term financing, central banks and other regulators have become more interested in them.

To appreciate the size and importance of the repo market, we can quote from a 2020 article from the Federal Reserve Bank of Richmond:

> On March 17 [2020], amid the market turbulence caused by the coronavirus pandemic, the Fed reintroduced its Primary Dealer Credit Facility, or PDCF. The Fed had first created the facility during the 2007-2008 financial crisis to alleviate severe strains in the "repo" market. While mostly invisible to the public at large, the repo market plays an important role in the transmission of monetary policy. It is also a critical source of financing for nonbank financial firms, including securities brokerage houses and real estate investment trusts that specialize in mortgages.... At the end of 2019, financial firms relied on the repo markets for over $4 trillion in borrowed funds to support their activities. The renewed PDCF is designed to make loans to primary dealers of U.S. Treasury securities, who are positioned to channel liquidity to

7. See CME Group, "What Is ICE LIBOR/What Is Eurodollar," Introduction to Eurodollars course, accessed June 21, 2021, https://www.cmegroup.com/education/courses/introduction-to-eurodollars/what-is-libor-what-is-eurodollar.html#.

8. See Neels Heyneke and Mehul Daya, *The Rise and Fall of the Eurodollar System* (Nedbank, September 2016), p. 3, https://www.nedbank.co.za/content/dam/nedbank-crp/reports/Strategy/NeelsAndMehul/2016/September/TheRiseAndFallOfTheEurodollarSystem_160907.pdf.

> repo markets in what policymakers expect to be a difficult economic environment.[9]

In September 2019 (well before the coronavirus panic), there was a sudden spike in (implicit) interest rates in the repo markets, where the rate on overnight loans jumped from 2.2 to 6 percent in two days. In response, the New York Fed announced that it would enter the repo market to provide its own financing (and hence suppress interest rates), pledging to provide up to $75 billion for overnight loans, and at least $30 billion for 14-day financing.[10]

Defenders of the Fed were quick to deny that these September 2019 repo actions were a restart of "QE," and instead described them as a mere technical operation to promote market efficiency. In any event, the episode at the very least underscored the continued fragility of the US financial sector, and the difficulty of removing the central bank's footprint after it had so heavily intervened following the 2008 crisis.

The BIS and the Basel Accords

The Bank for International Settlements (BIS) was established in 1930 and is headquartered in Basel, Switzerland. According to the BIS website, its mission is "to support central banks' pursuit of monetary and financial stability through international cooperation, and to act as a bank for central banks." Its website (as of summer 2021) also explains that "the BIS is owned by 63 central banks, representing countries from around the world that together account for about 95% of world GDP."

After the final collapse of the Bretton Woods system in 1971 (which we briefly discussed in chapter 2), the central bankers of the major powers wanted a new framework for regulating global finance. Consequently the BIS formed what is now called the Basel Committee on Bank Supervision (BCBS) in 1974, with the stated aim of enhancing "financial stability by improving supervisory knowhow and the quality of banking supervision worldwide."[11]

Over the years, the BCBS has provided three major updates on its guidance for central banks and governments. The first Basel Accord (or Basel I) was formally issued in 1988. Among other provisions, it recommended that banks operating internationally must maintain a capital-to-risk-weighted-assets ratio of at least 8 percent. Basel I also defined the types of "tier 1" and "tier 2" capital, designating the different sources of funding for the bank that

9. See: https://www.richmondfed.org/publications/research/econ_focus/2020/q1/federal_reserve.

10. See: https://www.newyorkfed.org/markets/opolicy/operating_policy_190920.

11. Much of the material on the Basel Accords in this section is drawn from James Chen, "Basel Accord," last modified on Mar. 10, 2021, https://www.investopedia.com/terms/b/basel_accord.asp.

could be used to satisfy this requirement. Tier 1 capital includes common shareholder equity, and is the most reliable source of funding, as it can't be "called" or withdrawn by the original contributors in the event of a market downturn. Tier 2 capital includes hybrid instruments, some of which—such as subordinated debt—mix characteristics of equity and debt.

Basel II was issued in 2004, and refined the definitions of various regulatory concepts used in Basel I, using the credit rating of certain assets to determine their risk weighting. It also introduced the notion of tier 3 capital, which is less reliable than tier 1 or tier 2. Basel III was published in 2010, and introduced further "stress test" requirements for bank strength in the wake of the financial crisis. It eliminated the use of the weakest (tier 3) capital for satisfying regulatory requirements and highlighted the danger of financial institutions that were "too big to fail."

It should be stressed that strictly speaking, the Basel Accords are merely *recommendations* or *guidelines*, portions of which the various governments and central banks around the world may adopt for their own domestic regulation of the financial sector. For example, although Basel III was published in late 2010, the Federal Reserve waited until late 2011 to announce that it would adopt most of the new guidelines, and even then, they would be phased in over the course of years.

Bank Reserves versus Bank Capital

As we explained in the previous section, one of the key takeaways from the Basel Accords was a strengthening of capital requirements for banks (and other important financial institutions). These are different from *reserve* requirements, which are covered in standard textbooks about money and banking. In this final section of the chapter we will illustrate this distinction through a simplified example.

Let us consider the hypothetical case of Acme Commercial Bank. When Acme is first formed legally, it takes in $5 million from investors who want to be shareholders of the new bank. It then opens its doors for business and accepts $95 million from customers who deposit those funds into their brand-new Acme checking accounts. Further suppose that all of the money transferred into Acme's possession comes in the form of checks written on preexisting checking accounts at other banks. When Acme submits these checks for processing, what ultimately happens is that the Federal Reserve debits the amount held by *other banks* (such as Bank of America, Citibank, etc.) in their accounts with the Federal Reserve and credits the corresponding amount to the account held by Acme.

At this point, the managers running Acme have $100 million in assets, which are in the form of electronic deposits reflected in Acme's account with the Federal Reserve. But Acme needs to have some of this money in the form of actual currency in its vaults (and ATMs), in case its customers want to withdraw some of their checking account balances. Therefore Acme requests $6 million in actual currency, which reduces its electronic balance with the Fed to $94 million. Of this, Acme then lends out $90 million to new homebuyers who request mortgages from Acme. (Assume that all of the money spent on the houses is deposited with clients of other banks.) When the dust settles from these operations, this is what Acme's balance sheet looks like:

Hypothetical Acme Bank's Balance Sheet

ASSETS	LIABILITIES AND SHAREHOLDER EQUITY
$6 million in vault cash	$95 million in customer checking account balances
$4 million electronic deposits with Fed	$5 million in shareholder equity (Acme's capital)
$90 million in residential mortgages (held by Acme Bank)	
TOTAL: $100 million	TOTAL: $100 million

In this simple example, Acme Bank would satisfy a 10 percent *reserve* requirement. Specifically, Acme's customers collectively have $95 million on deposit in Acme checking accounts. The traditional 10% reserve requirement—which in the United States was discontinued in 2020, as we explain in chapter 7—means that Acme must hold at least $9.5 million in the form of reserves, which include both currency in the vault *and* electronic deposits held at the Fed. As the balance sheet indicates, Acme actually holds $10 million in reserves ($6 million in vault cash and $4 million on deposit with the Fed). It thus satisfies the traditional reserve requirements, and even has $500,000 in *excess reserves*, which Acme would be allowed to lend out to new borrowers.

However, when we calculate the ratio of Acme's capital to total assets, we see that it is only 5 percent ($5 million / $100 million = 5%). If Acme is subject to a regulatory regime requiring at least an 8 percent capital ratio,[12] then

12. In the real world, the capital requirements contained in the Basel Accords and country-specific regulations typically measure capital against "risk-weighted" assets. In our example we are ignoring the risk of the mortgages to keep things simple.

it falls short. Even though Acme satisfies its reserve requirements, regulators could still say that Acme is "overleveraged" or "undercapitalized," because its portfolio of assets relies too heavily on money it obtained from depositors, rather than from investors. Consider: if real estate took an unexpectedly bad turn and the market value of Acme's mortgages fell a mere 5 percent (i.e., $4.5 million), then Acme's capital—defined as assets minus liabilities—would be almost completely wiped out. This is why, other things equal, the more capital a financial institution has, the better it can handle a plunge in asset values.

Chapter 6

Central Banking Since the 2008 Financial Crisis

In chapter 4 we reviewed the textbook analysis of how a central bank buys government debt in "open market operations" to add reserves to the banking system, with which commercial banks can then advance loans to their own customers. However, in the wake of the financial crisis of 2008, the Federal Reserve and other central banks around the world adopted new "tools" (the term often used) to influence economic activity.

In this chapter we will first elaborate on conventional monetary policy, and then explain why it had apparently "lost traction" after the fall of 2008. We will then summarize some of the major changes to the practice of central banking since the financial crisis. Although we will focus on the Federal Reserve, much of our commentary is applicable to other central banks.

Before proceeding, we should clarify for the reader that most of the discussion in this chapter will be standard, with many of the details coming from Federal Reserve publications. However, even though it is legitimate to rely on establishment sources to document *what* they did, it is more dubious to take at face value their explanations for *why* they did it. Some cynics, for example, might argue that particular changes in Fed policy—such as buying not just Treasurys but also mortgage-backed securities, or initiating the payment of interest on bank reserves—were implemented in order to benefit particular firms and coalitions with political influence, rather than out of concern for the general welfare. However, it lies outside the scope of the present volume to address the motivations behind the changes described in this chapter.

Federal Reserve Monetary Policy before the 2007–08 Crisis

In chapter 4 we introduced the mechanics through which a central bank that wished to engage in "looser" or "easier" monetary policy could (1) buy assets in so-called open market operations and thereby (2) increase commercial bank reserves that would normally (3) result in more commercial bank lending and thus (4) push down market interest rates. However, in actual practice, the Federal Reserve has historically adopted different *targets* that are the immediate object of its use of this conventional mechanism. Another way of stating this is that the Fed's *policy regime* has changed over time.

For example, economists believe that it was sometime in the 1980s that the Fed moved away from targeting the total amount of money and/or bank reserves, and instead began to use its powers to target interest rates.[1] Specifically, from the 1980s until the eve of the 2008 financial crisis, the Fed's official announcements of policy decisions concerned its target for the so-called *federal funds rate*.

The federal funds rate is the interest rate that commercial banks charge each other for overnight loans of reserves. Because of legal reserve requirements (which in the United States were abolished in the spring of 2020), commercial banks had to hold a certain quantity of reserves—which, recall, consist of either paper currency in the bank vault *or* electronic deposit balances with the Fed itself—to "back up" the outstanding demand deposits held with the bank by its own customers. For example, with a 10 percent reserve requirement, if Citibank's customers collectively hold $1 billion in their checking accounts, then Citibank must hold $100 million in reserves—perhaps $30 million in actual paper currency in Citibank's vaults and the remaining $70 million in Citibank's electronic account balance in the Fed's computer system.

Now when commercial banks had a reserve requirement (which was enforced at the end of each business day), if they made new loans, they might need to obtain more reserves in order to satisfy the requirement. To continue our example from above, if Citibank granted $10 million in loans to new borrowers, then immediately after crediting the $10 million to their checking accounts—but before they spent any of it—Citibank's new position would be: $1.01 billion in outstanding customer checking account balances, with $30 million still in the

1. It's actually difficult to pinpoint precisely *when* the Fed changed its approach, because it made no formal announcement, but an analysis of the transcripts of Fed meetings suggests that it was in 1982. See Daniel L. Thornton, "When Did the FOMC Begin Targeting the Federal Funds Rate? What the Verbatim Transcripts Tell Us" (Federal Reserve Bank of St. Louis working paper no. 2004–015B, Federal Reserve Bank of St. Louis, St. Louis, MO, Aug. 2004, rev. May 2005), available at https://papers.ssrn.com/sol3/papers.cfm?abstract_id=760518.

vault and $70 million still on deposit with the Fed. At the end of the business day, to avoid being assessed a penalty, Citibank would now need to have $101 million in reserves ($1.01 billion x 10% = $101 million). But at the moment it only has $100 million ($30 million + $70 million = $100 million). Being short $1 million in reserves, Citibank would go out into the federal funds market and borrow (overnight) $1 million in excess reserves from *other* commercial banks that have more reserves at that moment than they need to satisfy their own legal reserve requirements. The market-determined rate of interest (quoted on an annualized basis, even though the loan would only be for one day) on this overnight loan of $1 million would be the federal funds rate.

To reiterate, during the period from the 1980s up until the brewing crisis in 2007–08, when the Federal Reserve made an announcement, it would typically tell the world what it was doing *regarding its target for the federal funds rate*. When the *actual* federal funds rate in the market was higher than the Fed's target, the Fed would buy more assets, injecting new bank reserves into the system and thus push down the fed funds rate. On the other hand, when the Fed *raised* its target and wanted to push up the actual fed funds rate, it would do the opposite: it would sell off some of its assets, thereby draining bank reserves from the system and (since the quantity was now smaller) pushing up the interest rate that bankers themselves had to pay to other bankers in order to borrow reserves.

Another Old-School "Tool": The Discount Window

Although the use of open market operations to achieve its desired federal funds rate target was the primary "tool" that the Fed used from the 1980s up through 2008, another power that the Fed has held from its very inception is the ability to *directly* lend to financial institutions through the so-called discount window. As the Fed's website explains:

> When the Federal Reserve System was established in 1913, lending reserve funds through the Discount Window was intended as the principal instrument of central banking operations. Although the Window was long ago superseded by open market operations as the most important tool of monetary policy, it still plays a complementary role. The Discount Window functions as a safety valve in relieving pressures in reserve markets; extensions of credit can help relieve liquidity strains in a depository institution and in the banking system as a whole.[2]

2. See "The Federal Reserve Discount Window," Federal Reserve Discount Window and Payment Risk (website), last modified June 22, 2015, https://www.frbdiscountwindow.org/pages/general-information/the-discount-window.

For the purposes of an introductory text, the important thing to note is that when the Fed (tries to) push down interest rates through open market operations, *the Fed is NOT directly lending new reserves to the banks.* Instead, it is paying newly created reserves over to the sellers of financial assets in exchange for their property. When those new reserves are deposited into the banking system, the recipient *banks* lend them out to other banks and thereby (tend to) push down the fed funds rate.

In contrast, when a depository institution uses the discount window, it is *directly* borrowing newly created reserves from the Federal Reserve itself. In order to keep the discount window as a fallback option, the Fed typically sets the interest rate on its discount window lending—called the *discount rate*—above the federal funds rate.[3]

Out with Fed Funds Rate Targets, In with "QE"

The most obvious change in the conduct of monetary policy since 2008 was the de-emphasis on interest rates and the focus on the size (and composition) of asset purchases. Specifically, investors and the public at large began fretting over what the Fed would do with its various rounds of "quantitative easing" or simply "QE." (Note that the Federal Reserve itself has never officially used this popular term to describe its operations.)

Prior to the financial crisis most people probably never thought about—and the Fed itself certainly didn't emphasize—the fact that when the Fed cut or raised interest rates it didn't simply turn a dial but instead had to buy or sell assets, and thereby create or destroy dollar reserves in the financial system. But when the federal funds rate collapsed from 4 percent in late 2007 to just about *zero* percent by the end of 2008, it was clear that Fed officials could no longer announce additional rate cuts to show the world they were "helping." (To be clear, many Austrian economists would disagree that easier money is the solution to an ailing economy, as we explain in chapter 8.)

In this context, soon after the financial crisis struck, the Fed began announcing not merely its plans for the future path of the federal funds rate, but also its intentions for the scale, pace, and composition of its asset purchases. For example, in November 2010 the Federal Open Market Committee (FOMC) announced its plans for what the financial press would soon dub "QE2":

> To promote a stronger pace of economic recovery and to help ensure that inflation, over time, is at levels consistent with its mandate, the Committee decided today to expand its holdings of securities. The

3. Note that there are different rates the Fed charges based on the length of the loan and the creditworthiness of the borrower, and for all such discount lending the borrower must pledge collateral of adequate quality.

> Committee will maintain its existing policy of reinvesting principai payments from its securities holdings. In addition, the Committee intends to purchase a further $600 billion of longer-term Treasury securities by the end of the second quarter of 2011, a pace of about $75 billion per month.[4]

When this second round of quantitative easing didn't do the trick, the Fed in September 2012 announced what would be dubbed "QE3," in which it would buy $40 billion in additional mortgage-backed securities *per month.*[5] (Because there was not a set dollar-limit on the total plan, this program was also dubbed "QE-infinity" by some cynics.) A few months later, in December 2012, the Fed announced that it would also begin buying an additional $45 billion per month in (longer-term) Treasury securities, meaning that QE3 at that point consisted of adding $85 billion in new assets monthly to the Fed's balance sheet.[6]

And thus, what were once mechanical considerations kept behind the scenes now became front and center: the Fed no longer relied merely on interest rate targets to communicate its intentions to the public, but now announced detailed descriptions of its planned asset purchases. Since the federal funds rate had hit rock-bottom by late 2008, the subsequent rounds of quantitative easing allowed the Fed to show that it hadn't "run out of ammunition" and could continue to inject money in an attempt to boost spending through a "wealth effect" and reduced longer-term interest rates.

Another Major Innovation: Fed Begins Paying Interest on Reserves

Another significant change in Fed policy was its announcement in September 2008 that in October it would begin paying interest to commercial banks on the reserve balances that they kept on deposit (or "parked") with the Fed.

Because many commentators argue that this new policy was at least partially responsible for the failure of the Fed's extraordinary injections of new

4. See "FOMC Statement," Press Releases, Board of Governors of the Federal Reserve System, Nov. 3, 2010, https://www.federalreserve.gov/newsevents/pressreleases/monetary20101103a.htm.

5. See "Federal Reserve Issues FOMC Statement," Press Releases, Board of Governors of the Federal Reserve System, Sept. 13, 2012, https://www.federalreserve.gov/newsevents/pressreleases/monetary20120913a.htm.

6. See "Federal Reserve Issues FOMC Statement," Press Releases, Board of Governors of the Federal Reserve System, Dec. 12, 2012, https://www.federalreserve.gov/newsevents/pressreleases/monetary20121212a.htm.

reserves to lead to a comparable increase in bank lending and consumer price inflation, we will cover this topic in detail in chapter 13.

For our purposes in the present chapter, it is enough to note that the new policy of paying interest on reserves allowed the Fed to decouple its asset purchases from its target for the federal funds rate. Specifically, in October of 2008 the Fed wanted to (among other things) calm the panic in the financial sector by buying large quantities of mortgage-backed securities (which were then considered "toxic assets"). Normally, such large asset purchases would flood the system with new reserves and push down the federal funds rate. But since the Fed had not yet wanted the fed funds rate to sink to zero percent, it established a "floor" under the fed funds rate by paying commercial banks interest on the reserves that they kept on deposit with the Fed. The intuition here is that a commercial bank could always earn a guaranteed return from the Fed by keeping its excess reserves parked at the Fed rather than lending them to other commercial banks. Therefore, if a commercial bank needed to borrow excess reserves in order to satisfy its reserve requirements, it would have to offer at least as much as the prevailing rate that the Fed itself was paying on reserve balances.

At the other end of the cycle, when the Fed began "normalizing" its policy stance and finally began raising its target for the federal funds rate in December 2015, it did *not* do so by selling off some of its assets (and thereby draining reserves out of the banking system), as the textbook description of monetary policy would have it. Instead, the Fed maintained its outstanding stock of assets and caused the fed funds rate to increase by raising the interest rate that it paid to banks on their reserves kept at the Fed. In this way, the Fed could raise interest rates *without* selling off its large holdings of Treasury bonds and mortgage-backed securities, actions that may have jeopardized the still fragile recovery in financial markets.

To sum up, among other implications,[7] the new policy begun in October 2008 of paying interest on reserves allowed the Fed to decouple its asset purchases from its desired target for the market-clearing federal funds rate.

7. George Selgin has devoted an entire monograph to the (perhaps unintended) consequences of the Fed's decision to begin paying interest on reserves: "Floored! How a Misguided Fed Experiment Deepened and Prolonged the Great Recession" (Cato working paper, no. 50/CMFA no. 11, Center for Monetary and Financial Alternatives, Cato Institute, Washington, DC, Mar. 1, 2018, rev. Mar. 13, 2018), available at https://www.cato.org/sites/cato.org/files/pubs/pdf/working-paper-50-updated-3.pdf, published as Floored! How a Misguided Fed Experiment Deepened and Prolonged the Great Recession (Washington, DC: Cato Institute, 2018).

A Timeline of Additional "Tools" Added to the Fed's Kit

Drawing on the Federal Reserve's timeline, the following table summarizes some of the innovations in Fed policy introduced as the housing and credit markets began deteriorating in late 2007. (The descriptions in the second column are direct quotations from the St. Louis Fed timeline, with bold added by the present author.)

Date	Action
12/12/07	The Federal Reserve Board announces the creation of a Term Auction Facility (TAF) in which **fixed amounts of term funds will be auctioned to depository institutions against a wide variety of collateral**. The FOMC authorizes temporary reciprocal currency arrangements (swap lines) with the European Central Bank (ECB) and the Swiss National Bank (SNB).
3/11/08	The Federal Reserve Board announces the creation of the Term Securities Lending Facility (TSLF), which will **lend up to $200 billion of Treasury securities for 28-day terms against federal agency debt, federal agency residential mortgage-backed securities (MBS), non-agency AAA/Aaa private label residential MBS**, and other securities.
3/16/08	The Federal Reserve Board establishes the Primary Dealer Credit Facility (PDCF), extending credit to primary dealers at the primary credit rate against a broad range of investment grade securities.
3/24/08	**The Federal Reserve Bank of New York announces that it will provide term financing to facilitate JPMorgan Chase & Co.'s acquisition of The Bear Stearns Companies Inc. A limited liability company (Maiden Lane) is formed to control $30 billion of Bear Stearns assets** that are pledged as security for $29 billion in term financing from the New York Fed at its primary credit rate.
6/13/08	**The Federal Reserve Board authorizes the Federal Reserve Bank of New York to lend to the Federal National Mortgage Association (Fannie Mae) and the Federal Home Loan Mortgage Corporation (Freddie Mac)**, should such lending prove necessary.
9/16/08	The Federal Reserve Board authorizes the Federal Reserve Bank of New York to **lend up to $85 billion to the American International Group (AIG)** under Section 13(3) of the Federal Reserve Act.

Date	Action
9/18/08	The FOMC expands existing swap lines by $180 billion and authorizes new swap lines with the Bank of Japan, Bank of England, and Bank of Canada.
9/19/08	The Federal Reserve Board announces the creation of the Asset-Backed Commercial Paper Money Market Mutual Fund Liquidity Facility (AMLF) to extend non-recourse loans at the primary credit rate to U.S. depository institutions and bank holding companies **to finance their purchase of high-quality asset-backed commercial paper from money market mutual funds.** The Federal Reserve Board also announces plans to purchase federal agency discount notes (short-term debt obligations issued by Fannie Mae, Freddie Mac, and Federal Home Loan Banks) from primary dealers.
9/21/08	The Federal Reserve Board approves applications of investment banking companies Goldman Sachs and Morgan Stanley to become bank holding companies.
9/29/08	The FOMC authorizes a $330 billion expansion of swap lines with Bank of Canada, Bank of England, Bank of Japan, Danmarks Nationalbank, ECB, Norges Bank, Reserve Bank of Australia, Sveriges Riksbank, and Swiss National Bank. Swap lines outstanding now total $620 billion.
9/26/08	The Federal Reserve Board announces that **the Fed will pay interest on depository institutions' required and excess reserve balances** at an average of the federal funds target rate less 10 basis points on required reserves and less 75 basis points on excess reserves.
10/7/08	The Federal Reserve Board announces **the creation of the Commercial Paper Funding Facility (CPFF), which will provide a liquidity backstop to U.S. issuers of commercial paper** through a special purpose vehicle that will purchase three-month unsecured and asset-backed commercial paper directly from eligible issuers.
10/8/08	The Federal Reserve Board authorizes the Federal Reserve Bank of New York to borrow up to $37.8 billion in investment-grade, fixed-income securities from American International Group (AIG) in return for cash collateral.
10/21/08	The Federal Reserve Board announces creation of the Money Market Investor Funding Facility (MMIFF). Under the facility, the Federal Reserve Bank of New York provides senior secured funding to a series of special purpose vehicles to facilitate the purchase of assets from eligible investors, such as U.S. money market mutual

Date	Action
	funds. **Among the assets the facility will purchase are U.S. dollar-denominated certificates of deposit and commercial paper** issued by highly rated financial institutions with a maturity of 90 days or less.
10/29/08	The FOMC also establishes swap lines with the Banco Central do Brasil, Banco de Mexico, Bank of Korea, and the Monetary Authority of Singapore for up to $30 billion each.
10/10/08	The Federal Reserve Board and the U.S. Treasury Department announce a restructuring of the government's financial support of AIG....The Federal Reserve Board also authorizes the Federal Reserve Bank of New York to establish two new lending facilities for AIG: The Residential Mortgage-Backed Securities Facility will lend up to $22.5 billion to a newly formed limited liability company (LLC) to purchase residential MBS from AIG; **the Collateralized Debt Obligations Facility will lend up to $30 billion to a newly formed LLC to purchase CDOs from AIG (Maiden Lane III LLC).**
10/23/08	The U.S. Treasury Department, Federal Reserve Board, and FDIC [Federal Deposit Insurance Corporation] jointly announce an agreement with Citigroup to provide a package of guarantees, liquidity access, and capital. Citigroup will issue preferred shares to the Treasury and FDIC in exchange for protection against losses on a $306 billion pool of commercial and residential securities held by Citigroup. **The Federal Reserve will backstop residual risk in the asset pool through a non-recourse loan.**
11/25/08	The Federal Reserve Board announces the creation of the **Term Asset-Backed Securities Lending Facility (TALF)**, under which the Federal Reserve Bank of New York will lend up to $200 billion on a non-recourse basis to holders of **AAA-rated asset-backed securities and recently originated consumer and small business loans.**
11/25/08	**The Federal Reserve Board announces a new program to purchase direct obligations of housing related government-sponsored enterprises** (GSEs)—Fannie Mae, Freddie Mac and Federal Home Loan Banks—and MBS backed by the GSEs. Purchases of up to $100 billion in GSE direct obligations will be conducted as auctions among Federal Reserve primary dealers. Purchases of up to $500 billion in MBS will be conducted by asset managers.

Date	Action
12/22/08	The Federal Reserve Board approves the application of CIT Group Inc., an $81 billion financing company, to become a bank holding company.
1/16/09	The U.S. Treasury Department, Federal Reserve, and FDIC announce a package of guarantees, liquidity access, and capital for Bank of America. The U.S. Treasury and the FDIC will enter a loss-sharing arrangement with Bank of America on a $118 billion portfolio of loans, securities, and other assets in exchange for preferred shares. In addition, and if necessary, **the Federal Reserve will provide a non-recourse loan to back-stop residual risk in the portfolio**.
2/10/09	The Federal Reserve Board announces that is prepared to expand the Term Asset-Backed Securities Loan Facility (TALF) to as much as **$1 trillion and broaden the eligible collateral to include AAA-rated commercial mortgage-backed securities, private-label residential mortgage-backed securities**, and other asset-backed securities.
3/18/09	[T]he FOMC decides to **increase the size of the Federal Reserve's balance sheet by purchasing up to an additional $750 billion of agency mortgage-backed securities, bringing its total purchases of these securities to up to $1.25 trillion this year**, and to increase its purchases of agency debt this year by up to $100 billion to a total of up to $200 billion. **The FOMC also decides to purchase up to $300 billion of longer-term Treasury securities over the next six months** to help improve conditions in private credit markets. Finally, the FOMC announces that it anticipates expanding the range of eligible collateral for the TALF (Term Asset-Backed Securities Loan Facility).
3/19/09	The Federal Reserve Board announces an expansion of the eligible collateral for loans extended by the Term Asset-Backed Securities Loan Facility (TALF) to **include asset-backed securities backed by mortgage servicing advances, loans or leases related to business equipment, leases of vehicle fleets, and floorplan loans.**

Source: St. Louis Federal Reserve[8]

8. Table excerpted from "The Financial Crisis: A Timeline of Events and Policy Actions," Federal Reserve Bank of St. Louis, http://timeline.stlouisfed.org/index.cfm?p=timeline. This page is no longer live, but the Federal Reserve Archival System for Economic Research (FRASER) has preserved the timeline. See "Federal Reserve of St. Louis' Financial Crisis Timeline," FRASER, Federal Reserve Bank of St. Louis, accessed Feb. 24, 2020, https://fraser.stlouisfed.org/timeline/financial-crisis.

As the table above makes clear, the brewing crisis in the housing and credit markets in 2007–08 allowed for an extraordinary increase in the power of the Federal Reserve. This development led the present author to describe then chair of the Fed Ben Bernanke as "the FDR of central bankers."[9]

Were the Fed's Post-Crisis Asset Purchases Legal?

As explained in the previous section, since the advent of the financial crisis the Federal Reserve has drastically increased not merely the *amount* of assets that it purchases but also the *types* of assets. The figure below illustrates the dramatic expansion and change in composition of the Fed's balance sheet:

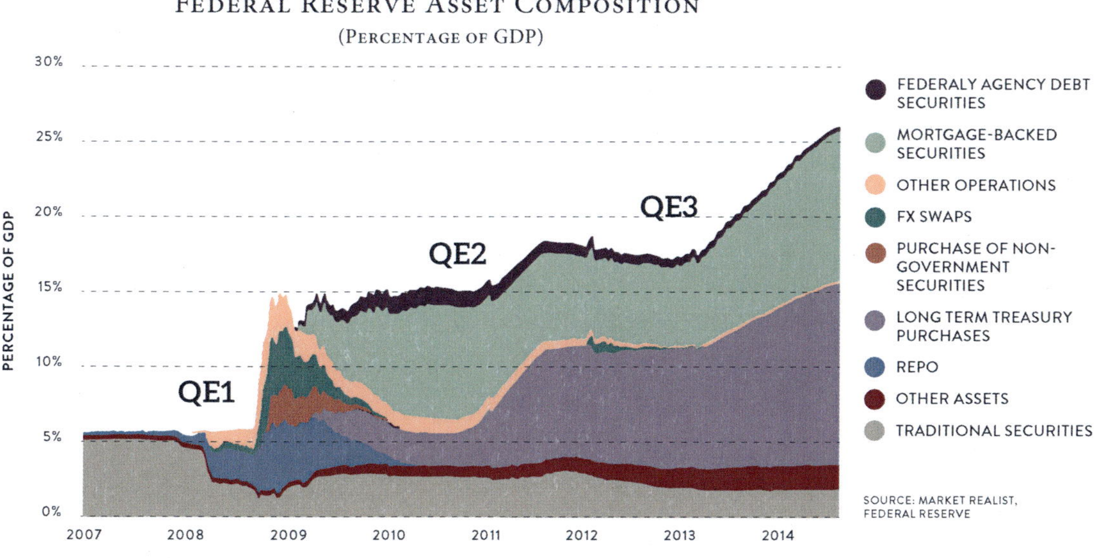

9. Robert P. Murphy, "Ben Bernanke, The FDR of Central Bankers," in *The Fed at One Hundred: A Critical View on the Federal Reserve System*, ed. David Howden and Joseph T. Salerno (London and New York: Springer, 2014), pp. 31–41.

In addition to the profound questions concerning the efficacy and wisdom of the Fed's dramatic new role in the economy, there is also the stark issue of whether the Fed's post-crisis actions were *legal.* In order to avoid the obvious invitation to corruption, the legislation authorizing the Federal Reserve put limits on what the US central bank could buy. After all, if the people running the New York Federal Reserve Bank could create money electronically with which to buy specific shares of Wall Street stock, there would be vast opportunities for abuse.

When justifying the new powers that it took after the financial crisis struck, Fed officials typically appealed to the section of the Federal Reserve Act giving it liberal powers to *lend* money to financial institutions. In practice, the Fed *lent* money to newly created Limited Liability Corporations (LLCs) named "Maiden Lane"—referring to the street in New York's financial district—that would then use the money borrowed from the Fed to purchase the desired assets.[10]

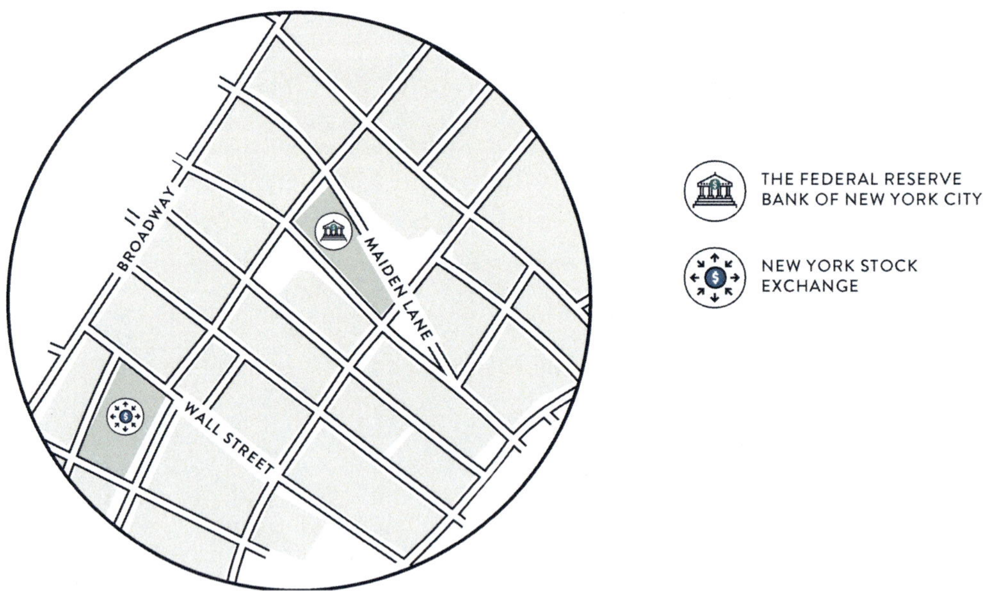

10. For an article discussing the dubious legality of this arrangement, see Alexander Mehra, "Legal Authority in Unusual and Exigent Circumstances: The Federal Reserve and the Financial Crisis," University of Pennsylvania *Journal of Business Law* 13, no. 1 (2010): 221–73, https://www.law.upenn.edu/journals/jbl/articles/volume13/issue1/Mehra13U.Pa.J.Bus.L.221(2010).pdf.

Chapter 7

The Fed's Policies Since the 2020 Coronavirus Panic

In chapter 6 we summarized some of the major changes in how central banks have operated since the 2008 financial crisis. In the present chapter, we detail some of the even more recent changes in Federal Reserve operations since the onset of the coronavirus panic in March 2020.

Size of the Fed's Balance Sheet

The most obvious change in Fed policy has been the dramatic expansion of its balance sheet since March 2020.

As Figure 1 indicates, the explosion in Fed asset purchases since March 2020 dwarfs even the three rounds of QE (quantitative easing) following the 2008 financial crisis. Indeed, from March 4, 2020, through March 3, 2021, the Fed increased its assets from $4.2 trillion to $7.6 trillion, an incredible *one-year jump* of $3.3 trillion (or 78 percent). Furthermore, as the graph reveals, the upward trajectory continues as of this writing.

Composition of the Fed's Balance Sheet

Besides the *quantitative* change in the Fed's asset purchases, there has been a *qualitative* change in the type of asset. In particular, the Fed is now buying large amounts of private sector corporate bonds (both individually and exchange-traded funds); as of the mid-May 2021 balance sheet report, the Fed's "Corporate Credit Facilities LLC" held almost $26 billion in assets.[1] This change

1. For the current summary of the Fed's balance sheet, see Board of Governors of the Federal Reserve System, "Factors Affecting Reserve Balances of Depository Institutions and Condition

Figure 1: Total Assets Held by the Federal Reserve

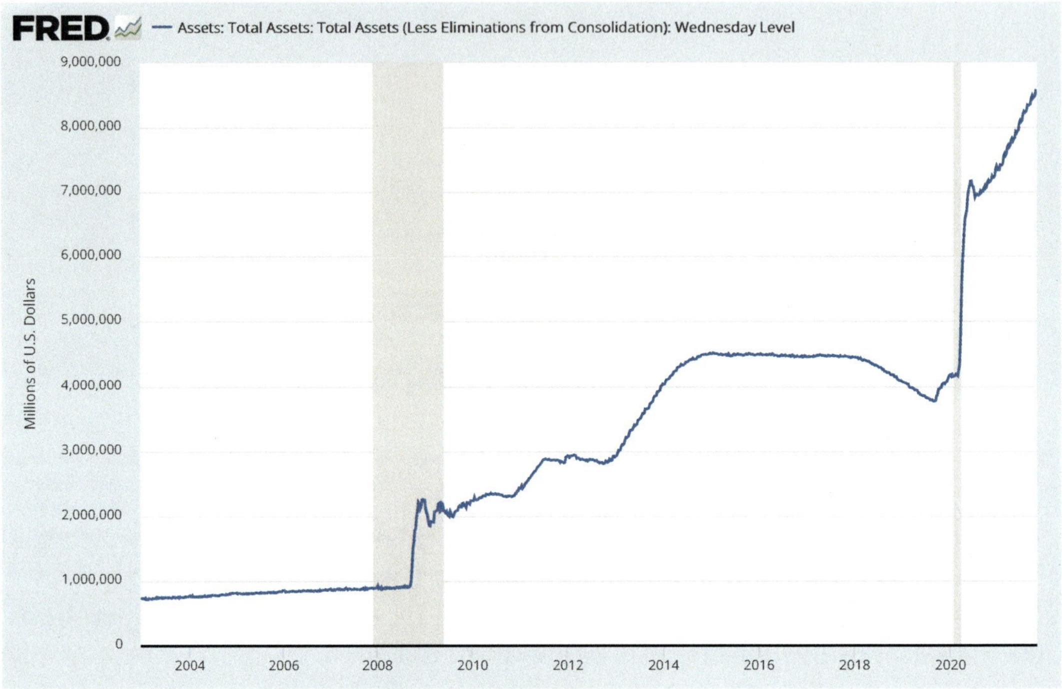

Source: Board of Governors of the Federal Reserve System (US)

in policy would have been extremely controversial (if only for the potential corruption) prior to the financial crisis, but it is now a seemingly natural outgrowth of the expansion of Fed discretionary power that began in the fall of 2008.

The Fed announced the creation of the Primary and Secondary Corporate Credit Facilities LLC in March 2020 (though it did not begin aggressively buying corporate debt—which had to have been rated "investment grade" before the pandemic hit—until June 2020[2]). At the same time, the Fed announced expansions of preexisting asset purchase programs, as well as the creation of a "Term Asset-Backed Securities Loan Facility (TALF), to support the flow of credit to consumers and businesses," which would "enable the issuance of asset-backed securities (ABS) backed by student loans, auto loans, credit card loans, loans guaranteed by the Small Business Administration (SBA), and certain other assets."[3]

Statement of Federal Reserve Banks," H.4.1 (Factors Affecting Reserve Balances) statistical release, May 27, 2021, https://www.federalreserve.gov/releases/h41/current/h41.pdf.

2. See Nancy Marshall-Genzer, "The Fed Starts Buying Corporate Bonds," Marketplace, June 16, 2020, https://www.marketplace.org/2020/06/16/the-fed-starts-buying-corporate-bonds/.

3. See the Fed's announcement of its new facilities in its March 23, 2020, press release: Board

At this point, the Federal Reserve now has the capability of influencing the credit markets not just for commercial banks, but for commercial and residential real estate, corporate bonds, commercial paper, cars, student loans, and even personal credit cards.

Abolition of Reserve Requirements for US Banks

In an emergency statement issued in the evening on Sunday, March 15, 2020, the Fed announced a host of new policies in light of the then emerging alarm over the coronavirus.[4] In addition to cutting the target for the federal funds rate back down to 0 percent (with a range of up to 0.25 percent) and pledging to increase the scale of its asset purchases, the Federal Open Market Committee (FOMC) statement concluded with this tantalizing paragraph:

> In a related set of actions to support the credit needs of households and businesses, the Federal Reserve announced measures related to the discount window, intraday credit, bank capital and liquidity buffers, **reserve requirements**, and—in coordination with other central banks—the U.S. dollar liquidity swap line arrangements. More information can be found on the Federal Reserve Board's website. (bold added)

The final word, "website," contained a hyperlink to the Fed's main website. Yet if one looked at the compilation of press releases, there was an additional item posted on March 15, 2020, titled "Federal Reserve Actions to Support the Flow of Credit to Households and Businesses," which was alluded to in the official FOMC statement.[5] For our purposes, we will highlight the last measure listed in this supplemental statement:

> **Reserve Requirements**
>
> For many years, reserve requirements played a central role in the implementation of monetary policy by creating a stable demand for reserves. In January 2019, the FOMC announced its intention to implement monetary policy in an ample reserves regime. Reserve requirements do not play a significant role in this operating framework.

---

of Governors of the Federal Reserve System, "Federal Reserve Announces Extensive New Measures to Support the Economy," press release, Mar. 23, 2020, last modified July 28, 2020, https://www.federalreserve.gov/newsevents/pressreleases/monetary20200323b.htm.

4. See the FOMC statement of March 15, 2020: Board of Governors of the Federal Reserve System, "Federal Reserve Issues FOMC Statement," press release, Mar. 15, 2020, https://www.federalreserve.gov/newsevents/pressreleases/monetary20200315a.htm.

5. The supplemental Fed posting from March 15, 2020, is Board of Governors of the Federal Reserve System, "Federal Reserve Actions to Support the Flow of Credit to Households and Businesses," press release, Mar. 15, 2020, https://www.federalreserve.gov/newsevents/pressreleases/monetary20200315b.htm.

> In light of the shift to an ample reserves regime, **the Board has reduced reserve requirement ratios to zero percent** effective on March 26, [2020,] the beginning of the next reserve maintenance period. This action eliminates reserve requirements for thousands of depository institutions and will help to support lending to households and businesses. (bold added)

Since the Fed's actions following the financial crisis of 2008, the US banking system as a whole has been awash with excess reserves (see the second chart in chapter 13). This is because following the Fed's injections of new reserves under the various rounds of quantitative easing, the commercial banks did not create new loans for their own customers to the maximum amount legally allowed. Therefore, the *immediate* impact of the Fed's 2020 decision to abolish reserve requirements should be minimal, since the original reserve requirements were not binding at the time of the change.

However, even though the US banking system had more than enough reserves to cover its requirements, it is still the case that the level of required reserves rose dramatically—quintupling from about $40 billion to more than $200 billion—since the financial crisis, as the following chart reveals:

Figure 2: Required Reserves of US Depository Institutions

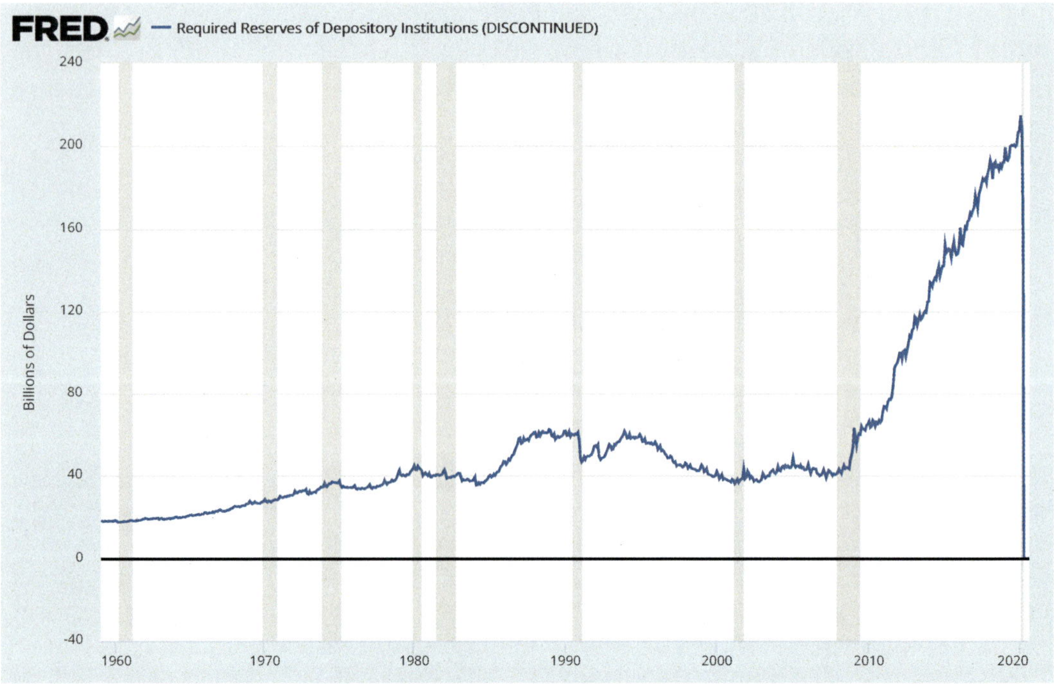

Source: Board of Governors of the Federal Reserve System (US)

(In Figure 2, the Required Reserves line falls vertically to zero at the end, because the Fed's policy change abolished reserve requirements.)

To avoid confusion, the reader should remember that in addition to the Fed's direct actions that caused the monetary base to soar, money "held by the public" (which we can summarize by the monetary aggregate M1) also dramatically increased following the 2008 crisis. Later in this chapter we will explain the redefinition of M1 in 2020, but the graph of M1 we present in chapter 13 shows the measure in its old definition; the reader can see that it rose steadily after 2008, and jumped sharply in 2020. To the extent that much of this increase in money held by the public took the form not of actual physical currency, but of checking account balances at commercial banks, the statutorily required reserves rose correspondingly—as reflected in the chart above.

Some analysts argue that the Fed's abolition of reserve requirements merely reflects the new realities of modern banking. With the 1994 introduction of retail "sweep accounts"[6] and especially in the post-2008 era of large central bank balance sheets, some have argued that reserve requirements are anachronistic and no longer influence commercial bank lending decisions, except to necessitate cumbersome maneuvers.[7]

Although the situation is no doubt nuanced, some of the more glib defenses of the new Fed policy prove too much. For example, the Fed's own explanation (quoted above) says, "This action eliminates reserve requirements for thousands of depository institutions and will help to support lending to households and businesses." If it were indeed the case that the reserve requirements did *not* constrain bank lending—as claimed by some of those dismissing the announcement as a bit of trivia—then abolishing the requirements wouldn't support lending to households and businesses.

To put it simply, if the abolition of reserve requirements really have no effect, then one wonders why the Fed decided to implement the move along with the other emergency measures activated at the onset of the coronavirus crisis. At the very least, abolishing the requirements will give the commercial

---

6. For the connection between sweep accounts and reserve requirements, see Richard G. Anderson and Robert H. Rasche, "Retail Sweep Programs and Bank Reserves, 1994–1999," *Review* 83, no. 1 (January/February 2001): 51–72, https://files.stlouisfed.org/files/htdocs/publications/review/01/0101ra.pdf.

7. For example, in his February 10, 2010, testimony before the House Committee on Financial Services, then Fed chair Ben Bernanke said that the "Federal Reserve believes it is possible that, ultimately, its operating framework will allow the elimination of minimum reserve requirements, which impose costs and distortions on the banking system." Benjamin Bernanke, "Federal Reserve's Exit Strategy" (statement before the Committee on Financial Services, US House of Representatives, Washington, DC, Feb. 10, 2010), quoted in Vijay Boyapati, "Why Credit Deflation Is More Likely Than Mass Inflation," *Libertarian Papers* 2, art. no. 43, (2010): 1–28, https://cdn.mises.org/-2-43_2.pdf.

banks freer rein to make loans down the road, if conditions return to a scenario where the original rules *would* have provided a check on additional bank credit inflation.

Redefinition of M1

On February 23, 2021, the Fed announced:

> As announced on December 17, 2020, the Board's Statistical Release H.6, "Money Stock Measures," will recognize savings deposits as a type of transaction account, starting with the publication today. This recognition reflects the Board's action on April 24, 2020, to remove the regulatory distinction between transaction accounts and savings deposits by deleting the six-per-month transfer limit on savings deposits in Regulation D. This change means that savings deposits have had a similar regulatory definition and the same liquidity characteristics as the transaction accounts reported as "Other checkable deposits" on the H.6 statistical release since the change to Regulation D. Consequently, today's H.6 statistical release combines release items "Savings deposits" and "Other checkable deposits" retroactively back to May 2020 and includes the resulting sum, reported as "Other liquid deposits," in the M1 monetary aggregate. This action increases the M1 monetary aggregate significantly while leaving the M2 monetary aggregate unchanged.[8]

In other words, in late April of 2020, the Fed removed some of the limits on savings deposits in a way that made them equivalent to checking account deposits. As such, savings deposits from May 2020 forward are now included in M1, whereas before they had been excluded from it. Yet either way, savings deposits were *always* included in M2. Consequently, we can look at the Fed's graphs of both M1 and M2 to isolate the impact of the reclassification, see Figure 3.

As the figure indicates, there was a massive spike in the official M1 measure in May 2020, *largely* (though not entirely) reflecting the reclassification of savings deposits as part of M1. However, note that M2 *also rose* sharply at exactly this time, reflecting a genuine increase in money held by the public because of the coronavirus panic and Fed policy. (Also remember that the M1 chart shown in chapter 13 was made based on the *original* M1 numbers, before the retroactive reclassification occurred. The chart in chapter 13 shows that M1, even according to the old definition, truly did spike in the spring of 2020.)

---

8. The block quotation is taken from the February 23, 2021, announcement available at this feed: Board of Governors of the Federal Reserve System, "Money Stock Revisions," H.6 (Money Stock Measures) statistical release, Mar. 23, 2021, https://www.federalreserve.gov/feeds/h6.html.

Figure 3: M1 and M2 Money Stock, Showing Effect of May 2020 Redefinition

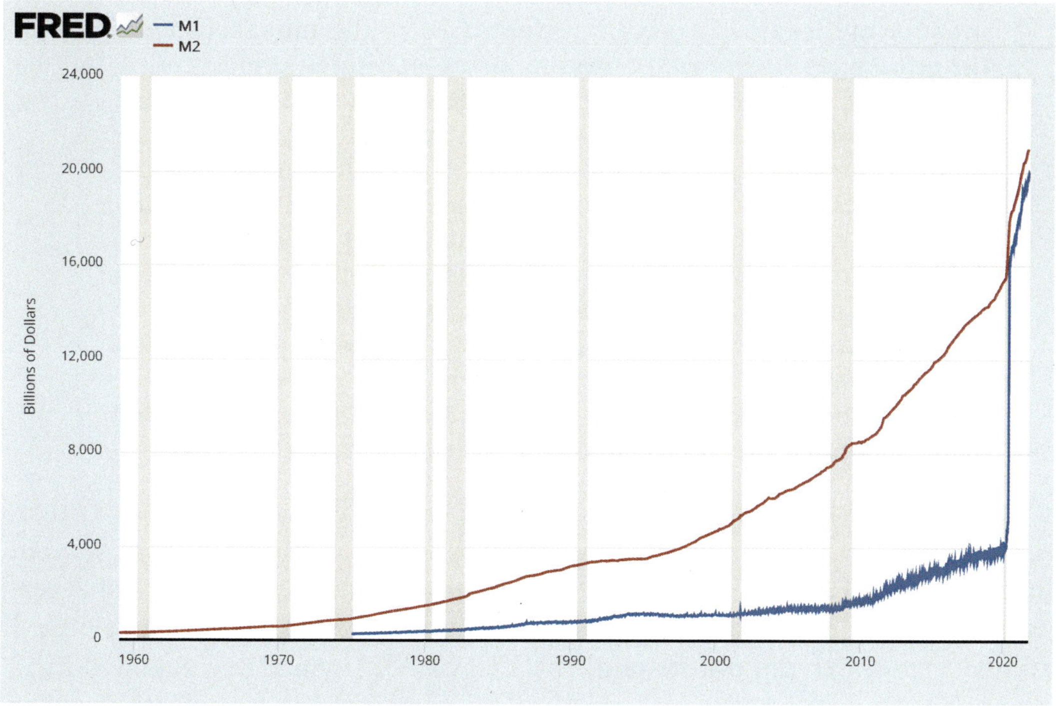

Source:Board of Governors of the Federal Reserve System (US)

Given the change in Regulation D, the reclassification of M1 made perfect sense. Some economists have speculated that the motivation for the Fed's decision to discontinue publication of certain monetary measures—which occurred at the same time as the retroactive M1 reclassification—may have been to obscure the large increase in US Treasury and foreign bank deposits with the Fed, as such data might fuel concerns that the Fed is acting to monetize US government spending.[9]

Switch to *Average* Inflation Targeting

On August 27, 2020, the Fed posted its "2020 Statement on Longer-Run Goals and Monetary Policy Strategy," which amended the original statement adopted back in 2012. The following excerpt highlights the major change in the 2020 amendment:

9. See the discussion and citation in Joseph T. Salerno, "The Fed's Money Supply Measures: The Good News—and the Really, Really Bad News," *Mises Wire*, Mar. 6, 2021, https://mises.org/wire/feds-money-supply-measures-good-news-and-really-really-bad-news.

> The inflation rate over the longer run is primarily determined by monetary policy, and hence the Committee has the ability to specify a longer-run goal for inflation. The Committee reaffirms its judgment that inflation at the rate of 2 percent, as measured by the annual change in the price index for personal consumption expenditures, is most consistent over the longer run with the Federal Reserve's statutory mandate. The Committee judges that longer-term inflation expectations that are well anchored at 2 percent foster price stability and moderate long-term interest rates and enhance the Committee's ability to promote maximum employment in the face of significant economic disturbances. In order to anchor longer-term inflation expectations at this level, **the Committee seeks to achieve inflation that averages 2 percent over time, and therefore judges that, following periods when inflation has been running persistently below 2 percent, appropriate monetary policy will likely aim to achieve inflation moderately above 2 percent for some time.** (bold added)[10]

Before the August 2020 change, the Fed had adopted a constant (price) inflation target, which reset anew each period. For example, if the Fed wanted inflation (in the Personal Consumption Expenditure index) to average 2 percent in 2020, but in actuality the desired inflation measure came in at only 1 percent, then under the old system, the Fed in 2021 would try again to hit 2 percent. But under the *new* system, the Fed might shoot for inflation of *2.5 percent* for both 2021 and 2022 to make up for the initial undershooting of the target back in 2020. (We are ignoring the complications of exponential growth to keep the arithmetic simple.) This is what the Fed authors mean by saying they are switching to an *average* inflation target: in our example, if the Fed undershoots the target in 2020, the average over the three-year period can only hit the target if the Fed overshoots in 2021 and 2022.

At the Jackson Hole monetary conference held in late August 2020, Fed chair Jay Powell gave the opening remarks. He first summarized some of the major changes in the global economy and central bank practice since 2012, and then explained the new Fed policy by saying:

> The key innovations in our new consensus statement reflect the changes in the economy I described. Our new statement explicitly acknowledges the challenges posed by the proximity of interest rates to the effective lower bound. By reducing our scope to support the economy by cutting interest rates, the lower bound increases downward risks to employment

10. See Board of Governors of the Federal Reserve System, "2020 Statement on Longer-Run Goals and Monetary Policy Strategy," Aug. 27, 2020, last modified Jan. 14, 2021, https://www.federalreserve.gov/monetarypolicy/review-of-monetary-policy-strategy-tools-and-communications-statement-on-longer-run-goals-monetary-policy-strategy.htm.

> and inflation. To counter these risks, we are prepared to use our full range of tools to support the economy.[11]

Specifically, Powell argued that the fall in real interest rates, as well as muted (price) inflationary expectations, made the "zero lower bound" a much more potent threat in 2020 than it had been a decade earlier. When short-term nominal interest rates hit 0 percent, it is difficult for the central bank to cut further; why would people lend out their money at a negative interest rate when they could just hold cash and earn 0 percent? According to some economists, at the zero lower bound conventional monetary policy loses traction and other measures are needed.

In theory, the switch to average inflation targeting can help alleviate the problem posed by the zero lower bound. Investors know that if the Fed runs into trouble during a sluggish year and inflation falls short of the target, then the Fed is required to let the economy "run hot" for a while in order to make up for the lost ground. Even if nominal interest rates stay at 0 percent, the increase in expectations of future inflation lower *real* interest rates and have the same impact as if the Fed had more room to cut nominal interest rates in the present.

In contrast to this optimistic interpretation of the Fed's new regime, a more cynical take is that Federal Reserve officials knew that their massive monetary expansion in 2020 would lead to higher price inflation, and they wanted to provide themselves with a framework to justify their failure to stay within their own guidelines.

11. Jerome H. Powell, "Opening Remarks: New Economic Challenges and the Fed's Monetary Policy Review" (speech given at the Navigating the Decade Ahead: Implications for Monetary Policy economic policy symposium, Jackson Hole, WY, August 2020), https://www.kansascityfed.org/documents/7832/JH2020-Powell.pdf.

Part III
Applications

Chapter 8

Ludwig von Mises's "Circulation Credit" Theory of the Trade Cycle

Starting with Carl Menger's undisputed role in the "marginal revolution," which ushered in subjective value theory, the Austrian school has made important contributions that have been absorbed into standard economic theory. However, the Austrian theory of the business cycle is still something unique to the school, differing not only from the Keynesian (see chapter 14) but also the market monetarist (see chapter 15) explanations.

Indeed, if someone asks, "Why study Austrian economics?," the present author answers that only the Austrian approach—with its emphasis on the economy's intricate capital structure and an appreciation for the guidance that market prices offer to entrepreneurs—can explain modern business cycles. Given the unprecedented actions of central banks following the 2008 financial crisis and now the 2020 coronavirus panic, it is more important than ever for investors and citizens to familiarize themselves with the Austrian perspective.

The present chapter summarizes the theory of the business cycle originally published in 1912 by Ludwig von Mises and elaborated by Friedrich Hayek (who would win a Nobel Memorial Prize in 1974 partly for this work[1]). This summary will be intuitive; the footnotes provide a list of further reading, both for newcomers and for advanced students of economics.[2]

1. See Friedrich Hayek's Nobel award notification here: "Friedrich August von Hayek – Facts," NobelPrize.org, May 11, 2020,

2. For beginners, here is a list of treatments of Austrian business cycle theory that are accessible yet comprehensive: Murray Rothbard's "Austrian Business Cycle Theory, Explained"

Mises's Framework for Money and Banking

Although Carl Menger founded the Austrian school in 1871 with his book *Principles of Economics*, in the twentieth century the acknowledged leader of the Austrians was Ludwig von Mises. Most modern fans associate him with his magnum opus, *Human Action* (first published in 1949), but Mises's pathbreaking work on money, banking, and the business cycle was contained in his 1912 German book, translated as *The Theory of Money and Credit*.[3]

(excerpted from his *America's Great Depression*), *Mises Wire*, July 9, 2019, available at: https://mises.org/wire/austrian-business-cycle-theory-explained; Mark Thornton's book *The Skyscraper Curse: And How Austrian Economists Predicted Every Major Economic Crisis of the Last Century* (Auburn, AL: Ludwig von Mises Institute, 2018), available at: https://mises.org/library/skyscraper-curse; Robert P. Murphy, *Choice: Cooperation, Enterprise, and Human Action* (Oakland, CA: Independent Institute, 2015), chap. 14; and Shawn Ritenour, *Foundations of Economics: A Christian View* (Eugene, OR: Wipf and Stock, 2010), chap. 13. For advanced readers, here are more technical expositions of the *Austrian approach: The collection of essays The Austrian Theory of the Trade Cycle*, ed. Richard M. Ebeling (Auburn, AL: Ludwig von Mises Institute, 1996), available at: https://mises.org/library/austrian-theory-trade-cycle-and-other-essays; Ludwig von Mises' collection of essays *The Causes of the Economic Crisis, and Other Essays before and after the Great Depression*, ed. Percy L. Greaves Jr. (Auburn, AL: Ludwig von Mises Institute, 2006), available at: https://mises.org/library/causes-economic-crisis-and-other-essays-and-after-great-depression; and Mises, *Human Action: A Treatise on Economics*, scholar's ed., (1949; Auburn, AL: Ludwig von Mises Institute, 1998), chap. 20, available at: https://mises.org/library/human-action-0. For the very technical work by Hayek, see his *Prices and Production*, second ed. (1935; repr., New York: Augustus M. Kelly Publishers, 1967), available at: https://mises.org/library/prices-and-production. Finally, to see the Hayekian vision expressed with the toolbox of mainstream economic theory, see Roger W. Garrison's *Time and Money: The Macroeconomics of Capital Structure* (New York: Routledge, 2001), as well as his excellent PowerPoint shows available at http://webhome.auburn.edu/~garriro/tam.htm.

3. The 2009 edition of *The Theory of Money and Credit* is available free from the Mises Institute at https://mises.org/library/theory-money-and-credit. See also the free study guide for the book

In this early book, before presenting his explanation of the business cycle (or what he called the "trade cycle"), Mises first offered a threefold classification of *types* of money: commodity money, fiat money, and credit money. What is fascinating to a modern reader is that Mises, writing in 1912, says of the second category:

> It can hardly be contested that fiat money in the strict sense of the word is theoretically conceivable. The theory of value proves the possibility of its existence. **Whether fiat money has ever actually existed is, of course, another question, and one that cannot off-hand be answered affirmatively.** It can hardly be doubted that most of those kinds of money that are not commodity money must be classified as credit money. But only detailed historical investigation could clear this matter up. [Mises 1912, p. 61, bold added.]

Besides reminding modern readers of the charming times when all major currencies were backed by the precious metals—such that Mises could not even be sure whether fiat money had ever existed—this passage is crucial to establish that **the Austrian theory of the business cycle isn't based on fiat money.** Indeed, Ludwig von Mises developed his explanation of the boom-bust cycle at a time when he didn't even think fiat money had ever been in use. So clearly, the Misesian theory of recessions isn't directly tied to the abandonment of the gold standard, and it's therefore not a problem for Austrians to explain depressions (or "panics") that occurred during the days of the classical gold standard.

Likewise, when it came to banking operations, in his 1912 book Mises distinguished between two types of credit transactions, namely *commodity credit* and *circulation credit*:

> Credit transactions fall into two groups...On the one hand are those credit transactions which are characterized by the fact that they impose a sacrifice on that party who performs his part of the bargain before the other does—the foregoing of immediate power of disposal over the exchanged good.... This sacrifice is balanced by a corresponding gain on the part of the other party to the contract—the advantage of obtaining earlier disposal over the good acquired in exchange...
>
> **The second group of credit transactions is characterized by the fact that in them the gain of the party who receives before he pays is balanced by no sacrifice on the part of the other party**.... In the credit transactions of the second group, the granter of the credit renounces for the time being the ownership of a sum of money, but

written by the current author at: *Study Guide to The Theory of Money and Credit* (Auburn, AL: Ludwig von Mises Institute, 2011), https://mises.org/library/study-guide-theory-money-and-credit.

> this renunciation (given certain assumptions that in this case are justifiable) results for him in no reduction of satisfaction. **If a creditor is able to confer a loan by issuing claims which are payable on demand, then the granting of the credit is bound up with no economic sacrifice for him....**
>
> It seems desirable to choose special names for the two groups of credit transactions in order to avoid any possible confusion of the concepts. For the first group the name Commodity Credit ... is suggested, for the second the name Circulation Credit... [Mises 1912, pp. 264–65, bold added.]

In a loan involving *commodity* credit, someone lends (say) 100 barrels of oil today in exchange for a promise of 110 barrels of oil delivered in a year's time. This credit transaction involves the renunciation of the oil for twelve months by the lender; he can't simultaneously lend it out and *still have* the oil. Likewise, it would also be an example of commodity credit if someone lent $100 in currency to a borrower who promised to pay back $110 in a year. Because the lender would no longer physically possess the currency, this would be a genuine deprivation, a sacrifice of present goods for the hope of obtaining a greater number of future goods, and hence would be considered commodity credit.

However, under the practice of "fractional reserve banking" (which we explained in detail in chapters 4 and 6), there is a sense in which a lender can lend out his funds *while still enjoying the benefits of holding the money*. For example, when a man deposits $100 in his checking account, upon which he earns interest because the bank then lends out $90 to a new borrower, even though this is a credit transaction, the original depositor still thinks that he has $100 in the bank. This is what Mises has in mind when he says that there are credit transactions in which the renunciation of the lender "results for him in no reduction of satisfaction." Thus, to the extent that bank loans involve *unbacked* claims to money, where the total customer deposits exceed the total reserves of actual money in the vaults, the loans constitute circulation credit in the Misesian framework.

It's significant that Mises himself didn't call his explanation "the Austrian theory of the business cycle," which is today's popular (yet somewhat generic) term. Rather, he used the more specific description "the monetary or circulation credit theory of the trade cycle."[4] We have explained Mises's terminology

4. In footnote 1 (p. 423) of the most recent edition of *The Theory of Money and Credit*, Mises writes: "Part III of the present book (pp. 261–366) is entirely devoted to the exposition of the trade-cycle theory, the doctrine that is called the monetary or circulation credit theory, sometimes also the Austrian theory." In his 1949 English-language work *Human Action*, Mises titles the crucial section in chapter 20 as "8. The Monetary or Circulation Credit Theory of the Trade Cycle."

to show that his theory was based on the fact that commercial banks could "create money" (in the broad sense of the term) by lending out deposits even though the depositors still thought they had the ability to immediately redeem "their" money.

To be sure, to this day one of the biggest controversies within Austrian circles concerns the validity (or lack thereof) of fractional reserve banking and the related question of whether Mises himself endorsed or opposed the practice.[5] But there is no doubt that Mises's theory of the business cycle is based on the ability of the private commercial banks to create money through the issuance of new loans using deposits that the depositors still think are in their checking accounts.[6]

It is true that central banks can influence these commercial bank practices in a harmful way, but the Misesian theory isn't about central banks (or fiat money) *per se*. It is thus no embarrassment for the Austrian theory that the United States suffered depressions and panics even before the formation of the Federal Reserve in 1913. Furthermore, when modern fans of Mises discuss the business cycle, they should be careful to avoid claiming that it *necessarily* starts with a central bank injecting new fiat money into the economy.

How Banks Cause the Business Cycle

In Mises's view, the economy relies on a sophisticated interlocking structure of capital goods that must reflect the preferences of the consumers over the *timing* of the flow of goods and services. For example, if most people in the community are very future oriented—economists would say they have *low time preference*—then they will save a large fraction of their income and interest rates (other things equal) will tend to be low, fostering long-term investment projects. In contrast, if most people in the community are present oriented—meaning they have *high time preference*—then they won't save much, and the corresponding high interest rates will be a signal to entrepreneurs "penalizing" long-term projects.

Now, because commercial banks enjoy the legal ability to create money by issuing loans in excess of their reserves in the vault—again, see chapters 4 and

5. For a discussion and links to further reading on the intra-Austrian debates on fractional reserve banking, see Robert P. Murphy, "More Than Quibbles: Problems with the Theory and History of Fractional Reserve Free Banking," *Quarterly Journal of Austrian Economics* 22, no. 1 (Spring 2019): 3–25, available at https://mises.org/library/more-quibbles-problems-theory-and-history-fractional -reserve-free-banking.

6. For example, after laying out his framework Mises says, "Our theory of banking, like that of the Currency Principle, leads ultimately to a theory of business cycles." *The Theory of Money and Credit*, trans. J.E. Batson (1912, 1953; repr., Auburn, AL: Ludwig von Mises Institute, 2009), p. 365.

6 for the details of this process—Mises argued that they could temporarily push the actual, market rate of interest below the "natural" rate corresponding to genuine consumer time preference and saving.[7] In effect, the banks can create new money and lend it out to borrowers even though there are no corresponding savers on the other end of the transaction.

In order to move the greater volume of loans, the banks have to cut interest rates, but this reduction isn't due to a genuine shift in household saving or preferences. Rather, the cut in interest rates merely reflects the commercial banks' willingness to reduce the amount of reserves they are holding to "back up" their existing customer deposits.

The influx of new credit and lower interest rates causes a boom. Entrepreneurs make calculations based on the "cheap credit" and start long-term projects, hiring workers and bidding up the prices of raw materials. So long as the cheap credit policy continues, people feel prosperous.

However, the boom can't last. Just because the commercial banks decide to lend out money—even though households haven't engaged in more saving—and cut interest rates, their actions don't actually create more barrels of crude oil, factory capacity, or inventory in warehouses. If the economy had originally been in a long-run equilibrium at the *higher* interest rate, it is now embarked on an unsustainable trajectory at the artificially *lower* interest rate.

In a typical boom, the banks eventually become skittish, perhaps because of rising prices or other indicators, and they abandon their cheap credit policy. That is, the banks stop injecting new amounts of unbacked money into the loan market, and the interest rate rises toward a more appropriate level. At this point, many entrepreneurs realize that they had been too ambitious, and they either scale back operations or shut down altogether. The workers who had been drawn into the unsustainable projects during the boom years must be laid off in order for their labor to (eventually) be reallocated to more sustainable outlets that are consistent with genuine consumer preferences and saving behavior.

---

7. In *The Theory of Money and Credit* Mises writes, "The issuers of the fiduciary media are able to induce an extension of the demand for them by reducing the interest demanded to a rate below the natural rate of interest, that is below that rate of interest that would be established by supply and demand if the real capital were lent in *natura* without the mediation of money" (pp. 306–07). However, in his exposition in *Human Action* Mises no longer uses this term, but instead contrasts the bank-distorted gross market rate of interest with the rate of "originary interest," which he defines as "the difference between the valuation of present and future goods" (p. 536).

Mises's Analogy of the Master Builder

In the preceding section we laid out the essence of Mises's theory of the business cycle. Yet in order to understand its implications, one of the most useful analogies was created by Mises himself. When responding to the claim that his was an "overinvestment" theory, Mises explained in *Human Action*:

> The whole entrepreneurial class is, as it were, in the position of a master-builder whose task it is to erect a building out of a limited supply of building materials. If this man overestimates the quantity of the available supply, he drafts a plan for the execution of which the means at his disposal are not sufficient. He oversizes the groundwork and the foundations and only discovers later in the progress of the construction that he lacks the material needed for the completion of the structure. **It is obvious that our master-builder's fault was not overinvestment, but an inappropriate employment of the means at his disposal**. [Mises [1949] 1998, p. 557, bold added.]

And thus we see that Mises doesn't say that the banks' injection of new money into the loan market causes *overinvestment*. Rather, he says that their policies cause *malinvestment*.

Imagine a builder working on a house. Thinking he has a certain quantity of materials—bricks, wood, glass, shingles, etc.—at his disposal, he draws up blueprints and assigns various skilled and unskilled workers to their tasks.

But suppose that the builder had overestimated how many bricks he originally had. In that case, the house depicted in his blueprints would be physically unattainable. The moment the builder realized his error—in other words, when he realized that his *actual* supply of remaining bricks was smaller than what his plans required—his immediate response would be to tell everyone on the work site to halt! Our master builder needs to revise the blueprints in light of the new information, and he doesn't want workers squandering scarce bricks or other materials until he knows the new plan.

This is a good metaphor for the market economy in the throes of a credit-induced boom-bust cycle. During the boom period, driven by the influx of unbacked money and artificially cheap credit, entrepreneurs begin various projects that are physically unsustainable: there is simply not enough "real" savings to carry all of the projects to completion.

The sooner the entrepreneurs realize their error, the better. That is, the sooner the banks end their cheap credit policy, the quicker they can nip the festering malinvestments in the bud.

In any event, whenever the boom ends and the entrepreneurs face reality, the immediate response is a slowdown in production. Factors of production, including workers' labor hours, must be rearranged. If everyone kept going to work and doing the same activities as during the boom years, there would eventually be an even bigger crisis.

In the Austrian view, paradoxically, the boom period is actually harmful, while the bust period, though unpleasant, is a healthy return to reality. According to Mises, the only way to permanently cure recessions is to stop letting banks foster the preceding artificial booms.

Chapter 9

Monetary Inflation and Price Inflation

This chapter explains the connection between the quantity of money and the height of prices quoted in that money. The chapter therefore deals with the phenomenon of "inflation," but as we shall see, the very meaning of this word changed during the twentieth century. (For clarity, we will distinguish the two concepts by using the more specific terms "monetary inflation" and "price inflation.") We will summarize some of the famous episodes of hyperinflation throughout history, showing the disaster that results when governments run the printing press too aggressively.

Finally, we will highlight the Austrian criticism of the so-called equation of exchange, nowadays usually written as $MV = PQ$. Although the equation is a tautology, this framework encourages thinking of money and prices in a mechanistic fashion rather than using the tools of subjective value theory. Although it is important to recognize that massive *price* inflation is always the result of massive *monetary* inflation, there isn't a stable relationship between the two; it's not the case that, say, a 50 percent increase in the quantity of money necessarily leads to a 50 percent increase in prices.

Changing Definitions: Monetary Inflation vs. Price Inflation

Nowadays when the media or government officials discuss "inflation" they mean "the increase in consumer prices." However, originally the term referred to an increase in the quantity of money (including bank credit). Here is how Ludwig von Mises, in a 1951 speech, discusses the semantic change and its implications:

> There is nowadays a very reprehensible, even dangerous, semantic confusion that makes it extremely difficult for the non-expert to grasp the true state of affairs. Inflation, as this term was always used everywhere and especially in this country [the United States], means increasing the quantity of money and bank notes in circulation and the quantity of bank deposits subject to check. But people today use the term "inflation" to refer to the phenomenon that is an inevitable consequence of inflation, that is the tendency of all prices and wage rates to rise. The result of this deplorable confusion is that there is no term left to signify the cause of this rise in prices and wages. There is no longer any word available to signify the phenomenon that has been, up to now, called inflation. It follows that nobody cares about inflation in the traditional sense of the term. As you cannot talk about something that has no name, you cannot fight it. Those who pretend to fight inflation are in fact only fighting what is the inevitable consequence of inflation, rising prices. Their ventures are doomed to failure because they do not attack the root of the evil.[1]

Precisely to avoid confusing modern readers while retaining the ability to diagnose cause and effect, in this chapter we use the more specific terms "monetary inflation" and "price inflation."

Famous Historical Episodes of Hyperinflation

Milton Friedman is often quoted as saying, "Inflation is always and everywhere a monetary phenomenon." To give more context, that quotation goes on to say "in the sense that [price inflation] is and can be produced only by a more rapid increase in the quantity of money than in output."[2] Although economists have debated the accuracy of Friedman's famous assertion, the historical record shows that episodes of *rapid* price inflation (almost) always go hand in hand with rapid *monetary* inflation.[3] In other words, if there is a genuine *hyperinflation*, then the government printing press is always involved. In this section we cover three famous historical examples.

---

1. Ludwig von Mises, *Economic Freedom and Interventionism: An Anthology of Articles and Essays*, ed. Bettina Bien Greaves (Irvington-on-Hudson, NY: Foundation for Economic Education, 1990), chap. 20, available at https://mises.org/library/economic-freedom-and-interventionism/html/p/123.

2. Milton Friedman, *Counter-Revolution in Monetary Theory*, Wincott Memorial Lecture, Institute of Economic Affairs, Occasional paper 33, 1970, quoted in John C. Williams, "Monetary Policy, Money, and Inflation" (presentation to the Western Economic Association International, San Francisco, CA, July 2, 2012), https://www.frbsf.org/our-district/press/presidents-speeches/williams-speeches/2012/july/williams-monetary-policy-money-inflation/.

3. Depending on our definitions, we could possibly find historical examples where a natural disaster or wartime measure caused such a widespread restriction of production that consumer prices skyrocketed, even in the absence of aggressive money printing. Yet even here, the effect would be nothing compared to examples of money-induced currency collapses.

The US Civil War

The United States' Civil War (or War between the States, as some prefer to call it) saw large-scale inflation in both the Union (Northern) and Confederate (Southern) economies, but it was particularly pronounced in the Confederacy. According to one estimate, fully one-third of the Confederate government's revenue came from the printing press, while only 11 percent came from tax receipts (with the rest covered by floating bonds). As a result, prices in the Confederate states increased rapidly: From early 1861 to early 1862, consumer prices *doubled*, and by the middle of 1863 they had risen by a factor of thirteen relative to the war's start. With military defeats in 1864 and 1865 sapping confidence in the Confederate currency, its value eventually collapsed—with prices rising some 9,000 percent cumulatively from the war's start—leading Southerners to use other monies or even barter. In the North, things were not nearly as bad, with consumer prices "only" rising about 75 percent from 1861 to 1865.[4]

The Weimar Republic

One of the more (in)famous examples of hyperinflation was the experience of Germany from 1921 to 1923. Because of its massive debts (including harsh reparations payments to the Allies, dictated by the Treaty of Versailles) following World War I, the German government resorted to the printing press to pay its bills. Yet because the war debts were denominated in "gold marks," this resulted in a vicious spiral, with each round of monetary inflation causing the German paper mark to depreciate against gold (and foreign currencies) even further, leading the German officials to print paper marks with higher denominations on each note in the next round in a vain attempt to stay ahead of the depreciation.[5] During the two-year hyperinflation, the total number of marks held by the public increased by a factor of more than 7 billion.[6] According to

4. Most Civil War statistics obtained from EH.net Encyclopedia of Economic and Business History, s.v. "The Economics of the Civil War," by Roger L. Ransom, Aug. 24, 2001, https://eh.net/encyclopedia/the-economics-of-the-civil-war/. The 9,000 percent Confederate inflation figure comes from: "Inflation in the Confederacy," *Dictionary of American History, Encyclopedia.com, last modified Jan. 13, 2021,* https://www.encyclopedia.com/history/dictionaries-thesauruses-pictures-and-press-releases/inflation-confederacy.

5. For the MMT (modern monetary theory) perspective, which argues that rising prices caused the monetary inflation in Weimar Germany rather than vice versa, see Phil Armstrong and Warren Mosler, "Weimar Republic Hyperinflation through a Modern Monetary Theory Lens," Gower Initiative for Modern Monetary Studies, Nov. 11, 2020, https://gimms.org.uk/wp-content/uploads/2020/11/Weimar-Republic-Hyperinflation-through-a-Modern-Monetary-Theory-Lens.pdf.

6. Michael K. Salemi, "Hyperinflation," Library of Economics and Liberty, accessed Jan. 28, 2021, https://www.econlib.org/library/Enc/Hyperinflation.html.

Hyperinflation in Germany during the 1920s.

Milton Friedman, money in the hands of the public increased at "the *average* rate of more than 300 percent a *month* for more than a year, and so did prices."[7]

In the single worst month of the German hyperinflation, October 1923, consumer prices (according to one estimate) rose 29,500 percent, or almost 21 percent *per day.*[8] The inflation was so severe that male workers would give their wages to their wives, who rushed to market, looking to exchange the rapidly depreciating paper for "real" goods that would better hold their market value. It was the Weimar Republic hyperinflation that gave us the iconic notion of workers being paid in wheelbarrows of cash, though that particular detail may be apocryphal. In any event, it is certainly true that everyday life changed, for example with restaurant patrons trying to pay their bill upfront rather than after eating because prices would rise during the course of the meal.[9]

Zimbabwe

A more recent (and severe) hyperinflation occurred in Zimbabwe, from 2007 to 2009. In the worst month, November 2008, prices increased more than 79 billion percent, or 98 percent *per day.*[10] As with other hyperinflations, in Zimbabwe too the connection between monetary and price inflation was evident:

---

7. Milton Friedman, *Money Mischief* (New York: Harcourt Brace, 1994), p. 194, italics in original.

8. See Steve Hanke, "R.I.P. Zimbabwe Dollar," Cato Institute, [Feb. 5, 2009], https://www.cato.org/zimbabwe. Note that the monthly and daily inflation rates are drawn from Hanke, who (in his table, which includes several countries) appears to be using thirty days per month for his calculations, even when (in the case of October 1923) the month in question had thirty-one days.

9. For an account of one researcher's attempt to verify the wheelbarrow story, see Keri Peardon, "Wheelbarrows of Money," *Vampires, Ladies, and Potpourri* (blog), June 1, 2013, https://keripeardon.wordpress.com/2013/06/01/wheelbarrows-of-money-and-the-weimar-republic/.

10. See Hanke, "R.I.P. Zimbabwe Dollar."

Figure 1: Inflation, Money Supply Rise in Tandem in Zimbabwe

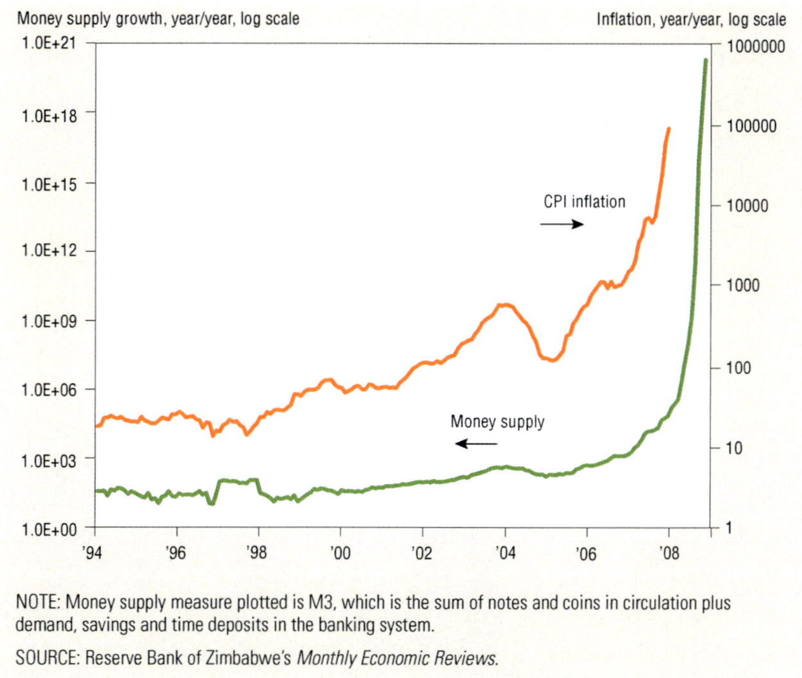

Source: Globalization and Monetary Policy Institute, "Hyperinflation in Zimbabwe," in 2011 Annual Report ([Dallas, TX]: Federal Reserve Bank of Dallas, 2011), chart 8, https://www.dallasfed.org/~/media/documents/institute/annual/2011/annual11b.pdf.

As with the German episode, in Zimbabwe the authorities continued to increase the denomination of the currency notes. That is why economics professors around the world can (cheaply) obtain large Zimbabwean notes on eBay to show their classes the dangers of hyperinflation:

One hundred trillion Zimbabwe dollars. Source: Getty Images. Credit: ppart. No. 478901066.

The Equation of Exchange, $MV = PQ$

It is standard for economists to handle the relationship between money and prices using the *equation of exchange*, credited to Irving Fisher, which is nowadays[11] often written as:

$$MV = PQ$$

where M is the quantity of money in the economy, V is the "velocity of circulation," meaning the average number of times a unit of money "changes hands" during the time period in question,[12] P is the "average price level," and Q is the total quantity of real output produced during the period.

The left side of the equation captures the total amount of money (dollars, in the United States) that is spent during the period. For example, if M is \$3 trillion and a dollar bill is used in a purchase on average four times per year, then there is a total of \$12 trillion of total spending on output during a year. (Notice that weighting is important when calculating V: when a hundred-dollar bill is used in a transaction, it contributes to V one hundred times more than when a one-dollar bill is used.)

At the same time, the right-hand side of the equation equals the total number of dollars received during the year. For example, if the "average price" of goods and services (P) is \$2/unit and the total real output (Q) during the year is 6 trillion units of goods and services, then the total amount received for the sale of goods and services is \$12 trillion. Either way we calculate, we should come up with the same answer, because the total number of dollars spent during the year must equal the total number of dollars received. A common way of describing the equation is that nominal spending (the left-hand side) equals nominal income (the right-hand side), where nominal income is expressed as the "price level" (P) times "real GDP" (Q).

Strictly speaking, the equation of exchange is a tautology or an identity; *given* the definitions of the four variables, it is necessarily true. In practice, however, it is often used as a way of illustrating the so-called quantity theory of money, which—as the name suggests—is a *theory* that might be wrong. There are different formulations of the quantity theory of money, but one simple version says that changes in the quantity of money go hand in hand proportionally with changes in the level of prices. To illustrate this statement using the

11. Originally, the equation of exchange was written as $MV = PT$, where T stood for the total number of transactions occurring during the time period.

12. Strictly speaking, for the equation to be correct, the V must refer to the velocity of money only in the applicable transactions. For example, if Q refers to real output, then V refers to the velocity of turnover of money in exchanges involving newly produced goods and services. In contrast, when someone spends \$1,000 on shares of corporate stock, this "turnover" of money would *not* go into the calculation of V.

equation of exchange, we could say, "If M doubles while V and Q stay the same, then P must also double."

What's Wrong with $MV = PQ$?

Economists in the Austrian tradition have criticized the equation of exchange.[13] In the first place, it seeks to explain economic phenomena in a mechanistic fashion, the way an engineer might write out an equation describing the flow of water through a pipe.

In contrast, the Austrians typically follow the approach of Mises by using the subjective preferences of an individual to explain his or her demand to hold a cash balance of a certain size. At any moment, there is no such thing as "money in circulation," as the equation of exchange leads us to believe. Rather, every unit of money is always held in an individual or organization's cash balance, and the Austrians typically use this perspective when tackling problems of monetary and price inflation. This "micro" method can then be scaled up to arrive at the *market* demand to hold money, which interacts with the total supply in order to explain the purchasing power of money. In this respect, the Austrian approach to explaining the "price" of money is the same subjective value theory used to explain the price of apples.

In light of the Austrian method, the variables of the equation of exchange are unhelpful or even nonsensical. No individual ever relies on the "average velocity of circulation" (V) of money when making decisions. The notion of a price level (or index), P, is also dubious, because it invites the false notion that changes in the quantity of money affect all prices uniformly. Yet in fact, when new money enters the economy in the real world, it isn't "neutral," but instead causes some prices to rise faster than others and in a sense transfers wealth from the rest of the community into the hands of the early recipients of the new money. The impact of this uneven process of price changes is called the *Cantillon effect*.[14]

Putting aside Cantillon effects, there is no reason for monetary inflation to necessarily have the same proportional impact on even the *average* index of prices. As Mises observed, once a hyperinflation is underway, injections of new

---

13. See for example Ludwig von Mises, *The Theory of Money and Credit*, trans. J. E. Batson (Auburn, AL: Ludwig von Mises Institute, 2009), pp. 131–36; Mises, *Human Action: A Treatise on Economics*, scholar's ed. (Auburn, AL: Ludwig von Mises Institute, 1998), pp. 395–97; and Murray Rothbard, *Man, Economy, and State with Power and Market*, 2d scholar's ed. (Auburn, AL: Ludwig von Mises Institute, 2009), pp. 831–42.

14. For a discussion, see Mark Thornton, review of *Money, Inflation, and Business Cycles: The Cantillon Effect and the Economy*, by Arkadiusz Sieroń, *Quarterly Journal of Austrian Economics 22*, no. 3 (Fall 2019): 503–05, https://mises.org/library/money-inflation-and-business-cycles-cantillon-effect-and-economy.

money may lead to *greater* than proportional increases in "the price level" (if such a concept made sense), as the community seeks to rid itself of the cash as quickly as possible in exchange for other goods.[15] For example, once a hyperinflation is underway, if the government doubles the quantity of money, then this action may result in *more* than a doubling of the typical price of a consumer good.

On the other hand, as the advanced economies experienced after the financial crisis of 2008, sometimes large injections of new base money do not correspond with comparable increases in consumer price indices. (We will cover this topic in greater detail in chapter 13.) Even if we restrict our attention to money in the hands of the public (using the aggregate M1 rather than the monetary base [M0]), it is still the case that there is no automatic connection between money and consumer prices:

Figure 2: M1 Money Stock vs Consumer Price Index

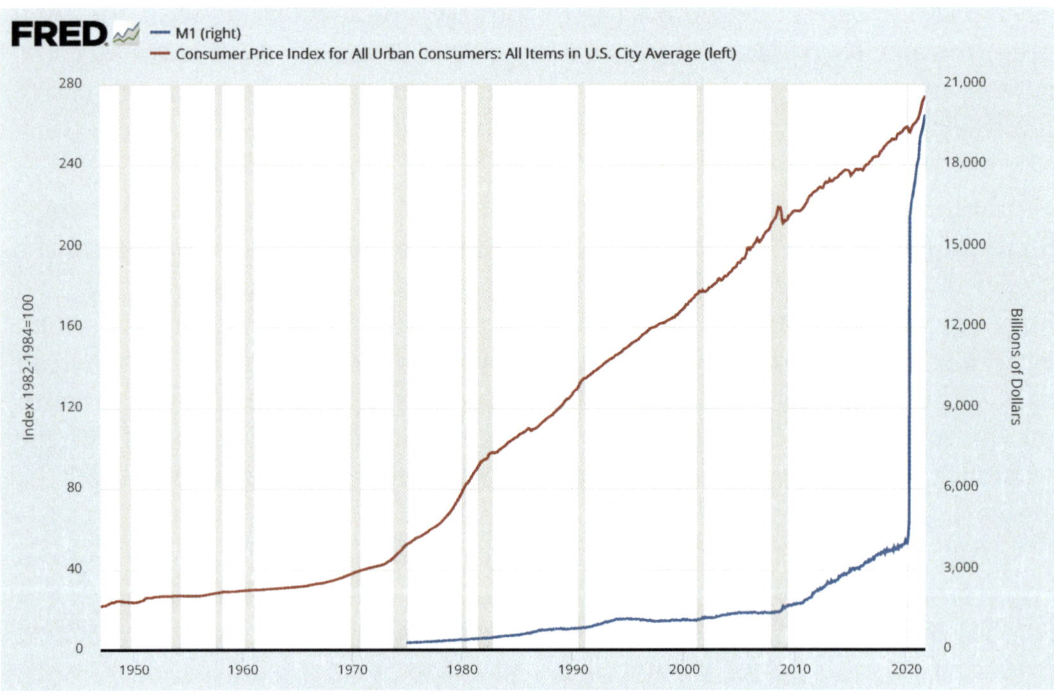

Source: Board of Governors of the Federal Reserve System (US)

15. Keep in mind that at any given moment *all* money must be held in the cash balances of various individuals or organizations. The community as a whole can't "get rid of" newly created money, but rather the desire to do so (at existing prices) causes the purchasing power of money to fall—meaning prices rise—until equilibrium is restored.

To reiterate, no matter *what* happens, the outcome can always be reconciled with the equation of exchange, because it is an identity rather than a falsifiable theory. If M doubles while prices and real output stay relatively constant, the "explanation" is that V suddenly fell in half. In a scenario like this, the objection to the equation of exchange isn't that it's wrong, but rather that it may mislead observers into thinking there is a simple relationship between monetary and price inflation.

Conclusion

Although the term "inflation" nowadays refers to rising consumer prices, historically it referred to increases in the quantity of money. There is a tight connection between monetary inflation and price inflation. Specifically, all examples of hyperinflation in prices involved comparable increases in the money stock. However, there are examples of large increases in the quantity of money that have not (thus far) resulted in comparable consumer price hikes. The equation of exchange, $MV = PQ$, is an identity and therefore must be true. Yet it invites a mechanistic view of the economy, rather than explaining prices on the basis of individual decisions to hold cash balances of a particular size.

Chapter 10

The Inverted Yield Curve and Recession[1]

The "yield curve" refers to a graph showing the relationship between the maturity length of bonds—such as one month, three months, one year, five years, twenty years, etc.—plotted on the x axis, and the yield (or interest rate) plotted on the y axis. In the postwar era, a "normal" yield curve has been upward sloping, meaning that investors typically receive a higher rate of return if they are willing to put their funds into longer-dated bonds. A so-called inverted yield curve occurs when this typical relationship flips, and *short*-dated bonds have a higher rate of return than long-dated ones.

Investors and financial analysts are very interested in this phenomenon, because an inverted yield curve (defined in a particular way) has been a perfect leading indicator of a recession going back at least fifty years. If we look at the last eight recessions, beginning with the downturn that began in December 1969, an appropriately defined yield curve inversion preceded all of them about a year ahead of time. Moreover, during this same fifty-one-year period the (appropriately defined) yield curve has only inverted when there would soon be a recession. (See the footnotes for citations to the scholarly literature.[2])

1. The material in this chapter draws on a forthcoming article to be published in the *Quarterly Journal of Austrian Economics* authored by Ryan Griggs and Robert P. Murphy.

2. Perhaps the first systematic exploration of the inverted yield curve's ability to forecast recessions was Campbell Harvey, "Recovering Expectations of Consumption Growth from an Equilibrium Model of the Term Structure of Interest Rates" (PhD diss., University of Chicago, 1986), https://faculty.fuqua.duke.edu/~charvey/Research/Thesis/Thesis.pdf. For a more recent discussion, see Arturo Estrella and Mary R. Trubin, "The Yield Curve as a Leading Indicator: Some Practical Issues," *New York Fed: Current Issues in Economics and Finance*,

The following chart illustrates the yield curve's apparent predictive power:

Figure 1: 10-Year Treasury Constant Maturity Minus 3-Month Treasury Maturity

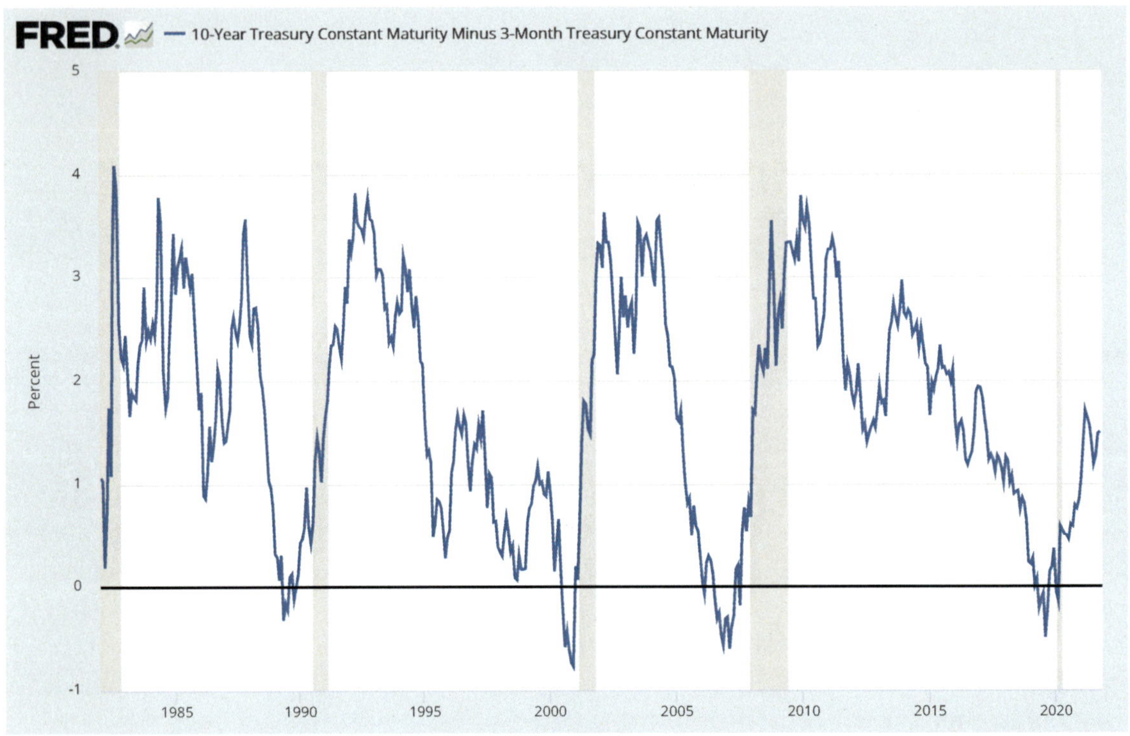

Source: Federal Reserve Bank of St. Louis (US)

In the above chart (which only goes back to the early 1980s and so doesn't cover the full extent of the yield curve's successful track record), we have charted the difference (or "spread") between the implicit interest rate on ten-year Treasury bonds and three-month Treasury bills. The normal state of affairs is for the yield on the longer ten-year security to be higher than the yield on the very short three-month security. (That's why the line in the chart is typically above the black horizontal line at the 0 percent notch.)

However, every once in a while the yield curve inverts, meaning that the line in the chart dips below the 0 percent threshold, corresponding to a situation in which the yield on three-month T-bills is actually higher than the yield on ten-year Treasury bonds. Notice in our chart that whenever that happens—and *only*

July/August 2006, pp. 1–7, https://www.newyorkfed.org/medialibrary/media/research/current_issues/ci12-5.pdf.

when that happens—the economy soon goes into a recession (indicated by the gray bars).

Economists have tried to explain the mechanism by which an inverted yield curve signals an impending recession. As we will see, the conventional attempts—such as the one offered by Paul Krugman—do not fit the actual facts. In contrast, the Misesian explanation of the business cycle quite easily explains the pattern we observe in interest rates during the "normal" boom time and shortly before the bust.

Paul Krugman on the Inverted Yield Curve

In his *New York Times* column and associated blogging platform, Paul Krugman over the years has clearly singled out investor expectations as the driving force behind the historical pattern. Here is Krugman in late 2008:

> **The reason for the historical relationship between the slope of the yield curve and the economy's performance is that the long-term rate is, in effect, a prediction of future short-term rates.** If investors expect the economy to contract, they also expect the Fed to cut rates, which tends to make the yield curve negatively sloped. If they expect the economy to expand, they expect the Fed to raise rates, making the yield curve positively sloped. (bold added)[3]

Then, in his column from mid-August of 2019—commenting on the then recent inversion of the two-year and ten-year yields, which was spooking investors—Krugman applied his framework to the data:

> An old economists' joke says that the stock market predicted nine of the last five recessions. Well, an "inverted yield curve"—when interest rates on short-term bonds are higher than on long-term bonds—predicted six of the last six recessions. And **a plunge in long-term yields, which are now less than half what they were last fall, has inverted the yield curve once again,** with the short-versus-long spread down to roughly where it was in early 2007, on the eve of a disastrous financial crisis and the worst recession since the 1930s.
>
> Neither I nor anyone else is predicting a replay of the 2008 crisis. It's not even clear whether we're heading for recession. **But the bond market is telling us that the smart money has become very gloomy about the economy's prospects. Why? The Federal Reserve basically controls short-term rates, but not long-term rates; low long-term yields**

3. See Paul Krugman, "The Yield Curve (Wonkish)," Paul Krugman blogs, *New York Times*, Dec. 27, 2008, https://krugman.blogs.nytimes.com/2008/12/27/the-yield-curve-wonkish/.

> **mean that investors expect a weak economy, which will force the Fed into repeated rate cuts.** (bold added)[4]

As the above quotations make clear, Krugman argues that the yield curve flattens/inverts before a recession because investors forecast trouble ahead. There are two problems with this approach.

First, why would an inverted yield curve spook investors if the *reason* it inverts is that investors already know a recession is coming?

Second and more significant: Krugman's explanation would make sense if yield curve inversions typically occurred when the long bond yield collapses. But in fact, as the following chart makes clear, the yield curve inverts primarily because the short rate spikes upward before a recession:

Figure 2: 10-Year Maturity Rate vs 3-Month Maturity Rate

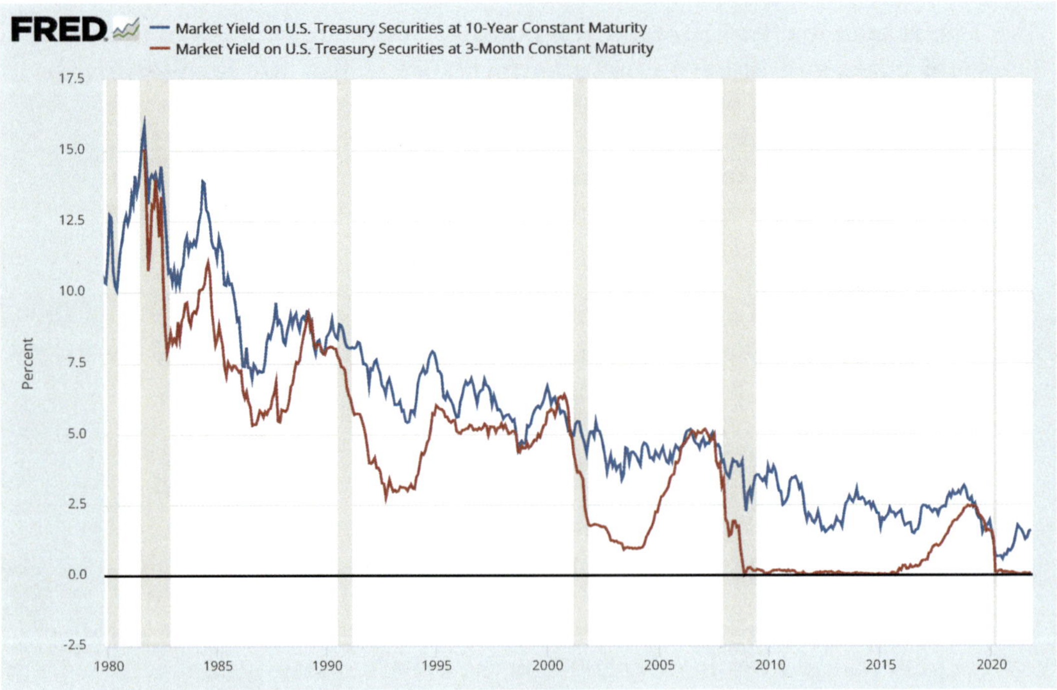

Source: Board of Governors of the Federal Reserve System (US)

In the above chart, particularly for the middle three recessions, it is clear that the yield curve inverted because the three-month yield (black line) rose rapidly to surpass the ten-year yield (green line). This is the *opposite* of what Krugman's readers would have expected to see.

4. See Paul Krugman, "From Trump Boom to Trump Gloom," *New York Times*, Aug. 15, 2019, https://www.nytimes.com/2019/08/15/opinion/trump-economy.html.

An Austrian Explanation

In contrast to Krugman's story, standard Austrian business cycle theory—which we explained in chapter 8—is quite compatible with the evidence presented in the above figure. In the Misesian framework, the unsustainable boom is associated with "easy money" and artificially low interest rates. When the banks (led by the central bank, in modern times) change course and tighten, interest rates rise and trigger the inevitable bust.[5] (It is standard in macroeconomics to assume that the central bank's actions affect short-term interest rates much more than long-term interest rates.)

In fact, as Ryan Griggs and the present author have demonstrated, changing growth rates in the Austrian "true money supply" (TMS) monetary aggregate correspond quite well with the spread in the yield curve:

Figure 3: Yield Spread vs TMS Growth

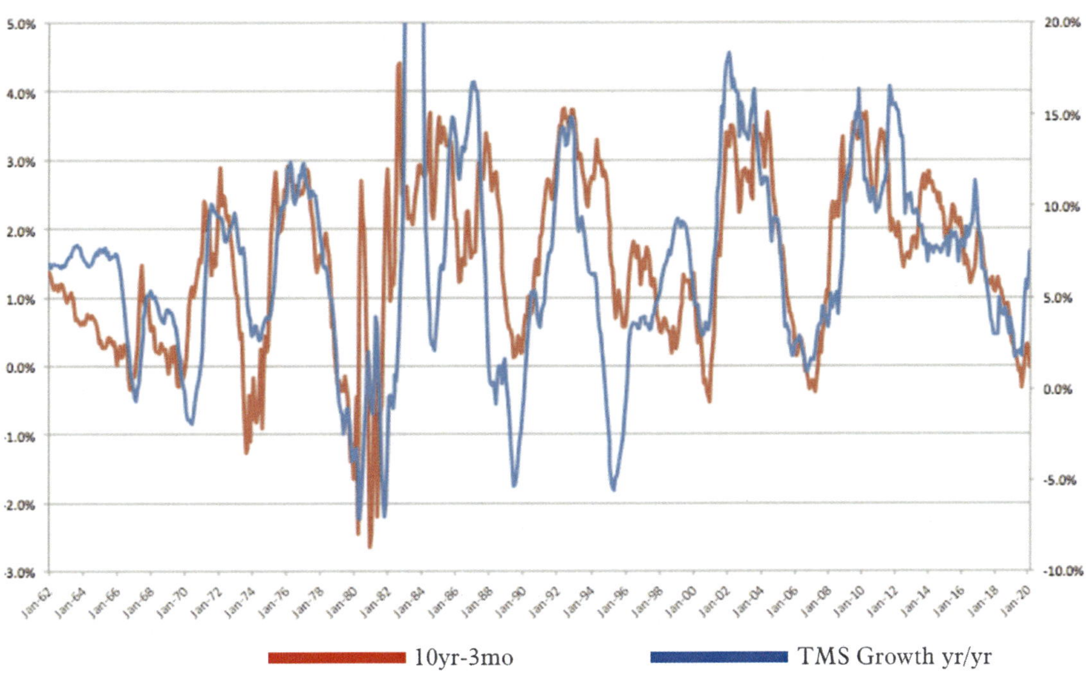

Source: Data from FRED.

In the above chart, the green line (corresponding to the left axis) is the difference between the ten-year Treasury bond yield and the three-month T-bill yield.

5. Paul Cwik's work explains the inverted yield curve's predictive power in light of Austrian business cycle theory. See for example Paul Cwik, "The Inverted Yield Curve and the Economic Downturn," *New Perspectives on Political Economy* 1, no. 1 (2005): 1–37; and "An Investigation of Inverted Yield Curves and Economic Downturns," (PhD diss., Auburn University, 2004).

The black line (corresponding to the right axis) is the twelve-month percentage growth in the true money supply as defined by Rothbard and Salerno (and which we briefly discussed in chapter 4).

As the chart indicates, these two series have a remarkably tight connection. Specifically, when the money supply grows at a high rate, we are in a "boom" period and the yield curve is "normal," meaning the yield on long bonds is much higher than on short bonds. But when the banking system contracts and money supply growth decelerates, then the yield curve flattens or even inverts. It is not surprising that when the banks "slam on the brakes" with money creation, the economy soon goes into recession.

In summary, the standard Austrian explanation of the business cycle has, as a natural corollary, a straightforward explanation for the apparent predictive power of an inverted yield curve.

Chapter 11

The Fed and the Housing Bubble/Bust

In chapter 8 we presented Ludwig von Mises's circulation credit theory of the trade cycle, or what is nowadays referred to as Austrian business cycle theory. In the present chapter, we will apply the general theory to the specific case of the US housing bubble and bust, which began sometime in the early 2000s and culminated in the financial crisis in the fall of 2008.

In a nutshell, the Austrian narrative recognizes the role that private sector miscreants can play in any particular historical boom but argues that these excesses were fueled by the easy money policy in the early 2000s enacted by then Fed chair Alan Greenspan. By flooding the market with cheap credit that came from the printing press rather than genuine saving, Greenspan pushed interest rates (including mortgage rates) down to artificially low levels. This caused (or at least exacerbated) the bubble in house prices and misallocated too many real resources to the housing sector. When the Fed got cold feet and began gently raising rates from mid-2004 onward, the bubble in house prices eventually tapered off and turned to a crash.

The present chapter draws on material developed in three separate articles that the author wrote for Mises.org in response to critics who tried to *exonerate the Federal Reserve from blame for the housing bubble.*[1] The chapter takes the standard

1. The three articles from which the charts in this chapter are drawn were all written by Robert P. Murphy for Mises.org: "Did the Fed Cause the Housing Bubble?," *Mises Daily*, April 14, 2008, https://mises.org/library/did-fed-cause-housing-bubble; "Evidence that the Fed Caused the Housing Boom," *Mises Daily*, Dec. 15, 2008, https://mises.org/library/evidence-fed-caused-housing-boom; and "Can Austrian Theory Explain Construction Employment?," *Mises Daily*, Jan. 19, 2011, https://mises.org/library/can-austrian-theory-explain-construction-employment.

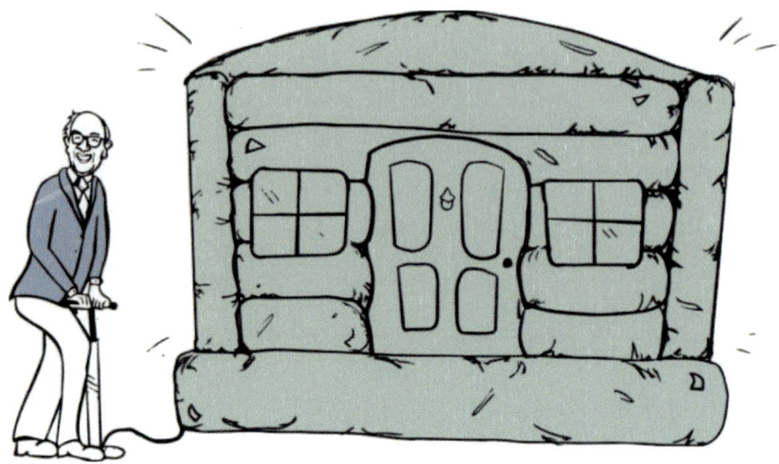

Austrian theory for granted—as it was already explained back in chapter 8—and provides empirical support for the application of the theory to the historical case of the US housing bubble and bust.

Link #1
Evidence That Changes in Interest Rates Affected Home Prices

To validate the Austrian explanation of the housing bubble, we must first establish that interest rates did indeed fall into unusually low territory during the boom phase, while they were hiked going into the bust. Figure 1 below shows the "real" (i.e., consumer price inflation–adjusted) federal funds rate, as a quarterly average from 1970–2006:

Figure 1: Real Federal Funds Rate

As Figure 1 indicates, the federal funds rate (which was the Fed's target variable at this time), taking account of price inflation, was pushed down to negative 2 percent by early 2004. This was the lowest it had been going back to the late 1970s. Then interest rates began rising after 2004.

It wasn't just short-term rates, but also mortgage rates, that fell during the peak years of the housing bubble. In Figure 2, we plot conventional thirty-year mortgage rates but also include year-over-year increases in the Case-Schiller Home Price Index (HPI).

Figure 2: Conventional 30-Year Mortgage Rates vs Year-Year Percentage Growth in Home Prices

Taking Figures 1 and 2 together, it is clear that interest rates—whether we look at the overnight fed funds rate or the thirty-year mortgage rate—really did fall significantly as the housing bubble accelerated. (It's not shown in Figure 2, but the trough for mortgage rates represented record-low rates going back at least through the 1970s.)

Moreover, notice by comparing Figures 1 and 2 that the bubbliest of the bubble years occurred when short-term rates were at their lowest, in 2004, and then home price appreciation began slowing as short rates were gradually hiked. To reiterate, this is perfectly consistent with the Austrian story of what happened.

Link #2
Evidence That Monetary Inflation Affected the Level of Interest Rates

In the previous section we established the fact that interest rates really did fall to historically low levels as the housing bubble intensified, while the cooling off of the boom went hand in hand with rising interest rates.

However, some apologists for the Fed argue that Alan Greenspan had nothing to do this. Why, it was *Asian saving* that explains what happened with US interest rates during the 2000s.

I have elsewhere directly rebutted the "Asian savings glut" explanation;[2] see the citation in the footnotes for the details. However, in this chapter let us clearly establish that changes in the growth of the US monetary base went hand in hand with movements in the federal funds rate, just as any economics textbook would suggest. We provide this data in Figure 3.

Figure 3: Year-Year Monetary Base Growth vs Federal Funds Target Rate

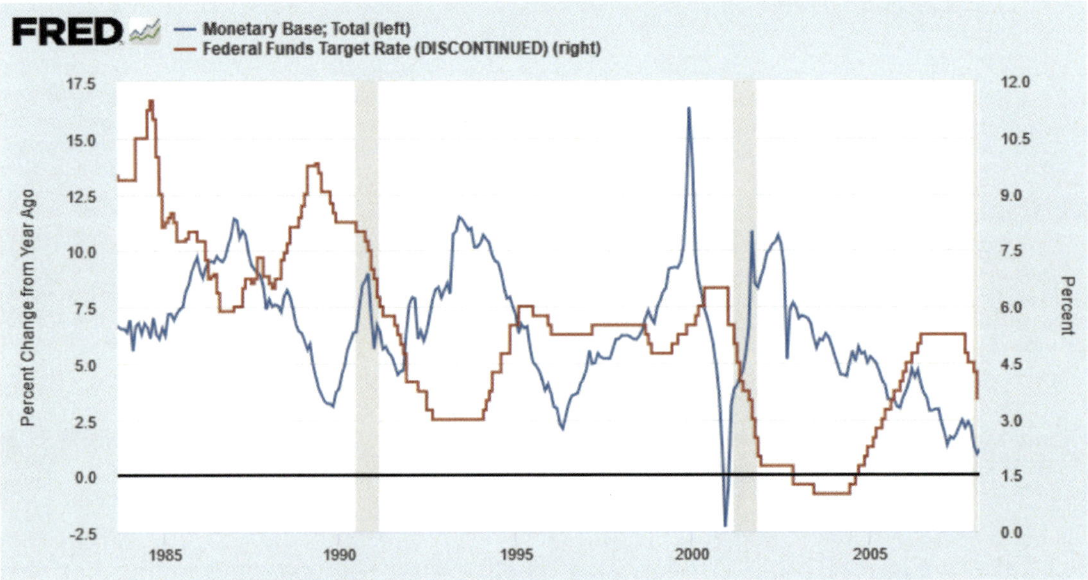

Source: Board of Governors of the Federal Reserve System (US)

Look at how the two lines in Figure 3 are (almost) mirror images of each other. Specifically, when monetary base growth is high, the federal funds rate is low. And vice versa, when the growth in the monetary base slows, the fed funds rate shoots up.

There is nothing mysterious about this. To repeat, this is the standard explanation given in economics textbooks—not just Austrian texts—to explain how a central bank "sets" interest rates. When the central bank wants to cut rates, it buys more assets and floods the market with more base money. And when

2. Robert P. Murphy, "Did the Fed, or Asian Saving, Cause the Housing Bubble?" *Mises Daily*, Nov. 19, 2008, https://mises.org/library/did-fed-or-asian-saving-cause-housing-bubble.

the central bank wants to raise rates, it slows the pace of monetary inflation (or even reverses course entirely and shrinks the monetary base).

Recall from chapter 4 that the "monetary base" consists of paper currency and member banks' deposits at the Fed. Therefore, the Federal Reserve has absolute control over the monetary base; those rascally Asians who have the gall to live below their means can't directly increase the US monetary base. As Figure 3 shows, when US interest rates fell sharply in the early 2000s, this occurred during a period of rapid growth in the monetary base. If the Fed *didn't* want interest rates falling so low in the early 2000s, it shouldn't have engaged in so much monetary inflation.

Link #3
Evidence That the Housing Bubble
Led to "Real" Problems in the Labor Market

Last, there are some economists—such as Scott Sumner, whose views on NGDP targeting we critique in chapter 15—who argue that the Austrians are wrong for thinking that the housing bubble had anything to do with the Great Recession. (See the articles in footnote 1 for more details on Sumner's perspective.) In this last section, we provide two additional charts to show that the Austrian explanation holds up just fine in this regard.

First, in Figure 4 we plot total construction employment against the civilian unemployment rate.

As with the previous charts, this one too is exactly the kind of picture Austrians would expect to see. Total construction employment surged from about 6.7 million in 2003 up to 7.7 million by 2006, but then began falling fast in mid-2007. This movement in construction employment was the mirror image of the national unemployment rate, which dropped from some 6 percent in 2003 to the low 4s in early 2007. After that, it began rising sharply, mirroring the crash in construction employment, hitting 10 percent in mid-2009.

Finally, let us plot the movement in total construction employment against an index of home prices (Figure 5).

As Figure 5 makes clear, the movement in total construction employment seems intimately related to the bubble in house prices. They both rose together from 2003, they both tapered off going into 2007, and they both began plummeting going into 2008.

Conclusion

In this chapter, we have applied the generic Austrian theory of the business cycle to the specific case of the US housing bubble and the ensuing financial crisis/Great Recession. Specifically, we showed that interest rates—including

Figure 4: All Employees-Construction (USCONS) vs Civilian Unemployment Rate (UNRATE)

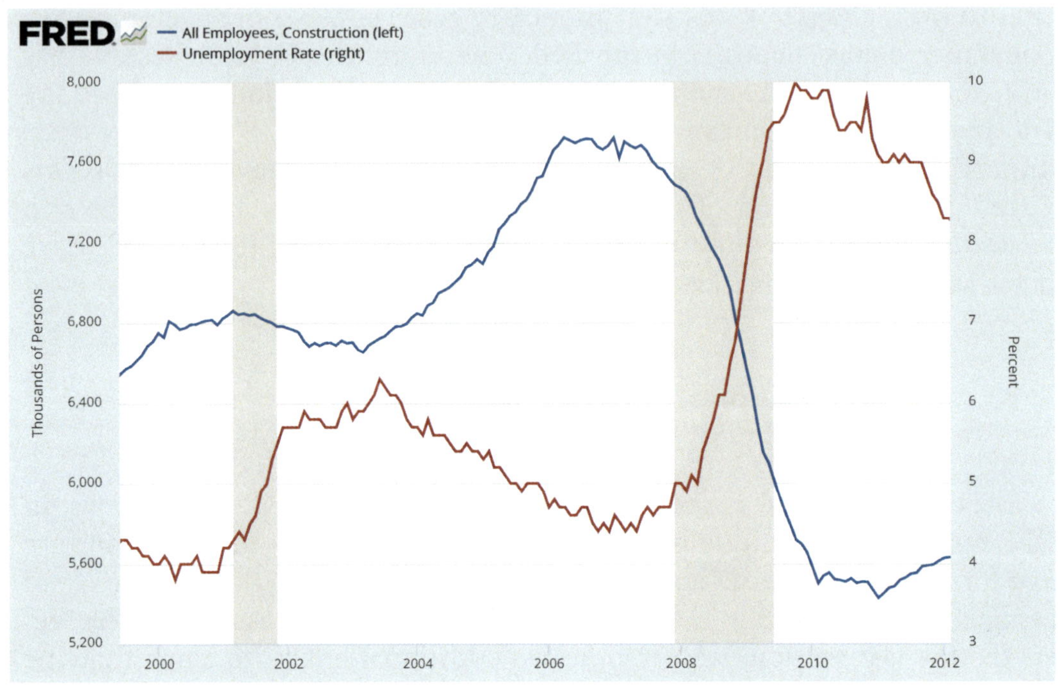

Source: U.S. Bureau of Labor Statistics (US)

Figure 5: All Employees-Construction (USCONS) vs House Price Index for the United States (USSTHPI)

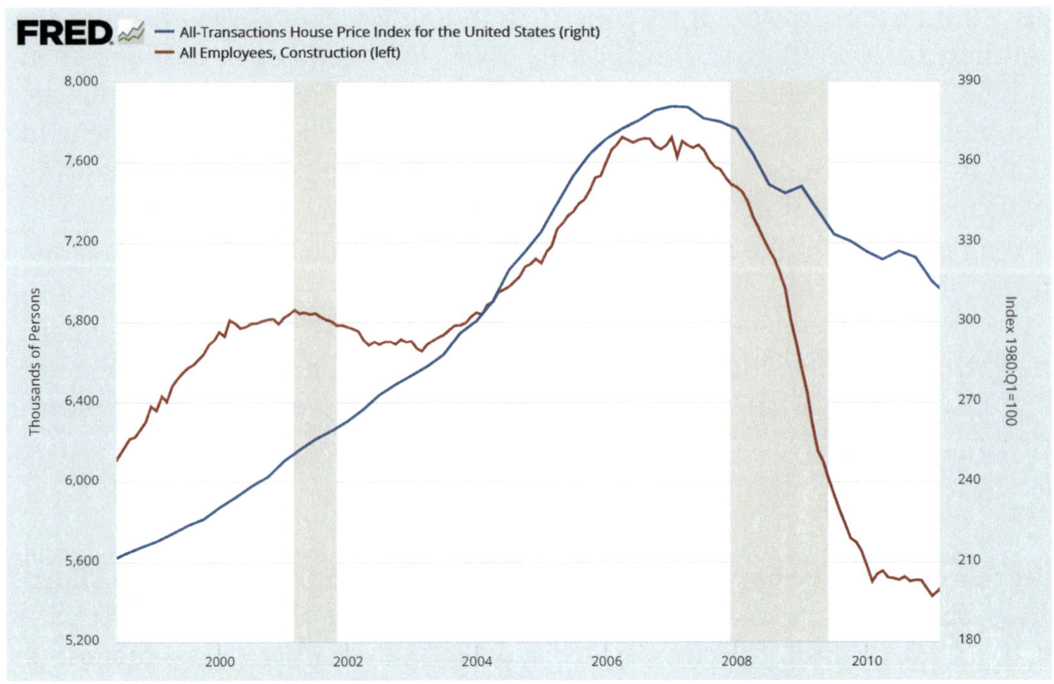

Source: US Federal Housing Finance Agency

not just short-term rates but also thirty-year mortgage rates—fell to historically low levels just as the housing bubble accelerated into high gear. We then showed that the fall and rise in interest rates corresponded with an increase and slowdown in the Fed's monetary inflation, just as any econ textbook would suggest.

Finally, we showed that the movement in home prices behaved as would be expected with respect to total construction employment and that this in turn tied up in the obvious way with the national unemployment rate. We have thus shown empirical evidence for each crucial link in the standard Austrian story of how "easy money" can fuel an unsustainable boom, which leads to an inevitable bust.

In closing, we should note that the Austrians didn't merely explain the Fed's role in the housing crash *after* the fact. On the contrary, in September 2003—five years before the financial crisis—Ron Paul testified before the House Financial Services Committee,[3] arguing that federal subsidies to housing, through such entities as Fannie Mae and Freddie Mac, were merely setting the country up for a housing crash. He also mentioned that the Fed's inflation would merely postpone the day of reckoning and make it that much more painful.

In the following year, 2004, Mark Thornton wrote a prescient article for Mises.org entitled "Housing: Too Good to Be True,"[4] in which he warned:

> It has now been three years since the U.S. stock market crash. Greenspan has indicated that interest rates could soon reverse their course, while longer-term interest rates have already moved higher. Higher interest rates should trigger a reversal in the housing market and expose the fallacies of the new paradigm, including how the housing boom has helped cover up increases in price inflation. Unfortunately, this exposure will hurt homeowners and the larger problem could hit the American taxpayer, who could be forced to bail out the banks and government-sponsored mortgage guarantors who have encouraged irresponsible lending practices.

Because Austrians tend to downplay the ability of economics to provide numerical predictions, its critics often mock the school as unscientific and useless for the investor. But the experience of the US housing bubble and bust shows that the Austrians, armed with Mises's theory of the business cycle, gave far better guidance than, say, Ben Bernanke.

---

3. Ron Paul, "Fannie and Freddie," LewRockwell.com, Sept. 10, 2003, https://www.lewrockwell.com/1970/01/ron-paul/fannie-and-freddie/.

4. Mark Thornton, "Housing: Too Good to Be True," *Mises Daily*, June 4, 2004, https://mises.org/library/housing-too-good-be-true.

Part IV
Challenges

Chapter 12

Do the Textbooks Get Money and Banking Backward?

In chapter 4 we reviewed the textbook analysis of how a central bank buys government debt in "open market operations" to add reserves to the banking system, with which commercial banks can then advance loans to their own customers. In this respect we merely summarized the textbook explanation that economists have given for decades. However, over the years a chorus of critics has alleged that this orthodox view is, if anything, *backward*, and that in reality commercial banks take the lead in making loans without regard to their reserves.

In order to have a concrete example of this rival perspective, we will draw on a 2014 report issued by the Bank of England entitled "Money Creation in the Modern Economy."[1] Coming from the UK's central bank—their counterpart to the United States's Federal Reserve—this is an authoritative example of the critique of the orthodox explanation for money and banking.

For our purposes in the present volume, we will select three of the alleged "myths" of money creation that the Bank of England report seeks to correct. (The serious student should of course read the original report for a full understanding of the challenge.) Our goal here is neither to affirm the orthodox explanation nor to concede its defeat, but rather to use the Bank of England's commentary as a springboard for ensuring that current readers truly understand how central banks and commercial banks work together in a fiat-based system to create money.

---

1. Michael McLeay, Amar Radia, and Ryland Thomas, "Money Creation in the Modern Economy," (Bank of England) *Quarterly Bulletin* 2014 Q1, pp. 14–27, available at https://www.bankofengland.co.uk/quarterly-bulletin/2014/q1/money-creation-in-the-modern-economy.

The Bank of England Wants to Overturn (Alleged) Textbook Myths

Below we provide two quotations from the Bank of England report to supply the fodder for the three (alleged) myths that we will discuss in this chapter:

> a common misconception is that the central bank determines the quantity of loans and deposits in the economy by controlling the quantity of central bank money—the so-called "money multiplier" approach. In that view, central banks implement monetary policy by choosing a quantity of reserves. And, because there is assumed to be a constant ratio of broad money to base money, these reserves are then 'multiplied up' to a much greater change in bank loans and deposits. For the theory to hold, the amount of reserves must be a binding constraint on lending.... **While the money multiplier theory can be a useful way of introducing money and banking in economic textbooks, it is not an accurate description of how money is created in reality.** Rather than controlling the quantity of reserves, central banks today typically implement monetary policy by setting the price of reserves—that is, interest rates.
>
> **In reality, neither are reserves a binding constraint on lending**, nor does the central bank fix the amount of reserves that are available. As with the relationship between deposits and loans, **the relationship between reserves and loans typically operates in the reverse way to that described in some economics textbooks. Banks first decide how much to lend** depending on the profitable lending opportunities available to them—which will, crucially, depend on the interest rate set by the [central bank]. It is these lending decisions that determine how many bank deposits are created by the banking system. **The amount of bank deposits in turn influences how much central bank money banks want to hold in reserve...which is then, in normal times, supplied on demand by the [central bank].** [McLeay, Radia, and Thomas 2014, p. 15, bold added.]

And then later in the report the authors argue, "A related misconception is that banks can lend out their reserves. Reserves can only be lent *between* banks, since consumers cannot have access to reserves accounts at the [central bank]" (ibid., p. 16, italics in original).

(Alleged) Myth No. 1 Banks Lend Out Reserves

This particular "myth" is largely a matter of semantics, but the Bank of England treatment might mislead some readers. Here we will attempt to clarify what really happens when banks make new loans.

Suppose Acme Bank starts in a position where its existing customers have a total of $100 million on deposit with the bank. In other words, if you added up the checking account balances of all of Acme Bank's customers the total would be $100 million.

At the same time, Acme Bank starts off with $10 million in reserves. These reserves consist of (a) $2 million in vault cash and (b) $8 million in Acme's own account held with the Federal Reserve.

Now Acme Bank decides to grant new loans to business owners to the tune of $5 million. At the moment of granting these new loans, Acme Bank sets up the new customers with checking accounts, and the total amount on deposit in these accounts is $5 million. That means Acme's total outstanding deposits now stand at $105 million.

It is certainly true that the act of granting new loans did not *itself* reduce the amount of Acme's reserves. The bank still has $2 million in currency in its vaults, and the Fed still reports that Acme's account with it contains $8 million.

However, the whole point of the public getting loans from Acme Bank is to *spend the borrowed money*. That is, the business owners who just got new loans from Acme will go around the community buying items for their businesses. They will either write out paper checks or swipe a plastic card tied to their new checking accounts with Acme.

In practice, some of the merchants and employees who receive these payments will *themselves* also be clients of Acme Bank. In that case, the spending of the newly loaned funds will not affect Acme's overall accounts; it will just involve changing the numbers to reflect how Acme's $105 million in total customer deposits is distributed among its customers.

However, *most* of the recipients of the new spending will typically be customers of *other* banks. Suppose that of the newly created $5 million, 80 percent of it—that is, $4 million—gets spent on goods and services provided by people who bank somewhere *other* than Acme. After Acme and the other banks in the community engage in clearing operations, Acme must "settle up" with them and transfer $4 million in its reserves, which we can assume happens by the Fed transferring the reserves in Acme's account to the accounts of the other banks.

When the dust settles after this first round of spending, Acme Bank will only have $101 million in total customer deposits (because the other $4 million is now in the personal checking accounts of people who don't bank with Acme), and Acme's total reserves will only be $6 million. These $6 million in reserves consist of the original $2 million in vault cash but now only $4 million on deposit in Acme's own account with the Fed ($8 million – $4 million = $4 million).

This type of process is what the textbook writers had in mind when they claimed that a bank would "lend out its excess reserves" by making new loans. There is a definite sense in which Acme's decision to grant new loans to the public will—soon enough—lead to a drain of reserves *from Acme*.

Now, in fairness, the authors of the Bank of England study could clarify that even in our hypothetical story, *the banking system as a whole* didn't "lend out reserves." Remember, in our story the total reserves in the system were just rearranged among Acme and the other banks. When Acme granted $5 million in new loans, that action simply increased Acme's outstanding deposits. And when $4 million of those newly created deposits were spent on clients of other banks, Acme simply transferred $4 million of its original reserves *to those other banks*, not to individuals in the community.

However, we can make just one little tweak to the story to show that there is an even more direct sense in which a commercial bank can "lend out its reserves." Suppose that one of the business owners, after receiving a new loan from Acme, wants to withdraw *actual currency* in order to give several of her employees "petty cash" that they will need for their duties. (Perhaps these employees are going to an industry convention and need to be able to pay for cabs, tip the bellboy at the hotel, buy pizza and get it delivered to the hotel room, etc.) More specifically, suppose that after being granted a new loan from Acme and seeing how much she has in her new checking account, the business owner goes to the bank teller and withdraws a total of $10,000 in the form of five hundred $20 bills.

In this case, Acme's vault cash—which, remember, started out at $2 million—has dropped to $1,990,000. That means that Acme's total reserves have dropped by the $10,000 that its client withdrew from the bank after being granted a new loan. This is an even more direct way in which a commercial bank can "lend out its reserves."

Now it's true that even here the authors of the Bank of England study could object that *we don't call it* "reserves" when a member of the public holds currency, even though those same $20 bills were considered reserves when they sat in Acme's vault.

But this is obviously a matter of semantics, not economics. For an analogy, consider this puzzle: Would it be wrong to say that a department store "sells its inventory" to members of the public? After all, we only call it "inventory" when the *store* owns it—the "inventory" turns into "merchandise" when the customer walks out of the store. But clearly, there is nothing wrong economically with saying that a department store sells its inventory to the public. Likewise, there is nothing wrong with saying that a commercial bank, in granting new loans, lends out some of its reserves.

(Alleged) Myth No. 2
Banks Worry About Reserve Requirements When Making Loans

When disentangling this issue, again we must distinguish things from the perspective of an individual bank versus the entire banking system. As we showed in our hypothetical story above, it *is* true that an individual bank can grant a new loan simply by crediting a new checking account for a borrower. This action will increase the bank's total outstanding deposits.

Now if the government/central bank has formal reserve requirements (which was true in the United States up until they were dropped in March 2020, amid the coronavirus panic[2]), an individual bank must ensure that it has enough reserves to meet the legal requirement. If the bank is short, it must go to the federal funds market and borrow the necessary reserves from other banks. Remember that the "federal funds rate" is the interest rate that banks charge each other for overnight loans of reserves. (These principles were described in chapters 4 and 6.)

So although any individual bank can go to the federal funds market and borrow enough reserves to satisfy its individual requirements, *the banking system as a whole* can't create new reserves. If Acme Bank borrows $4 million in the federal funds market to replenish the $4 million in reserves that it lost in our story above, those reserves must have come from other banks that had excess reserves. When the commercial banks lend money among themselves, these actions don't have the power to alter the total amount of paper currency or bank deposits with the Fed itself. In other words, only the Fed (in conjunction with the Treasury) has the legal power to create US dollars as part of the monetary base.

In any event, to show why, historically, the economics textbook writers assumed that under normal circumstances the banks would keep making new loans until the total amount of "excess reserves" dwindled away, consider the following chart:

2. The Federal Reserve announced that it would abolish formal reserve requirements effective March 26, 2020. See "Federal Reserve Actions to Support the Flow of Credit to Households and Businesses," Press Releases, Board of Governors of the Federal Reserve System, Mar. 15, 2020, https://www.federalreserve.gov/newsevents/pressreleases/monetary20200315b.htm.

Figure 1. Total and Required Reserves of US Depository Institutions, January 1959–February 2007

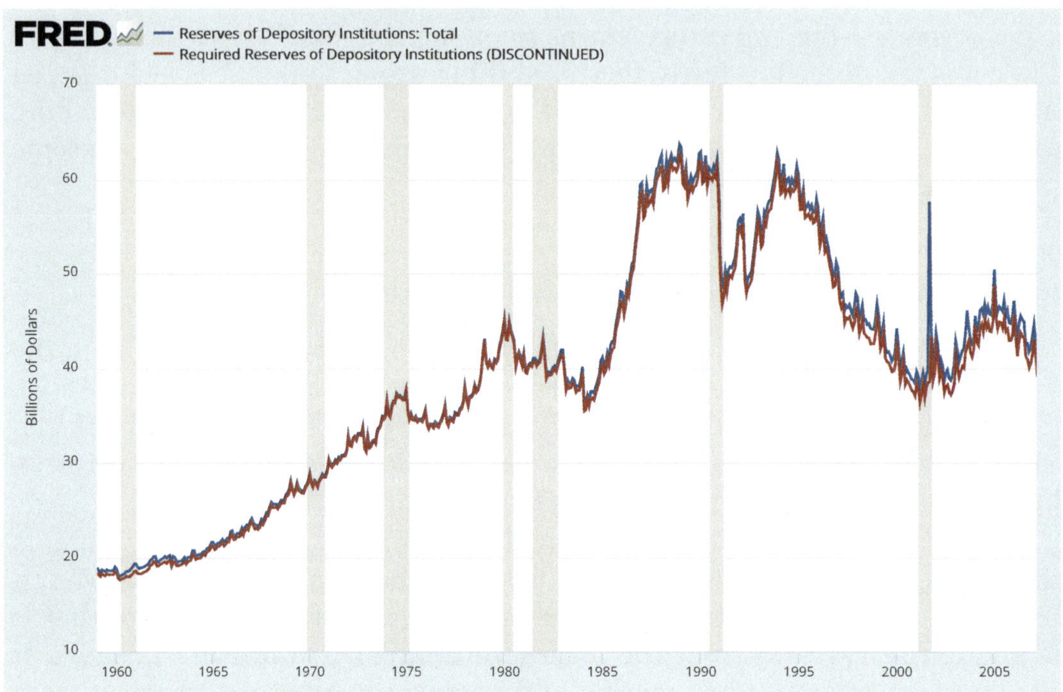

Source: Board of Governors of the Federal Reserve System (US

As Figure 1 shows, it was typical in the US for the banks to hold *actual* reserves very close to their legally required amount. And since the Fed itself ultimately controlled the quantity of actual reserves, the standard textbook story of open market operations was quite sensible.

However, the Bank of England authors are correct when they say that this textbook story assumes that banks make new loans up until the point when all of the excess reserves have been squeezed out of the system. In particular, we can see that since the financial crisis of 2008, the US banking system has been awash in excess reserves:

Figure 2. Total and Required Reserves of US Depository Institutions, February 2007–February 2020

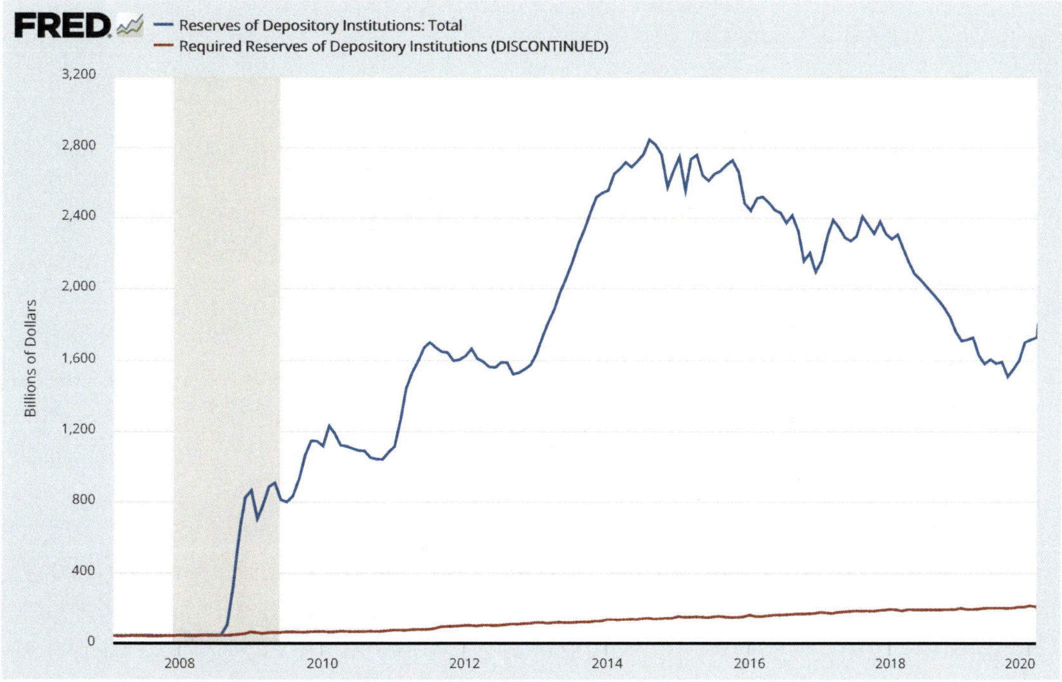

Source: Board of Governors of the Federal Reserve System (US)

What Figure 2 shows us is that in the wake of the massive rounds of QE (quantitative easing) following the financial crisis, US banks had the legal ability—at least with respect to formal reserve requirements—to create many trillions of dollars' worth of new loans for customers. But they chose not to do so (for various reasons, some of which we will discuss in chapter 13), hence the amount of "excess reserves" in the entire system skyrocketed. We show this in Figure 3:

Figure 3. Excess Reserves of US Depository Institutions, February 1984–February 2020

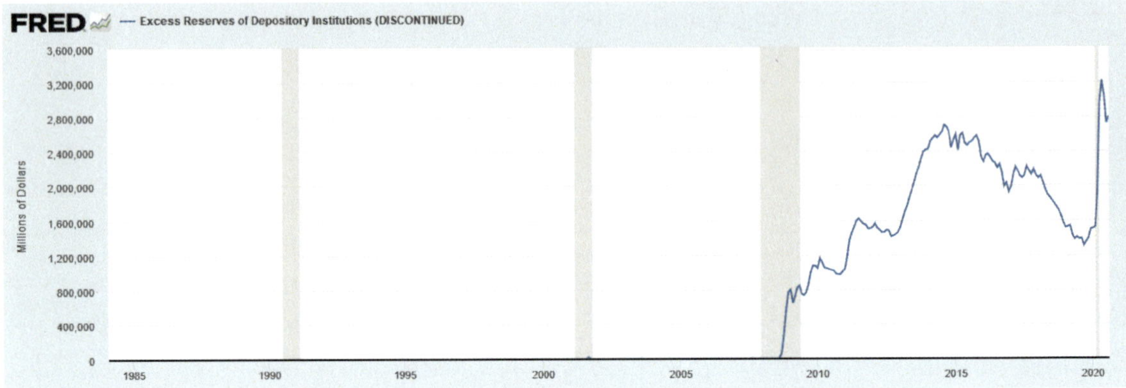

Source: Board of Governors of the Federal Reserve System (US)

As Figure 3 indicates, for most of the Fed's history, the amount of excess reserves in the system was close to zero. (Technically this chart only goes back to 1984, but Figure 1 shows that the pattern holds back to 1959, and in fact it holds even further back.)

Although it is beyond the scope of the present volume, when discussing reserve requirements there are two other complicating factors: one is that governments/central banks may impose not only *reserve* requirements but also *capital* requirements; these regulations also influence how banks operate when making loans and holding certain assets.

A second complicating factor is that commercial banks need to hold reserves even when there is no legal requirement to do so. For example, banks need to honor the typical customer request to withdraw money from an ATM or at the bank counter, and so *some* vault cash—which counts as part of the bank's reserves—must always be on hand, regardless of whether government regulations insist upon it.[3]

3. Some economists argue that with the adoption of "sweep accounts" by US banks in the 1990s, the formal reserve requirements became inconsequential as banks could sweep their client deposits into non-reserve-required accounts each night. In practice, the banks could keep their reserves at whatever their vault cash needs dictated, and then use sweep accounts to reduce their apparent outstanding deposits such that their actual reserves (consisting mostly of vault cash) satisfied their postsweep reserve requirements. See George Selgin, "Floored! How a Misguided Fed Experiment Deepened and Prolonged the Great Recession" (Cato working paper, no. 50/CMFA no. 11, Center for Monetary and Financial Alternatives, Cato Institute, Washington, DC, Mar. 1, 2018, rev. Mar. 13, 2018), p. 10, available at https://www.cato.org/sites/cato.org/files/pubs/pdf/working-paper-50-updated-3.pdf, published as Floored! How a

(Alleged) Myth No. 3 The Central Bank Controls the Amount of Base Money

With this final (alleged) myth, the dispute is again largely one of semantics. Here is what the Bank of England authors have in mind:

Before the financial crisis of 2008, a central bank would typically set policy by picking a target for the interest rate that banks charge each other for overnight loans of reserves—in the US, we would say that the Fed set a target for the federal funds rate.

Suppose the Fed target is 5 percent. If the economy is on an upswing and the commercial banks spot numerous profitable lending opportunities, they begin advancing more loans to new borrowers. Other things equal, more and more banks would find that they need extra reserves in order to satisfy their reserve requirements (or simply to bolster vault cash to accommodate the increased activity from more customer deposits).

If the Fed didn't take any action, then the banks' increased clamoring for reserves would push up the market interest rate on overnight loans of those reserves, perhaps to 6 percent. In other words, in an environment where the banks perceive new lending opportunities, their activity would tend to push the *actual* federal funds rate above the Fed's desired *target* federal funds rate.

In order to maintain its target, the Fed would have no choice but to engage in open market operations, in which it would buy new assets and create more reserves, thus pushing the actual fed funds rate back down to the desired 5 percent target. *This* is the kind of mechanism that the authors of the Bank of England study have in mind, in which the central bank passively responds to the banks' "needs" for reserves.

However, this is largely a matter of semantics. It is still the case that the central bank controls the total quantity of base money, and that the commercial banks can't create new reserves. The textbook description is still correct: When the fed funds rate is 6 percent and the Fed wants to push it down to 5 percent, the Fed must buy assets and inject new reserves into the system.

Summary

After reading the orthodox discussion of money creation given in chapters 4 and 6 of the present volume, readers may find it helpful to read the alternative description given by critics of that textbook view. In this chapter, we have reviewed the critique offered by writers for the Bank of England.

Although most of the dispute hinges on semantics, there are some sub-

---

Misguided Fed Experiment Deepened and Prolonged the Great Recession (Washington, DC: Cato Institute, 2018).

stantive differences in perspective. To avoid confusion and achieve better comprehension of the actual mechanics of central and commercial bank activities, readers should read both descriptions and understand the extent to which they are each correct.

Chapter 13

Crying Wolf on (Hyper)Inflation?

In chapter 9 we explained the connection between monetary inflation and price inflation, and warned that there is no simple one-to-one relationship. This fact has been very relevant in the wake of the various rounds of quantitative easing (QE) that the Federal Reserve implemented after the financial crisis of 2008. The following chart shows the huge increase in the monetary base since 2008:

Figure 1: Monetary Base

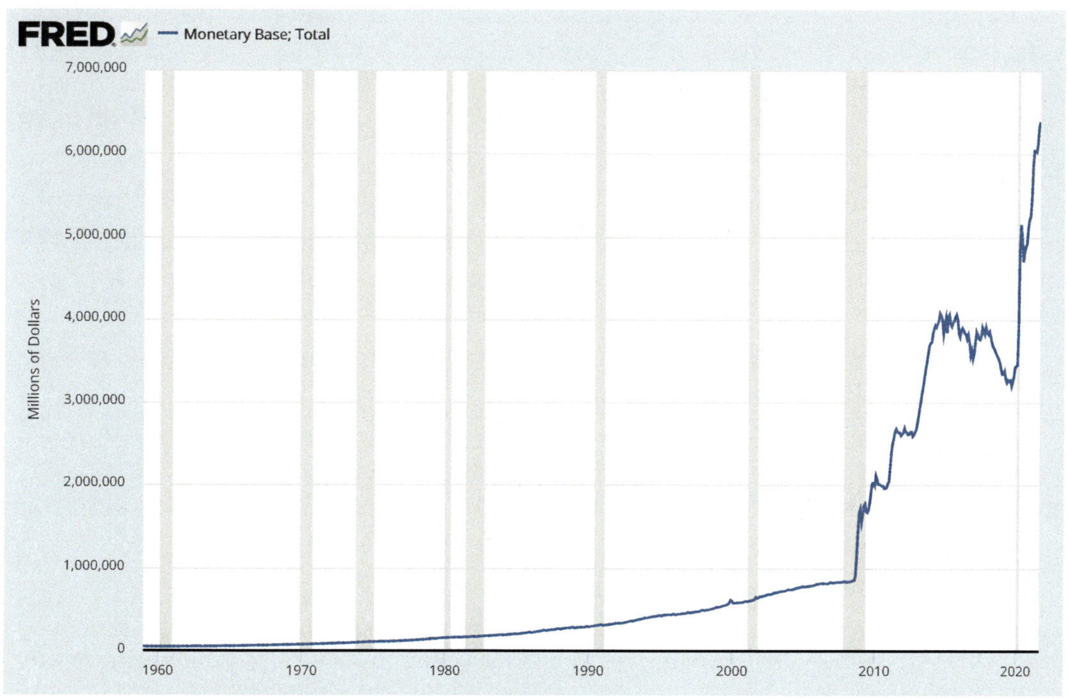

Source: Board of Governors of the Federal Reserve System (US)

In the early years of QE, many economists—including the present author[1]—warned that the Fed's unprecedented monetary inflation would cause a significant increase in consumer prices. Some pundits went so far as to warn of actual hyperinflation, reminding Americans of the terrible experiences of Weimar Germany and modern Zimbabwe. Yet years passed by without the "inflation time bomb" exploding. This led the *proponents* of the Fed's policies to mock the warnings as crying wolf.

In this chapter, we'll assess several popular explanations for why the Fed's monetary inflation since 2008 hasn't generated a comparable increase in price inflation. Because this book is intended to be educational rather than polemical, we will merely mention some of the pros and cons for each possibility, rather than arguing which are correct and which should be rejected.

"The government's CPI measure vastly understates price inflation."

The benefit of this type of explanation is that it focuses proper cynicism on data produced by government agencies, which are not renowned for their unwavering devotion to truth.

However, the problem with this explanation is that many critics of QE were warning of *significant* price inflation that could not have been hidden through statistical tricks. Americans were able to fill up their vehicles in 2010 (say) and for most drivers the price was $3 or less per gallon of gasoline. If some of the more serious warnings of price inflation had proved correct, this would not have been possible.

Keep in mind that the official government measures showed twelve-month CPI (Consumer Price Index) inflation hit a whopping 14.6 percent in March 1980. Had the government told Americans at that time that inflation were under 2 percent, it would have been an obvious lie. So although the conventional measures may be significantly understating the rising cost of living

1. Specifically, the present author lost public wagers to (free market) economists David R. Henderson and Bryan Caplan on whether twelve-month CPI increases would exceed 10 percent by January 2013 and January 2016, respectively. For a discussion from various economists on why their price inflation predictions turned out right or wrong, see Brian Doherty, Peter Schiff, David R. Henderson, Scott Sumner, and Robert Murphy, "Whatever Happened to Inflation?," *Reason*, December 2014, https://reason.com/2014/11/30/whatever-happened-to-inflation/.

since 2008, the mismatch between the extreme warnings and reality can't be explained *entirely* by reference to data fudging.

"Inflation won't be a problem while we still suffer from an output gap / idle resources."

According to both Keynesians and proponents of MMT (modern monetary theory), increased government spending—even if financed by monetary inflation—won't generate large increases in consumer prices so long as the economy is operating below its capacity. In more technical terms, they argue that so long as real GDP is below potential GDP, increases in nominal spending serve to boost real output rather than prices. The intuitive idea is that the unemployed and other idle resources will absorb new spending first, before tightening labor and resource markets cause wages and other prices to begin rising.

On the plus side, the Keynesians and MMT camp were correct when they said the various rounds of QE since 2008 would *not* cause extreme price inflation, let alone hyperinflation. Since some of their opponents *did* predict such a result, the Keynesians and MMTers can understandably claim vindication.

However, there are numerous problems with this explanation. For one thing, the Keynesians didn't *merely* predict a lack of significant price inflation; many of them predicted price *de*flation. For example, Paul Krugman in a blog post in early 2010 posted a graph of collapsing CPI inflation, warned that the disinflation could soon turn to outright deflation, and ended with, "Japan, here we come."[2] (Japan had experienced sustained reductions in CPI.)

Five months later, Krugman admitted that the standard Keynesian tool of the Phillips curve—which models a tradeoff, at least in the short run, between unemployment and (price) inflation—hadn't worked so well in the aftermath of the financial crisis. As Krugman acknowledged in a post entitled, "The Mysteries of Deflation (Wonkish)," coming into the Great Recession, "the inflation-adjusted Phillips curve predict[ed] not just deflation, but *accelerating* deflation in the face of a really prolonged economic slump" (italics in original).[3] And since that hadn't happened, the Keynesians too had to tinker with their model in light of reality. To generalize, in 2009 the conservative economists had predicted accelerating inflation, while the progressive economists had predicted accelerating deflation.

---

2. Paul Krugman, "Core Logic," Paul Krugman blogs, *New York Times*, Feb. 26, 2010, https://krugman.blogs.nytimes.com/2010/02/26/core-logic/.

3. Paul Krugman, "The Mysteries of Deflation (Wonkish)," Paul Krugman blogs, *New York Times*, July 26, 2010, https://krugman.blogs.nytimes.com/2010/07/26/mysteries-of-deflation-wonkish/.

Another serious problem with the no-inflation-until-full-employment doctrine is that it was disproved in the so-called stagflation of the 1970s. The Keynesian mindset of the postwar era had originally led policymakers to believe that they had to choose between *either* high unemployment *or* high inflation in consumer prices. It should not have been possible for the economy to suffer through *both* evils at the same time.

And yet, once Richard Nixon killed the last vestiges of the gold standard in 1971 (which we explained in chapter 2), the remainder of the decade saw unusually high levels of both. For example, in May 1975 the unemployment rate was 9 percent while the twelve-month change in CPI was 9.3 percent. In light of the US experience of the 1970s, simple rules such as "the economy can't overheat while there are still idle resources" can't be the full story.

"Yes, the money supply increased dramatically after mid-2008, but the demand to hold it increased as well."

On the plus side, this explanation is necessarily correct; *every* fact about prices can be handled in a supply-and-demand framework. The "price" of money refers to its purchasing power; how many units of goods and services can a unit of money fetch on the market? If we hold the demand for money constant and vastly increase its supply (through rounds of QE, for example), then the "price of money" falls, meaning the currency becomes weaker, meaning that the prices of goods and services quoted in that money go up. This is of course just another way of describing price inflation.

However, in practice other things might not remain equal; the demand for money might increase too, especially during a financial crisis. Remember that the "demand to hold money" isn't the same thing as a desire for more *wealth*. If someone has (say) $100,000 in liquid wealth, it will generally be diversified among several assets, including stocks, bonds, precious metals, life insurance, cryptocurrencies, and some in actual money (whether literal cash on hand or money on deposit in a checking account). During times of great uncertainty, the advantages of holding actual money become more important to many people, and so they adjust their portfolios to hold a greater share of their wealth in the form of money. This is what it means to say the "demand to hold money" increases.

After the fact, because we didn't observe an unusual drop in the purchasing power of the US dollar from 2008 onward, we can confidently say that the demand to hold US dollars increased to offset the increase in US dollars orchestrated by the Federal Reserve. This is necessarily true.

However, the downside of this explanation is that we can only be sure to apply it correctly *in hindsight*. If we want to assess what will happen to the path of price inflation in the future, we need to forecast changes on both the supply and demand sides, and of course we might be *wrong* about our forecasts. This becomes especially problematic if changes in the supply of money *directly cause* an increase in the demand to hold it, a possibility we discuss in the next section.

"Of course QE wasn't inflationary. Since the economy was stuck in a liquidity trap, the Fed's bond purchases were just an asset swap."

As we explain in chapters 6 and 14, Keynesian economists argued that once the Fed had slashed nominal interest rates to zero in the wake of the 2008 financial crisis, the US economy was in a "liquidity trap," where conventional monetary policy no longer had traction. At this point, so the story went, the Fed had to switch to so-called quantitative easing, where the emphasis was on the size of the central bank's asset purchases (rather than its target for the relevant interest rate). In the Keynesian view, the relative impotence of monetary policy during a liquidity trap was the justification for government budget deficits (i.e., fiscal policy) as a means of boosting aggregate demand.

One offshoot of this typical Keynesian framework was the argument that the Fed's purchase of Treasury securities looked like a mere asset swap. (It should be noted that Chicago school economist and Nobel laureate Eugene Fama *also* made this argument, not just Keynesians.[4]) It was true that the Fed's bond purchases "created money out of thin air" and injected it into the economy, as the critics warned. But in so doing, the Fed took government debt securities *out* of the economy as well. And to the extent that US Treasury securities earning (close to) 0 percent are similar to bank reserves parked at the Fed (which also earned close to 0 percent), the inflationary impact of the QE programs was significantly muted. A $10 billion purchase injected $10 billion of base money into the financial sector, but it simultaneously removed $10 billion of "near money."

The benefit of this explanation is that it is an important caveat to a naïve supply-and-demand analysis; it would be foolish to focus merely on increases in the supply of money *if the very process that created the money* also boosted the demand for cash (by removing "near money" substitutes dollar for dollar).

---

4. The entire debate lies outside the scope of the present book, but readers should be aware that some prominent Keynesians—in particular Paul Krugman and Brad DeLong—changed sides on this issue. See Scott Sumner, "Brad Delong, Sounding Unusually Market Monetarist, Calls a Nobel Prize-Winning Believer in Liquidity Traps a 'Dumbass,'" *Money Illusion* (blog), October 30, 2013, https://www.themoneyillusion.com/brad-delong-sounding-unusually-market-monetarist-calls-a-nobel-prize-winning-believer-in-liquidity-traps-a-dumbass/.

The downside of this analysis is that it ignores the influence central bank policy has on asset prices. For an exaggerated example, suppose the Federal Reserve announced a new plan of buying any model year 2010 Ford pickup truck for $100,000. This announcement would immediately cause the "market price" of such trucks to jump to $100,000. At the moment of sale, the Fed would be engaged in a mere asset swap; it would provide $100,000 in new bank reserves in exchange for a truck valued at $100,000. Yet, clearly, our hypothetical truck-buying program would distort the used vehicle market and would financially benefit the lucky owners of 2010 Ford trucks. In the same way, even though at the moment of purchasing Treasury bonds the Fed is engaging in an asset swap, the "market" price of those Treasury bonds might be propped up by the Fed's purchase itself.

"The Fed's new policy of paying interest on reserves arrested the usual money multiplier."

As we explained in chapter 6, in October 2008 the Fed implemented a new policy of paying interest on bank reserves parked at the Fed. From an individual commercial bank's perspective, the interest payment offered an incentive to *refrain* from making new loans to customers. Because of the massive QE purchases, plenty of newly created bank reserves flooded the system. Yet even though commercial banks had the legal ability to pyramid trillions of dollars of newly created loans on top of the Fed's injections, they largely remained on the sidelines. Figure 2 of "excess" bank reserves illustrates this unprecedented development.

As Figure 2 indicates, prior to the financial crisis it was typical for the banking system as a whole to be (nearly) "fully loaned up," meaning that excess reserves were close to $0. In other words, the normal state of affairs—prior to 2008—was for banks to make loans to their own customers until the point at which all of their reserves were "required reserves," meaning that they legally couldn't lend more money and still satisfy their reserves requirements.

Yet after 2008, as the Fed injected new reserves into the system through its three rounds of QE, the commercial banks did not lend out (several multiples of) these new reserves, as a standard textbook treatment would suggest. As the chart shows, at the (local) peak in mid-2014, excess reserves were just shy of $2.7 *trillion*. Could the policy of paying interest on reserves, begun in October 2008, explain this pattern?

The introduction of interest payments was indeed an important innovation in Fed policy, giving the central bank a means of divorcing its open market operations from interest rate targets. (For example, when the Fed began raising its policy interest rate in late 2015, its balance sheet remained constant for about two years thereafter. The Fed steadily raised rates during this period by

Figure 2: Excess Reserves of Depository Institutions

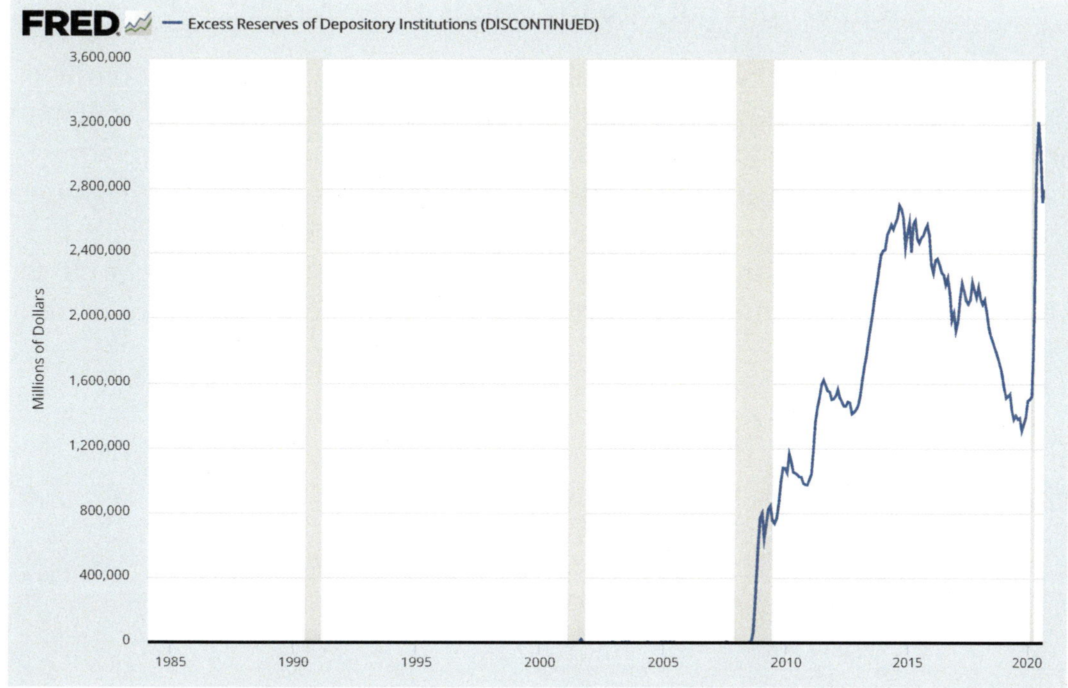

Source: Federal Reserve Bank of St. Louis (US)

hiking the interest rate paid on reserves, *not* by selling off Fed assets.) When trying to understand commercial bank loan activity from late 2008 onward, the Fed's new policy is definitely an important consideration.

However, when answering the question, "Why didn't the Fed's QE programs cause significant consumer price inflation?" the new policy of interest on reserves seems inadequate to bear the full weight of the explanation. After bouncing around (but never rising above 1.15 percent) in the first few months after its introduction, the interest rate paid on excess reserves settled at 0.25 percent by mid-December 2008. It stayed at that near-zero level for a full seven years, being raised to 0.50 percent in mid-December 2015.

It seems unlikely that a mere twenty-five basis points can explain why nearly $2.7 trillion in excess reserves piled up in the banking system rather than being funneled into new loans. Presumably, even *without* the extra inducement of a guaranteed 0.25 percent, commercial banks would have kept most of their new reserves safely parked at the Fed from 2008 through 2015.

"The new money stayed bottled up in the banks; it never got out into the hands of the public."

Whether tied to the Fed's policy of paying interest on reserves, a common explanation for the lack of significant consumer price inflation is that the newly injected money never got into the hands of the general public.

The benefit of this insight is that it correctly takes note of the huge increase in excess reserves (shown in the chart above). Yet it fails to account for the fact that M1, which includes currency held by the public as well as checking account balances, *did* begin a rapid increase in the wake of the financial crisis:

Figure 3: M1 Monetary Stock

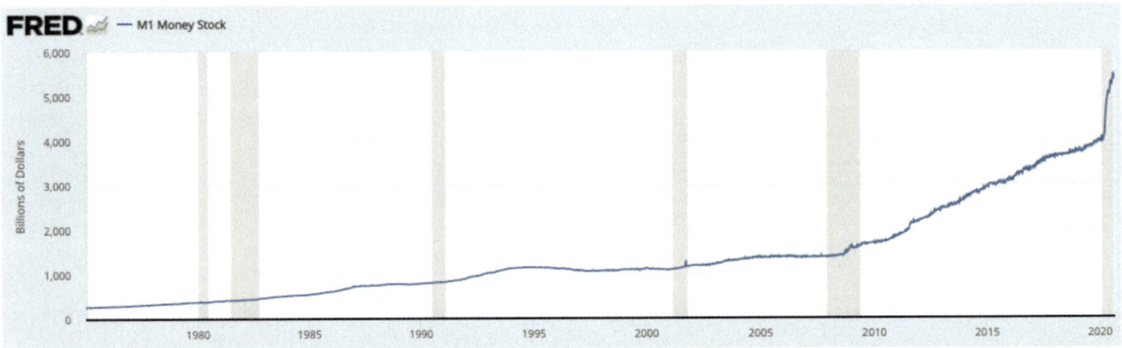

NOTE: The above chart was created before the Fed in February 2021 changed its M1 money stock series retroactively back to May 2020. (For details see the discussion in chapter 8.) In particular, the spike shown in the spring of 2020 existed even with the original definition of M1; it shows an actual increase in money held by the public, and is not an artifact of the Fed's 2021 statistical revision.

As the chart shows, the M1 money stock was virtually flat from early 2005 through early 2008. Yet it began steadily rising from late 2008 onward (and of course spiked dramatically during the coronavirus panic in 2020). We can't explain the lack of high CPI inflation by claiming there was no new money held by the public, because this simply isn't true.

"The new money went into the stock market, real estate, and commodities, not into retail goods."

The benefit of this type of explanation is that it underscores the arbitrariness of the conventional public discussions about money and prices. Why should the particular metric of the Consumer Price Index, as tabulated by the Bureau of Labor Statistics with its controversial techniques of "hedonic" adjustments, be the default measure of "inflation"? Indeed, academic economists have long argued that on a theoretical level, rising asset prices can be indicative of "easy money" just as surely as rising consumer prices.[5] For an obvious example, rising home prices are relevant to "the cost of shelter" along with real estate *rental* prices, even though only the latter are currently included in the CPI.

The danger in this type of explanation is that it often misconstrues what actually happens when new money is injected into the economy. In reality, it is not the case that some money is "in" the stock market, while other portions of the money stock are "in" consumer goods. At any given time, all units of physical currency are held in cash balances, located in people's wallets (or home safes), or inside of commercial bank vaults. If someone buys one hundred shares of a stock at $10 per share, it's not that money "goes into the stock market." Rather, what typically happens is that $1,000 is debited from the checking account of the buyer, while an equal amount is credited to the checking account of the seller. If the buyer and seller are clients of different banks, their transaction might cause some reserves to transfer from one bank to the other, but nobody looking at the money after the fact would be able to tell that it "had gone into the stock market."

"Those warning of significant price inflation will eventually be proven right."

During the housing bubble years in the early and mid-2000s, a growing number of alarmists warned that home prices were rising to absurd levels and that Americans should prepare for a giant crash in real estate and stocks. While the bubble was still inflating, the conventional wisdom dismissed these warnings as baseless fearmongering. It was only *after* the crash that most people recognized that the doomsayers had been correct.

Likewise, it is possible that the US dollar will crash against other currencies, interest rates on US Treasurys will spike, and official CPI inflation will rise well above the Fed's target of 2 percent. If this happens, those early critics of the Fed's QE policies could plausibly claim, "We were right about the impact, just not about the timing."

On the downside, the problem with this explanation is that most of those warning of significant price inflation led their audiences to believe that it would

5. The classic paper is Armen Alchian and Benjamin Klein, "On a Correct Measure of Inflation," *Journal of Money, Credit, and Banking* 5, no. 1 (February 1973): 173–91. For a nontechnical summary, see Robert P. Murphy, "Fed Policy and Asset Prices," *Mises Daily*, Oct. 26, 2011, https://mises.org/library/fed-policy-and-asset-prices.

be hitting within a few years at the latest. If they had coupled their initial warnings with the caveat "CPI inflation won't be a problem for a decade but *then* it will get out of hand," the reaction to their analyses would have been different.

Chapter 14

Keynesians on the Cause of, and Cure for, Depressions

In chapter 8 we presented Ludwig von Mises's explanation of how bank credit expansion causes the boom-bust cycle, what is now known as Austrian business cycle theory. However, the reigning view today in both academia and the popular media is the *Keynesian* explanation, derived from John Maynard Keynes's famous 1936 book *The General Theory of Employment, Interest, and Money*.

In contrast to the Austrians, Keynes viewed depressions as something that could naturally plague market economies when total spending ("aggregate demand") was insufficient to support full employment. Keynes argued that markets didn't possess a self-correcting mechanism and that left to their own devices, markets could be mired in depression for years on end. Only with wise oversight by central banks and government officials could we hope to achieve steady economic growth.

This chapter will summarize the Keynesian view and then challenge it from an Austrian perspective.

The Rhetorical Framing of *The General Theory*

It would be difficult to overstate the extent to which the Keynesian approach has permeated modern society. Although Keynes wasn't the first to blame business downturns on a lack of spending, his 1936 book—released in the midst of an unending global depression—appeared to offer a sophisticated diagnosis of the problem, and furthermore seemed to explain why the traditional economic remedies had failed.

The very *title* of the book reflects Keynes's clever rhetorical framing and helps us nowadays to understand why this book captivated so many of its readers. Keynes himself explains it well in the (very brief) first chapter of the book:

> I have called this book the *General Theory of Employment, Interest and Money*, placing the emphasis on the prefix general. The object of such a title is to contrast the character of my arguments and conclusions with those of the *classical* theory of the subject, upon which I was brought up and which dominates the economic thought, both practical and theoretical, of the governing and academic classes of this generation, as it has for a hundred years past. **I shall argue that the postulates of the classical theory are applicable to a special case only and not to the general case,** the situation which it assumes being a limiting point of the possible positions of equilibrium. *Moreover, the characteristics of the special case assumed by the classical theory happen not to be those of the economic society in which we actually live*, with the result that its teaching is misleading and disastrous if we attempt to apply it to the facts of experience. (Keynes 1936,[1] p. 11, bold added)

It would have been presumptuous and provoked defensiveness for Keynes to argue that his predecessors were complete buffoons and totally wrong. Instead, as the introductory chapter explains, Keynes argued that their "classical" approach was correct *under certain conditions* (namely, when the economy is at full employment) but that *in general* those conditions might not be fulfilled.

1. In this chapter, references to *The General Theory* use the pagination contained in this (free) online version of the book: John Maynard Keynes, *The General Theory of Employment, Interest, and Money* (1936; ETH Zurich International Relations and Security Network, n.d.), https://www.files.ethz.ch/isn/125515/1366_KeynesTheoryofEmployment.pdf.

In that case—such as the world faced in 1936—Keynes proposed a more *general* theory that could handle all possible scenarios.

Thus, Keynes was proposing to do for economics what Albert Einstein had done for physics: Einstein's theory of relativity didn't say that the classical mechanics of Isaac Newton were totally wrong. Instead, Einstein proposed equations that described the behavior of matter and energy under more general circumstances. Then, *in the special case* when the objects moved at only a small fraction of the speed of light, Einstein's system "reduced to" the more familiar Newtonian system. This explained to physicists why Newton's model had initially seemed so successful but also demonstrated the superiority of Einstein's approach.

To be sure, there are serious problems with Keynes's rhetorical framing. For one thing, it was a misnomer to use the term "classical," when that phrase already had a well-established meaning among economists, to refer to the doctrines based on the labor theory of value that were dominant before the so-called Marginal Revolution of the 1870s. Even more serious, Keynes was wrong to claim that his predecessors "assumed" full employment. As an obvious example, which we discussed in chapter 8, Mises developed his own theory of the business cycle in 1912—two decades before Keynes!

Despite these problems, Keynes's rhetorical framing surely helps to explain the impact of his book. Another common explanation is that the Keynesian framework provided a seemingly scientific justification for increased government spending and intervention in markets, which was music to the ears of many academics and political officials. Ironically, Keynes himself acknowledged this affinity in the 1936 preface to the German edition when he wrote:

> [T]he theory of output as a whole, which is what the following book purports to provide, is much more easily adapted to the conditions of a totalitarian state, than is the theory of the production and distribution of a given output produced under conditions of free competition and a large measure of laissez-faire. (Keynes 1936, p. 6)

The Paradox of Thrift

Perhaps the quickest way to illustrate the divide between Keynesian and "orthodox" economics is the so-called paradox of thrift. According to conventional wisdom as well as a straightforward application of economic principles, when the community saves more, this allows for more investment spending, and is thereby the path to growing productivity and rising living standards. Yet as Keynes explained in the 1939 preface to the French edition of his book:

> **Quite legitimately we regard an individual's income as independent of what he himself consumes and invests. But this, I have to point out, should not have led us to overlook the fact that the demand arising out of the consumption and investment of one individual is the source of the incomes of other individuals, so that incomes in general are not independent, quite the contrary, of the disposition of individuals to spend and invest....** It is shown that, generally speaking, the actual level of output and employment depends, not on the capacity to produce or on the pre-existing level of incomes, but on the current decisions to produce which depend in turn on current decisions to invest and on present expectations of current and prospective consumption. Moreover, as soon as we know the propensity to consume and to save ... *we can calculate what level of incomes, and therefore what level of output and employment, is in profit-equilibrium with a given level of new investment*; out of which develops the doctrine of the Multiplier. Or again, it becomes evident that **an increased propensity to save will ceteris paribus contract incomes and output**; whilst an increased inducement to invest will expand them. (Keynes 1936, p. 9, bold added)

The above excerpt is a good distillation of the entire enterprise of *The General Theory*. Rather than viewing the economy from the perspective of an individual household or firm—where we start each time period with a particular level of income out of which consumption and investment are financed—Keynes reversed causality. Individual and business decisions to consume or invest, driven by psychological considerations, *determine* the level of income in the community.

Under the "paradox of thrift," when hard times hit, the seemingly rational thing for households and businesses is to tighten their belts and eliminate superfluous spending. But from a Keynesian perspective, this leads to disaster, as the drop in spending only further reduces the income in the economy. This is why government budget deficits—a form of negative saving—are called for, as they can more than pay for themselves through the "multiplier."

Even though the economic models and arguments have been refined over the decades, this basic Keynesian attitude survives to this day. The hostility to saving is apparent in the writings of economists like Paul Krugman, but also among central bankers such as Ben Bernanke, who justified his unprecedented actions as Fed chair by reference to the dread of "deflation" (by which he meant falling prices). And the popular press toes the Keynesian line as well: amid the COVID-19 crisis, a CNN headline declared, "New threat to the economy: Americans are saving like it's the 1980s."[2]

The Keynesian Understanding of the Great Depression

According to Keynes, the persistence of the Great Depression showed the failure of "classical" economic doctrines and policies. If the market economy had a self-corrective mechanism, why had the world been mired in high unemployment for years on end?

According to Keynes, his orthodox colleagues were unable to explain persistent unemployment. As he argues in chapter 2, the orthodox school had to believe that if unemployment were excessively high, then market forces would eventually bring down the wage rate, at least as measured in "real" terms (i.e., adjusted for price inflation). The falling (real) wage rate would reduce the number of people looking for work, and it would increase the amount of workers that employers wanted to hire. Thus, any "glut" in the labor market should be quickly eliminated according to the orthodox economists.

Keynes pointed out two flaws with this argument. First, it simply didn't fit the facts: workers strongly resisted cuts in the actual money wages they received, but they didn't respond the same way if their "real" wages fell because of a general increase in prices. Therefore, Keynes argued, the orthodox explanation—in which workers rationally supplied labor hours according to the height of the real wage—was simply not true. (This real-world behavior on the part of workers is sometimes explained as "money illusion.")

Second, Keynes argued that even if the workers collectively *wanted* to reduce their (real) wage demands, they might be powerless to do so, for if workers agreed to even a significant pay cut—measured in nominal, actual money terms—the lowered costs of production would then lead firms to reduce the prices they charged for their products, meaning that in real terms the wage rate wouldn't have fallen so much after all.

2. See Matt Egan, "New Threat to the Economy: Americans Are Saving like It's the 1930s," CNN Business, May 12, 2020, https://www.cnn.com/2020/05/12/investing/jobs-coronavirus-consumer-spending-debt/index.html?fbclid=IwAR09Du7nf1OKE9-VpOgayFNTIDeKJis-VivSlOR-rYtKoxQw9H8MwcIU49FM.

Thus Keynes thought it was obvious that something external to the labor market caused the massive increase in unemployment during the Great Depression years. Any attempt to fit the facts of the 1930s into the orthodox framework would seem contrived. As he wryly observed, "Labour is not more truculent in the depression than in the boom—far from it. Nor is its physical productivity less. These facts from experience are a *prima facie* ground for questioning the adequacy of the classical analysis" (Keynes 1936, p. 14).

Line to get into a soup kitchen in Chicago, November 1916. Source: Getty Images. Credit: RollsPress/Popperfoto, Popperfoto Collection, No. 80752202.

In the Keynesian approach, it wasn't that workers in the 1930s were suddenly more insistent on being paid a high wage or that their productivity had somehow slumped. Rather, the economy became stuck at a point of high "involuntary unemployment," because aggregate spending by the private sector was too low. After the initial shocks to the system in the early years—characterized by stock market crashes and (especially in the United States) massive bank failures—individuals and businesses understandably hunkered down and cut their spending even more. Yet this merely led to a vicious downward spiral, as these decisions lowered the total income available to the community. And contrary to the alleged doctrines of the classical approach, there was no reason to suppose that the market economy would quickly bounce back; it could be stuck in an "equilibrium" with high levels of involuntary unemployment.

In this context, Keynes argued that government budget deficits could provide relief. (We are here omitting his more complex discussion on interest rates.) To drive home his shocking perspective, Keynes actually argued:

> If the Treasury were to fill old bottles with banknotes, bury them at suitable depths in disused coal mines which are then filled up to the

> surface with town rubbish, and leave it to private enterprise on well-tried principles of *laissez-faire* to dig the notes up again ...there need be no more unemployment and, with the help of the repercussions, the real income of the community, and its capital wealth also, would probably become a good deal greater than it actually is. It would, indeed, be more sensible to build houses and the like; but if there are political and practical difficulties in the way of this, the above would be better than nothing. (Keynes 1936, p. 68)

Needless to say, in the orthodox approach, diverting labor power into burying money and then digging it up again is hardly the way to help a distressed economy.

The Austrian Critique of Keynesianism

There are entire books (cited in the footnotes[3]) devoted to the refutation of Keynesian theory and its treatment of the Great Depression, so our discussion here will be brief.

On theoretical grounds, the Austrians provide a much more satisfactory explanation of the business cycle, as laid out in chapter 8. Contrary to Keynes, workers *aren't* as productive when the boom collapses into a bust, at least not when we take into account the overall structure of production.

To use an exaggerated illustration: if during the boom period the economy produced nothing but hammers and no new nails, eventually a crisis would emerge. Even though carpenters would possess the same skills, their physical productivity would clearly plummet once the last nail in inventory had been used. A massive drop in "real output" would be necessary at that point, while the economy retooled (literally). No amount of deficit spending or money printing could paper over such basic material facts. The fact that the Austrian approach accords with common sense is evidence in its favor, and the amusing *reductio ad absurdum* that Keynes himself invented for his own theory should be a strike against it.

Empirically, we note that during the 1930s, governments and central banks around the world engaged in the most Keynesian policies in history to that

---

3. Murray N. Rothbard's *Man, Economy, and State* (Princeton, NJ: D. Van Nostrand, 1962), https://mises.org/library/man-economy-and-state-power-and-market, contains a scathing critique of Keynesian thought as it stood in the early 1960s. Henry Hazlitt wrote a point-by-point critique of Keynes in his book *The Failure of the "New Economics"* (Princeton, NJ: D. Van Nostrand, 1959), https://mises.org/library/failure-new-economics-0. For an Austrian explanation of the Great Depression, see Murray N. Rothbard's *America's Great Depression* (Princeton, NJ: D. Van Nostrand, 1963), https://mises.org/library/americas-great-depression, and for a newer version that specifically critiques modern Keynesian arguments, see Robert P. Murphy, *The Politically Incorrect Guide to the Great Depression and the New Deal* (Washington, DC: Regnery Publishing, 2009).

date. In the United States, for example, the Hoover administration—despite disinformation to the contrary—cajoled big business to prop up wage rates and ran unprecedented peacetime budget deficits.[4] For its part, the Federal Reserve in the early 1930s expanded the monetary base and slashed interest rates to then record lows.

Now, to be sure, modern-day Keynesians acknowledge these awkward facts as "too little, too late." But even so, their admission raises the obvious question: If the fundamental Keynesian explanation for the Great Depression is that governments were too timid when it came to deficit spending, then why didn't the Great Depression happen *earlier*, when everybody admits that governments did even less during financial panics?

No, a much more sensible explanation of the historical record is staring us in the face: the depressions (or "panics") of the nineteenth and early twentieth centuries played out according to the theory developed by Ludwig von Mises. Yet during those crises, governments largely remained aloof, and that's why the economy recovered. In contrast, it wasn't until government and central bank officials became serious about helping with "countercyclical" policies in the 1930s that an initial crash blossomed into a Depression that wouldn't go away.

4. To see the truth about the Hoover record, consult Rothbard's America's Great Depression, or start with the online article from Robert P. Murphy, "Did Hoover Really Slash Spending?," *Mises Daily*, May 31, 2010, https://mises.org/library/did-hoover-really-slash-spending.

Chapter 15

The "Market Monetarists" and NGDP Targeting

In addition to the Keynesian perspective (covered in chapter 14), a relatively new challenge to the Austrian framework comes from the "market monetarists" and their endorsement of a central bank policy of "level targeting" of nominal gross domestic product (sometimes abbreviated as NGDPLT[1]). Although not as widespread as the Keynesian paradigm, market monetarism is arguably a more serious competitor to the Austrian school when it comes to monetary theory and business cycle analysis, because many of the leaders of the new approach are self-described libertarians with positions at free market organizations.

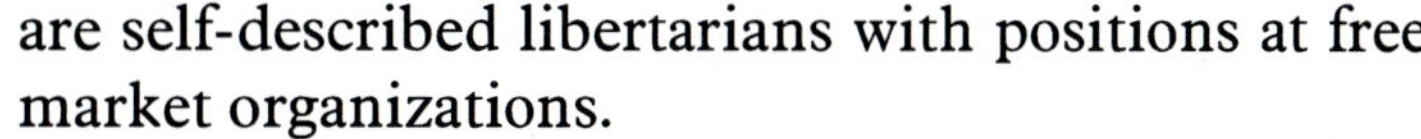

Scott Sumner

The most obvious example is Scott Sumner—the undisputed leader of the market monetarists—who has an economics PhD from the University of Chicago and occupies (as of this writing) the Ralph G. Hawtrey Chair of Monetary Policy at the Mercatus Center at George Mason University. In addition, Sumner is one of a handful of regular contributors at Liberty Fund's popular economics blog, *EconLog*.

Although Sumner himself is modest and points to precursors in the academic literature, in his

1. See, for example, David Beckworth, "Facts, Fears, and Functionality of NGDP Level Targeting: A Guide to a Popular Framework for Monetary Policy" (Mercatus Special Study, Mercatus Center at George Mason University, Arlington, VA, September 2019), https://www.mercatus.org/publications/monetary-policy/facts-fears-and-functionality-ngdp-level-targeting.

online writings over the years he almost single-handedly convinced many fans of the free market that the severity of the Great Recession was *not* the inevitable fallout from malinvestments made during the housing boom, but instead was due to the Federal Reserve's *tight* monetary policy from 2008 onward.

In light of the standard Austrian view of the business cycle in general (summarized in chapter 8) and the housing boom in particular (summarized in chapter 11), it would be an understatement to say that the market monetarist approach differs dramatically in both its diagnosis and prescription. Inasmuch as the market monetarists have gained supporters who might otherwise have endorsed the Austrian view of recessions, it is important for the current volume to critically assess this new paradigm. For concreteness, this chapter focuses specifically on Sumner's work, but the treatment is applicable to the entire market monetarism approach.

The Legacy of Milton Friedman's Monetarism

In order to understand Sumner's approach—including the very label "market monetarism"—it is necessary to first review some of the work of Milton Friedman, the famous Chicago school economist closely associated with monetarism.[2]

After the Great Depression, the standard Keynesian view (as we explained in chapter 14) was that aggressive monetary policy—at least as conventionally conceived—had been tried but had failed. After all, during the early 1930s central banks rapidly expanded their asset purchases while slashing interest rates to very low levels. Yet this apparently "easy money" policy didn't resuscitate aggregate demand and restore full employment, leading the Keynesians to conclude that the global economy was stuck in a "liquidity trap" requiring budget deficits to escape. In the famous metaphor, the Keynesian assessment of the Great Depression was that central banks had been "pushing on a string."

Anna Schwartz and Milton Friedman

Milton Friedman and Anna Schwartz overturned this consensus with their famous 1963 book *A Monetary History of*

2. See Bennett T. McCallum, "Monetarism," Library of Economics and Liberty, accessed Mar. 9, 2020, https://www.econlib.org/library/Enc/Monetarism.html.

the United States, 1867–1960. The chapter in the book dealing with the Great Depression years was also published as a separate volume entitled *The Great Contraction: 1929–1933*.

In contrast to the standard view that the Fed had tried a loose monetary policy that was impotent, Friedman and Schwartz argued that the Federal Reserve had actually adopted a *tight* policy. Specifically, even though the Fed expanded the monetary base by some 20 percent from 1929–33,[3] a broader measure of money—M2—had nonetheless *declined by a third* over this period. (Recall that this was a period of bank runs, when depositors were rushing to withdraw their funds from the banks. In a fractional reserve system, mass withdrawals from banks will cause M1 and M2 to decline, even if the central bank doesn't itself "tighten.") It is not surprising, Friedman and Schwartz argued, that consumer prices and real output collapsed when the Fed allowed the overall money stock (used by the public) to drop so rapidly.

Just as the low interest rates of the 1930s were not a sign of loose money, Friedman argued that high interest rates were not necessarily a sign of tight money, either. In a 1997 article for the *Wall Street Journal*,[4] he recommended that the Bank of Japan increase the rate of monetary growth to stimulate its lackluster economy, and then argued:

> Initially, higher monetary growth would reduce short-term interest rates even further. However, as the economy revives, interest rates would start to rise. That is the standard pattern and explains why it is so misleading to judge monetary policy by interest rates. **Low interest rates are generally a sign that money has been tight, as in Japan; high interest rates, that money has been easy** [Friedman 1997, bold added].

Friedman then tied the lesson back to his view of the Great Depression:

> The Fed [in the early 1930s] pointed to low interest rates as evidence that it was following an easy money policy and never mentioned the quantity of money. The governor of the Bank of Japan...referred to the "drastic monetary measures" that the bank took in 1995 as evidence of "the easy stance of monetary policy." He too did not mention the quantity of money. Judged by the discount rate, which was reduced to 0.5% from 1.75%, the measures were drastic. Judged by monetary

3. See Sumner's summary of Friedman and Schwartz's view of the Great Contraction: Scott Sumner, "Milton Friedman Argued That the Great Depression Occurred Despite Massive QE," *EconLog* (blog), Library of Economics and Liberty, Apr. 3, 2015, https://www.econlib.org/archives/2015/04/milton_friedman_15.html.

4. Milton Friedman, "Rx for Japan: Back to the Future," *Wall Street Journal*, Dec. 17, 1997, available at https://miltonfriedman.hoover.org/friedman_images/Collections/2016c21/WSJ_12_17_1997.pdf.

> growth, they were too little too late, raising monetary growth from 1.5% a year in the prior three and a half years to only 3.25% in the next two and a half.
>
> After the U.S. experience during the Great Depression, and after inflation and rising interest rates in the '70s and disinflation and falling interest rates in the '80s, **I thought the fallacy of identifying tight money with high interest rates and easy money with low interest rates was dead. Apparently, old fallacies never die** [Friedman 1997, bold added].
>
> Being trained at the University of Chicago himself, Scott Sumner is an expert on the legacy of Milton Friedman. Sumner believes that he is doing for the interpretation of the Great Recession what Friedman (and Schwartz) did for the Great Depression.

Scott Sumner's Market Monetarism

As we documented in chapter 6, after the global financial crisis struck in the fall of 2008, the Fed unveiled a variety of new lending programs, slashed its policy rate to virtually zero, and *doubled* the monetary base—all in a matter of months. In light of these unprecedented actions, both economists and the general public understandably concluded that the Fed was engaged in a very easy money policy.

Yet Scott Sumner—starting at his lonely blog—managed to eventually convert a large portion of the profession to his startling claim that the Great Recession was caused by *tight money.* A full account of his argument is linked in the footnotes,[5] but we can summarize his argument as follows:

- ➔ Just as Milton Friedman taught, it is misleading to look at the Fed's (virtually) zero percent interest rates, or massive expansion of the monetary base, as indicating easy money from late 2008 onward.
- ➔ Instead, we should look at a much better indicator, namely the growth rate of nominal gross domestic product (NGDP). That is, economists should look at the growth in final spending on goods and services (*without* adjusting for price inflation) to assess whether monetary policy has been too easy or too tight. As Sumner argued in mid-2009:

5. Sumner lays out his position in a 2009 *Cato Unbound* series of essays: "The Real Problem Was Nominal," "Almost on the Money: Replies to Hamilton, Selgin, and Hummel," "From Discretion to Futures Targeting, One Step at a Time," "Score-Keeping with Selgin," "Clearing Up Some Miscommunication," "Defining the Stance of Monetary Policy Is Harder Than It Looks," "We Can't Agree on Everything, George [Selgin]...," and "Final Thoughts and Thanks," all in *Cato Unbound*, September 2009, https://www.cato-unbound.org/issues/september-2009/monetary-lessons-not-so-great-depression.

> Between the early 1990s and 2007, NGDP grew at just over five percent per year. Because the real GDP growth rate averaged nearly three percent, we ended up with a bit more than two percent inflation, which was widely believed to be the Fed's implicit target. Beginning around August 2008, however, NGDP slowed sharply, and then fell at a rate of more than four percent over the following several quarters. Indeed the decline in NGDP during 2009 is likely to be the steepest since 1938. This produced what may end up being the deepest and most prolonged recession since 1938 [Sumner 2009].[6]

- ➔ The reason Sumner believes that a drop in the growth rate—let alone an actual decline—in "nominal spending" is so damaging, is that wages and some other prices are "sticky," at least in the short to medium run. In Sumner's words:

> as of early 2008 the U.S. economy featured many wage and debt contracts negotiated under the expectation that NGDP would keep growing at about five percent per year. Because nominal GDP is essentially total national gross income, if it falls sharply it becomes much harder for debtors to repay loans, and much harder for companies to pay wages and salaries. The almost inevitable consequence is that unemployment rises sharply, and debt default rates soar [Sumner 2009].

- ➔ Rather than focus on interest rate or monetary growth targets, Sumner instead recommends that the Fed adjust policy such that NGDP grows at 5 percent per year. In a typical year, this 5 percent growth would be composed of 3 percent real GDP growth and 2 percent price inflation. However, if there were a recession and real output dropped by a percentage point (i.e., real GDP growth of –1 percent), then Sumner would still insist that total nominal spending grow by 5 percent that year, meaning that now price inflation would have to be 6 percent.
- ➔ Furthermore, Sumner advocates a "level target," meaning that if the Fed misses its target and NGDP grows at, say, only 3 percent in one year, then it must grow at 7 percent the next in order for the *level* of NGDP in the second year to catch up to where it should have been. Hence the official title of Sumner's proposal: NGDPLT.
- ➔ The final subtlety is that Sumner argues that the right time to gauge Fed policy is *immediately*, according to the *market's* expectation. In other words, Sumner doesn't want the Fed to look backward over the course of twelve months to see if NGDP in fact grew at the target

---

6. The Sumner quotation is from the 2009 *Cato Unbound* opening essay: "The Real Problem Was Nominal," *Cato Unbound*, September 2009, https://www.cato-unbound.org/2009/09/14/scott-sumner/real-problem-was-nominal.

5 percent. Rather, Sumner wants Fed officials to look at a "futures market" in NGDP contracts to see what investors predict the level of NGDP will be *twelve months from now*. If the expected growth rate of NGDP is different from the 5 percent target, then the Fed can "passively" expand or contract its balance sheet in order to move expected future NGDP in the right direction.

→ Because of Sumner's similarity to Friedman, and because of his proposal to use a futures market in NGDP contracts to effectively automate Fed policy, Sumner's framework was eventually dubbed (by a fan) "market monetarism."

It would be difficult to overstate Sumner's personal role in elevating market monetarism from a heretical notion in late 2008 to a set of ideas being seriously discussed by central bankers (as well as economics bloggers). Indeed, after a press conference in which Fed chair Ben Bernanke announced (what would be called) the beginning of QE3 and mentioned NGDP targeting, George Mason University economist Tyler Cowen declared it "Scott Sumner day."[7]

Problems with Market Monetarism

For the purposes of this primer on money mechanics, we will only sketch some of the problems with the market monetarist framework. The following considerations are not offered as an exhaustive critique.

Problem No. 1
Monetary Growth Accelerated after the 2008 Crisis

Remember that the original Friedman and Schwartz revisionism concerning the causes of the Great Depression was their observation that the Fed, though it expanded the monetary base after the 1929 stock market crash, didn't inflate *enough* to offset the bank runs. According to them, the Fed's blunder was allowing M2 to collapse by a third from 1929–32.

But there is no analogy between this critique of the Fed's behavior regarding the 2008 crisis, and the ensuing Great Recession. First, let's document just how aggressively the Fed expanded the monetary base when the crisis struck in the fall of 2008:

7. Tyler Cowen, "It's Not Just Monetary Policy, It's Scott Sumner Day," *Marginal Revolution* (blog), Sept. 13, 2012, https://marginalrevolution.com/marginalrevolution/2012/09/its-not-just-monetary-policy-its-scott-sumner-day.html.

Figure 1: Monetary Base

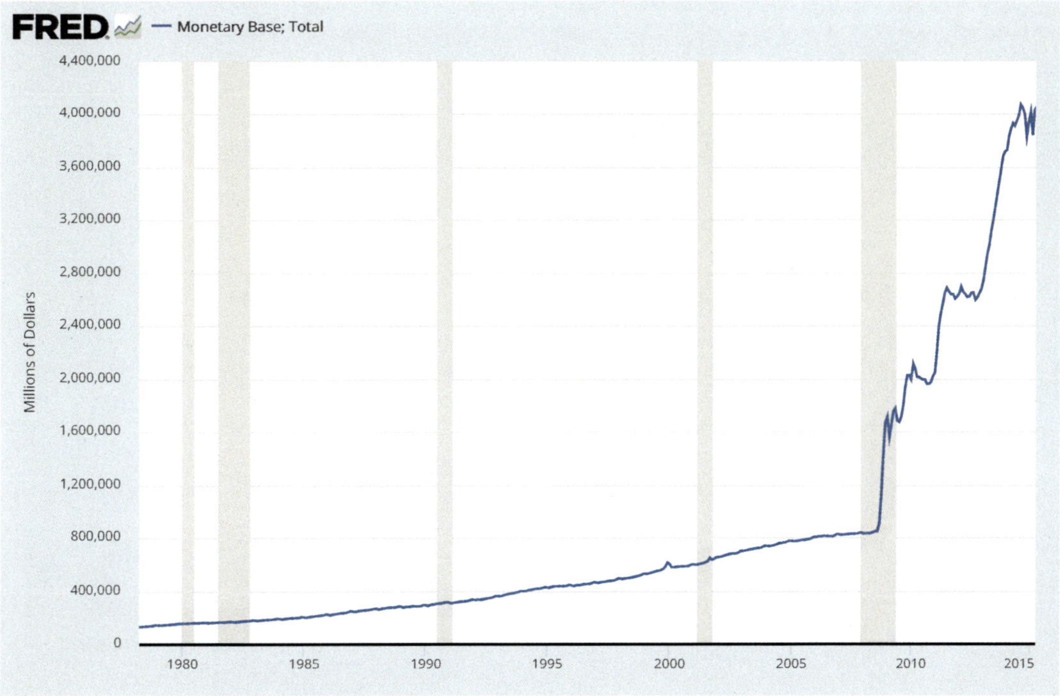

Source: Board of Governors of the Federal Reserve System (US)

Not only did Bernanke's Fed engage in a jaw-dropping injection of base money in response to the panic, but the admittedly tepid base growth in 2007 is not something that most observers would have predicted would lead to a global financial panic. (Although not shown on this cart, the monetary base actually shrank in the early 1960s—in contrast, its twelve-month growth never went negative in 2007 or 2008—and yet this didn't lead to the worst crisis since the Great Depression.

Nothwithstanding the Fed's handling of the monetary base, one might suppose that M1 and M2 collapsed on Bernanke's watch—just as Friedman and Schwartz pointed out happened in the early 1930s. Yet on the contrary, both the M1 and M2 measures of the money stock continued to grow after the crisis struck, particularly M1:

Figure 2: M1 Money Stock

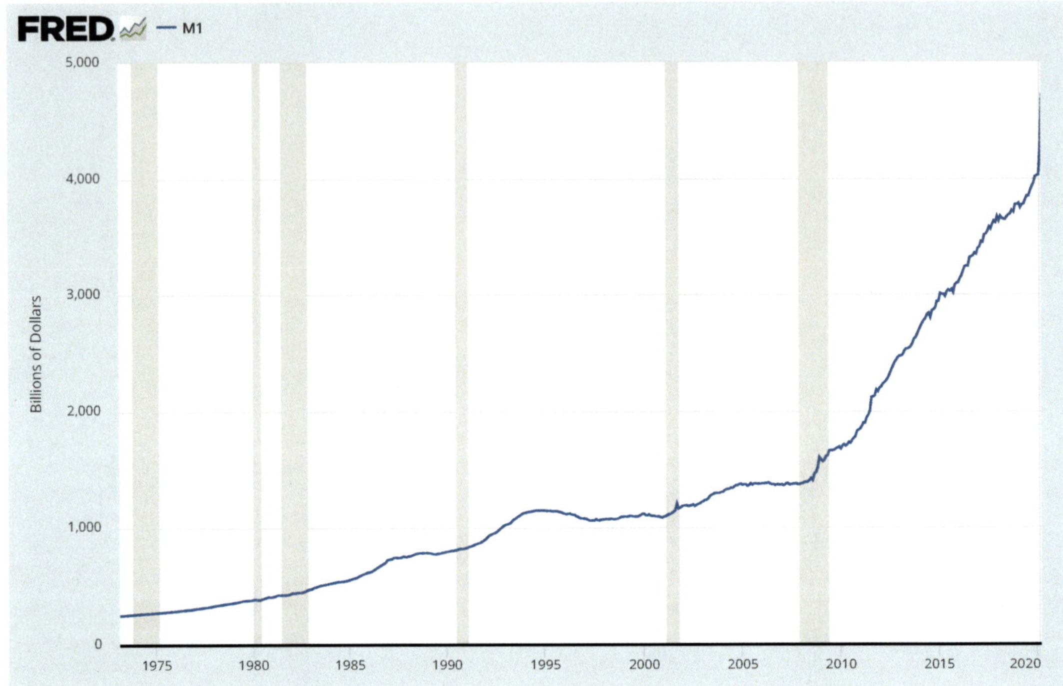

Source: Board of Governors of the Federal Reserve System (US)

Figure 3: M2 Money Stock

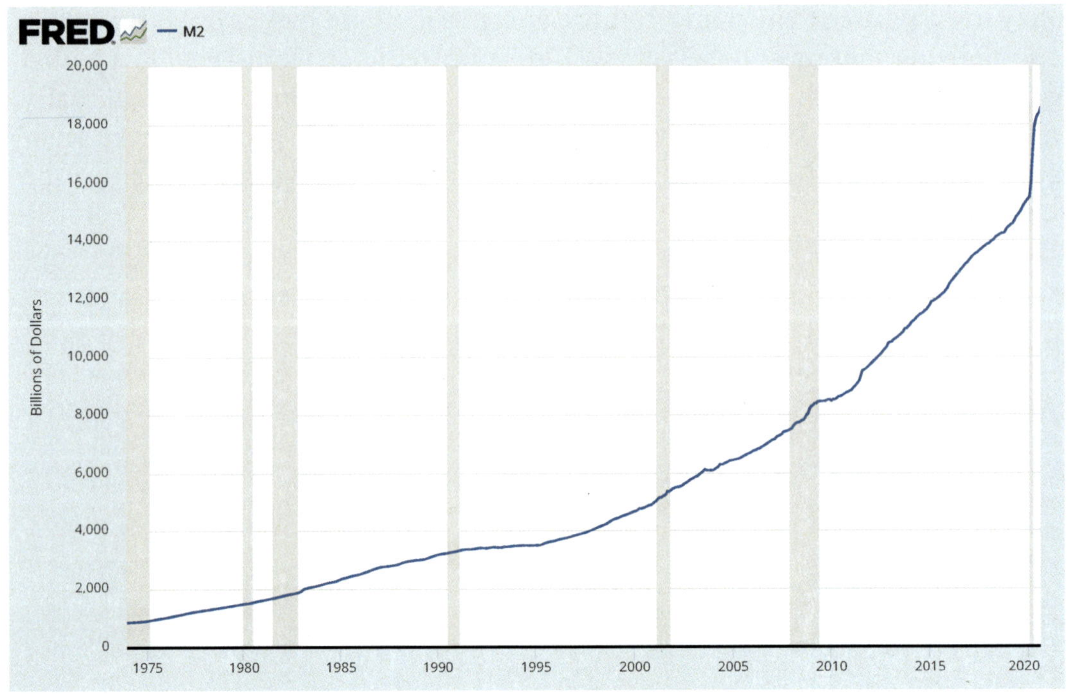

Source: Board of Governors of the Federal Reserve System (US)

Finally, let us chart the precise metric that Friedman and Schwartz used when giving their "monetarist" explanation of the Great Depression—that the growth in M2 collapsed, and in fact went sharply negative. Do we see anything comparable with the financial crisis of 2008?

Figure 4: One-Year Growth Rate in M2

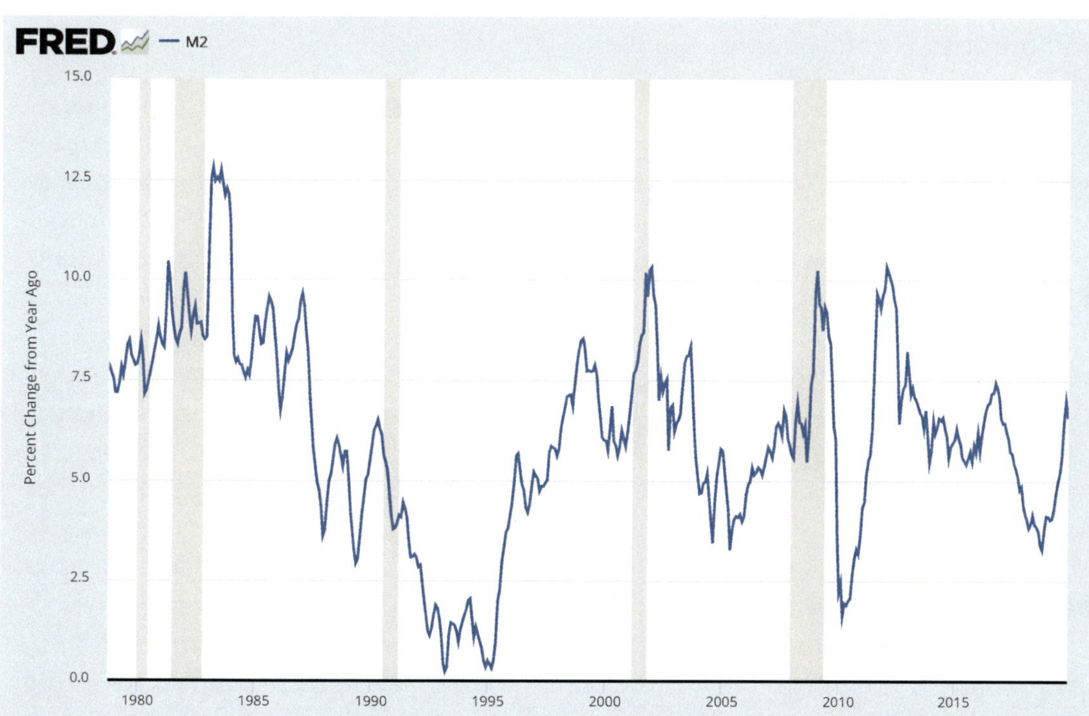

Source: Board of Governors of the Federal Reserve System (US)

The above chart shows the twelve-month percentage change in the M2 monetary aggregate. It clearly shows that there was nothing unusual about the "growth rate of money in the hands of the public" before or during the crisis, with the M2 growth rate only dropping sharply *after* the Great Recession had officially ended (i.e., to the right of the gray bar).

Furthermore, the above chart shows that the M2 growth rate *really did* fall substantially in the early 1990s. If one were to adopt the Friedman and Schwartz framework—which explained the Great Depression as a collapse in M2 growth—then this modern chart would lead to the "obvious" conclusion that the financial crisis and ensuing Great Recession began *in 1995*. And yet, that obviously didn't happen.

As the above charts indicate, Scott Sumner's explanation for the financial crisis and Great Recession shouldn't be labeled "monetarist" at all. There is no sense in which these events can be blamed on Bernanke's unwillingness to boost the money stock, however measured. (And for what it's worth, in 2008 Anna Schwartz herself blamed the financial crisis on the Fed for blowing up the housing bubble![8])

Problem No. 2
Sumner's "NGDP Growth" Criterion Is Vacuous and (Almost) Nonfalsifiable

Of course, Sumner and other market monetarists would object to the discussion in the previous section by explaining that their preferred criterion for assessing the Fed's "tightness" or "looseness" is not any particular monetary aggregate, but instead the growth rate of nominal GDP. Since the Fed allowed NGDP growth to (eventually) collapse, Sumner argues that by *definition* this is a "tight" central bank policy.

The fundamental problem with this definition is that it assumes Sumner's conclusion. One of *the very issues under dispute* is whether aggressive monetary expansion by the central bank is medicine or poison for an economy entering recession. If the Austrian analysis of boom-bust cycles (given in chapter 8) is correct, then the Fed's actions from 2008 onward only generated another unsustainable boom. Sumner's rhetorical device of framing inadequate NGDP growth as "tight money" *by definition* would make it impossible to learn whether his policy advice is simply *wrong*.

Consider a medical analogy: suppose a patient is suffering from fever, running a temperature of 103 degrees. One group of doctors recommends injecting the patient with substance M, in order to cure the fever. Yet another group of doctors argues that *past* injections of substance M are what made the patient sick in the first place.

Now, if they are to have any hope of resolving this dispute, how should the doctors *measure* the amount of substance M being injected into the patient? Most people would argue that the doctors should look at absolute physical measurements, involving the volume and/or rate of injection. And so, for example, if they injected the patient with more M than had ever been administered to any patient in the history of that hospital, it would be odd if the patient's chart read, "Received a very restrictive treatment of M."

Indeed, imagine if the doctors who think that substance M is a helpful medicine wanted to *define* the M treatment in terms of the fever. That is, if after they had injected the patient with unprecedented amounts of M, whether

8. Sumner acknowledges Schwartz's apparent about-face and late found agreement with the Austrians: "Friedman and Schwartz vs. the Austrians," The Money Illusion (blog), Jan. 16, 2020, https://www.themoneyillusion.com/friedman-and-schwartz-vs-the-austrians/#more-203.

the fever had stayed the same or even gone up, the doctors declared, "We just made the patient sicker with our shift to restrict the M treatment." This would be Orwellian and obviously would make it virtually impossible to figure out whether more or less M was what the patient needed.

As a final demonstration of how Sumner's framework is (virtually) nonfalsifiable, consider his January 2020[9] declaration in a blog post:

> **We are entering a golden age of central banking, where the Fed will become *more effective* and come closer to hitting its targets than at any other time in history. Over the next few decades, inflation will stay close to 2% and the unemployment rate will generally be relatively low and stable....**
>
> In fact, Fed policy is becoming more effective because it is edging gradually in a market monetarist direction...
>
> If they continue moving in this direction, then NGDP growth will continue to become more stable, the business cycle will continue to moderate, inflation will stay in the low single digits, and unemployment will stay relatively low and stable....
>
> As an analogy, when I was young I would frequently read about airliners crashing in the US...After each crash, problems were fixed and planes got a bit safer.
>
> **Recessions and airline crashes: They are getting less frequent, and for the exact same reason** [Sumner 2020, bold added].

Most Austrian readers would view Sumner's predictions as incredibly off the mark. And yet, it will be hard for Sumner's rosy compliments for the Fed to be falsified.

For example, suppose that at some point the economy crashes and the unemployment rate surges while the Fed engages in continued rounds of QE to "fix it." In particular, suppose that in an especially terrible year unemployment jumps to 20 percent, real (i.e., inflation-adjusted) GDP drops by 15 percent, and the official Consumer Price Index (CPI) surges by 10 percent. In the midst of such terrible "stagflation," the Austrians run victory laps, arguing that underlying "structural" malinvestments can't be fixed by the printing press. The combination of high unemployment and high consumer price inflation shows—so our Austrians would claim—that loose money sinks economies.

Yet in our hypothetical scenario, Sumner would *also* claim victory. He would point out that when real GDP drops 15 percent while the price level

---

9. See Sumner, "Fed Policy: The Golden Age Begins," The Money Illusion (blog), Feb. 17, 2009, https://www.themoneyillusion.com/fed-policy-the-golden-age-begins/.

only rises by 10 percent, nominal GDP falls by (roughly) 5 percent. Since Sumner recommended that the Fed keep NGDP *growing* at 5 percent, this horrible fall in NGDP—so Sumner would claim—was the culprit. Once again, Sumner would argue, the Fed's "tight money" had caused another economic disaster.

Problem No. 3
Market Monetarists Take Their (Simplistic) Model Too Seriously

One illustration of this problem is the tendency for market monetarists to conflate "NGDP" with "total spending," at least in the way they discuss their framework in essays for the public.[10] Yet there is much more "total spending" in the economy than what is spent *on final goods and services*. Even if we put aside the entire financial sector—and note that the standard Sumnerian model doesn't have a stock market or even banks, with Sumner actually arguing that putting banks in a model of the business cycle will only confuse matters[11]—the bulk of "total spending" in the economy is actually on *intermediate* purchases of goods, which are ignored in calculations of GDP in order to avoid "double counting."

Normally, the conflation of "total spending" with "spending on final goods and services" might not be a huge problem in terms of policy advice, though it's conceivable that a change in economic organization (perhaps with industries becoming more or less "vertically integrated") could render the Fed's stance "tight" according to one metric but "easy" according to the other. The more fundamental problem is that Sumner's model ignores the entire capital structure of the economy, which blinds him to the very possibility of the Austrians being right.

Another illustration of the market monetarists taking their model too seriously is Sumner's continued claims that participants in the market had expectations about NGDP growth. For example, when explaining why the Fed's (allegedly) tight policy in 2008 caused the crisis, he argues that "as of early 2008

---

10. For example, Sumner himself refers to "nominal spending" as the item that the Fed allowed to collapse in his original *Cato Unbound* essay, while George Selgin in his initial response essay writes, "Like [Sumner], I believe that monetary policy should strive, not to achieve any particular values of interest rates, employment, or inflation, but simply to maintain a steady growth rate of overall nominal spending." To be sure, these are sharp economists who know the formal definition of NGDP—and that it is smaller than "total spending" —but nonetheless, these quotations are what they actually wrote. See Sumner, "The Real Problem Was Nominal," and George Selgin, "Between Fulsomeness and Pettifoggery: A Reply to Sumner," *Cato Unbound,* September 2009, https://www.cato-unbound.org/2009/09/18/george-selgin/between-fulsomeness-pettifoggery-reply-sumner.

11. Sumner literally titled a blog post, "Keep banks out of macro." See "Keep Banks out of Macro," *The Money Illusion* (blog), Jan. 22, 2013, https://www.themoneyillusion.com/keep-banks-out-of-macro/.

the US economy featured many wage and debt contracts negotiated under the expectation that NGDP would keep growing at about five percent per year."

This is obviously a false claim. Barely anybody in the US knew what NGDP was in early 2008; they certainly didn't accept job offers or take out mortgages with expectations of NGDP growth in mind. To be sure, Sumner could rehabilitate his claim in terms of individual expectations of *personal* income growth, but the point still stands that Sumner has an unfortunate habit of confusing his (simplistic) model of the economy for the real world. This makes it difficult for him to even see contrary evidence.

Problem No. 4
Central Bank Actions Distort Relative Prices and Have "Real" Impacts

From an Austrian perspective, the previous objections are mere quibbles; the *fundamental* problem with the market monetarist approach is that its policy recommendations would simply perpetuate the boom-bust cycle.

Sumner quite consciously eschews analysis of interest rates, viewing them as "misleading" indicators of the stance of monetary policy. Yet if the Austrians are correct, then if the Fed reacts to a downturn (which normally would go hand-in-hand with a fall in NGDP growth) with monetary expansion, then, besides the impact on aggregate nominal variables, this action will also distort *relative* prices. In particular, short-term interest rates will typically be pushed below their "natural" levels, giving the wrong signal to entrepreneurs and setting in motion another unsustainable boom.

Even on Sumner's own terms, it is unclear how his recommended policies are supposed to fix the alleged problem. For example, Sumner claims that in late 2008, the collapse in nominal income growth meant that millions of workers—stuck in employment contracts and mortgages with "sticky" numbers in them—no longer had enough money coming in each month to pay their bills. So if in response the Fed creates trillions of new dollars in base money by buying government bonds and other financial assets, *how exactly does this help those millions of wage earners*? Injecting new money into the hands of the financially savvy and politically connected, if anything, makes those humble wage earners even *worse* off, as commodity prices instantly respond to the rounds of QE while the workers' "sticky" hourly wages do not rise nearly as quickly.

Indeed, the entire "sticky prices" boogeyman is a red herring. During the 1920–21 depression, consumer prices collapsed more rapidly than in any twelve-month stretch during the Great Depression.[12] Yet the 1920s were not a

12. For more on the 1920–21 depression and how it explodes the monetarist explanation of the Great Depression, see: Robert P. Murphy, "The Depression You've Never Heard of: 1920–

decade of economic stagnation. Blaming the worst economic crises in US history on "deflation" and "sticky prices" doesn't fit the facts.[13]

1921," Foundation for Economic Education, Nov. 18, 2009, https://fee.org/articles/the-depression-youve-never-heard-of-1920-1921/.

13. Sumner himself disputes the claim that the 1920-21 depression is somehow embarrassing to the market monetarist framework. When prices fell faster than wages in 1921, unemployment soared, and then when wages followed suit, unemployment fell. Thus, Sumner believes the data of the 1920-21 depression adhere to his model quite well.

Chapter 16

Bitcoin and the Theory of Money

In a modern primer on money mechanics, it is necessary to provide at least an introduction to Bitcoin.[1] Consequently, in this chapter we will first give a basic explanation of what Bitcoin is and how it works. Then we will place Bitcoin in the framework of money that we developed in chapter 1, seeking to answer the fundamental question: Is Bitcoin money?" Finally, we will relate Bitcoin to an important component in the Austrian school's discussion of money, namely Ludwig von Mises's "regression theorem."

Explaining Bitcoin with an Analogy[2]

"Bitcoin" encompasses two related but distinct concepts. First, individual bitcoins (lowercase *b*) are units of (fiat)[3] digital currency. Second, the *Bitcoin*

---

1. For concreteness, in this chapter we will refer specifically to Bitcoin. However, much of what we say will be applicable to other cryptocurrencies.

2. Much of the material in this chapter is reproduced from Silas Barta and Robert P. Murphy, *Understanding Bitcoin: The Liberty Lover's Guide to the Mechanics and Economics of Crypto-Currencies*, version 1.11 (self-pub., CreateSpace, 2017), available at understandingbitcoin.us/wp-content/uploads/2017/12/2017.11-Understanding-Bitcoin-v1.11.pdf.

3. Many Bitcoin enthusiasts would vehemently object to classifying it as a fiat currency, because the Bitcoin network is completely voluntary and doesn't rely on state-enforced legal tender laws or other methods of suppressing competition. However, in monetary economics the term *fiat* has a very precise meaning, under which (we argue) bitcoins would qualify. (See Ludwig von Mises's *The Theory of Money and Credit* for a scholarly treatment.) In particular, it is simply not true that the state can merely declare "through fiat" that something is money. In our judgment, it is more important for the beginner to understand that there is no other commodity or asset "backing up" bitcoins—and this is the sense in which it is a fiat currency—rather than to avoid the possibly negative connotations from our use of a term that is usually reserved for low-quality money issued by modern states.

protocol (uppercase *B*) governs the decentralized network through which thousands of computers across the globe maintain a "public ledger"—known as the *blockchain*—that keeps a fully transparent record of every authenticated transfer of bitcoins from the moment the system became operational in early 2009. In short, Bitcoin encompasses both (1) an unbacked digital currency and (2) a decentralized online payment system.

According to its official website: "Bitcoin uses peer-to-peer technology to operate with no central authority; managing transactions and the issuing of bitcoins is carried out collectively by the network."[4] Anyone who wants to participate can download the Bitcoin software to his or her computer and become part of the network, engaging in "mining" operations and helping to verify the history of transactions.

To fully understand how Bitcoin operates, one needs to learn the subtleties of public-key cryptography, which we briefly discuss in a later section. For now, we focus instead on an analogy that captures the economic essence of Bitcoin, while avoiding the need for new terminology.

Imagine a community where the money is based on the integers running from 1, 2, 3, … up through 21,000,000. At any given time, one person "owns" the number **8**, while somebody else "owns" the number **349**, and so on.

In this setting, suppose Bill wants to buy a car from Sally, and the price sticker on the car reads "Two numbers." Bill happens to be in possession of the numbers **3** and **12**. So Bill gives the two numbers to Sally, and Sally gives Bill the car. The community recognizes two facts: first, the title to the car has been transferred from Sally to Bill, and second, Sally is now the owner of the numbers **3** and **12**.

Further suppose that in this fictitious community an industry of thousands of accountants maintains the record of ownership of the 21 million integers. Each accountant keeps an enormous ledger in an Excel file. The columns run across the top, from 1 to 21 million, while the rows record every transfer of a particular number. For example, when Bill bought the car from Sally, the accountants who were within earshot of the deal entered into their respective Excel files "Now in the possession of Sally" in the next available row, in the columns for **3** and **12**. In these ledgers, if we looked one row above, we would

4. See http://bitcoin.org.

see "Now in the possession of Bill" for these two numbers, because Bill owned these two numbers before he transferred them to Sally.

Besides documenting any transactions that happen to be within earshot, the accountants also periodically check their own ledgers against those of their neighbors. If an accountant ever discovers that his neighbors have recorded transactions for other numbers (i.e., for deals for which the accountant in question was not within earshot), then the accountant fills in those missing row entries in the columns for those numbers. Therefore, at any given time, there are thousands of accountants, each of whom has a virtually complete history of all transactions involving all 21 million numbers.

Explaining the Analogy

We hope our analogy gives a decent first pass in explaining how Bitcoin works. In our hypothetical story, the people in the community kept track of which person "owned" an abstract, intangible number. Of course, you can't physically hold the number 3, but because the people in the community had adopted a convention where the accountants' Excel files kept track of which person was "matched" with the number 3, there was a sense in which the person owned it. And then, as our story showed, a person could transfer his claim to a number in order to buy real goods, such as a car.

To keep things simple, in our analogy, we assumed that the community had already reached the end state after all of the bitcoins have been "mined." In the real world, this will occur at some point after the year 2100, when (virtually) all of the 21 million bitcoins will be in the hands of the public.[5] After that time, there will be no more "mining" operations; the total number of bitcoins will be fixed at 21 million, forever.

Just as in our story, when people in the real world want to buy something using Bitcoin, they transfer their ownership of a certain amount of bitcoins (or fractions of a bitcoin, for smaller purchases) to other people in exchange for goods and services. This transfer is effected by the network of computers performing computations, and changing the *public* key to which the "sold" bitcoins are assigned. (This is analogous to the accountants in our story entering a new person's name in the column for a given integer.) Rather than physically handing over an object—such as a $20 bill or a gold coin—to the seller, the buyer who uses Bitcoin engages in the necessary electronic operations in order to command the network of computers to edit the blockchain to reflect the transfer of ownership/control of the relevant bitcoins to the seller.

Where Does Cryptography Come In? The Problem of Anonymous Owners

The present book deals with *economics*, not computer science, and consequently we will only provide a brief sketch of what's going on during a Bitcoin transaction. (Interested readers can refer to the footnotes for a fuller explanation.[6]) But we can't really apply economic concepts to something like Bitcoin, if we don't have a decent understanding of what it is and how it *works*.

We should first clarify that though you may often hear the term *encryption* in this context, Bitcoin doesn't actually use encryption. Indeed, the whole point is to provide a *public* ledger, recording all of the Bitcoin transactions that have ever occurred. It would defeat the purpose to hide the transaction messages with encryption. Rather, what we want is a way to securely *authenticate* the transactions involving transfers of bitcoins.[7]

5. Strictly speaking, the total quantity of mined bitcoins will never quite reach 21 million; the protocol ensures that eventually the reward for mining a new block will be rounded down to literally zero bitcoins (sometime around the year 2140). But it is currently projected that by the year 2108 mining from that point onward will only bring into circulation ever smaller fractions of the 21 millionth bitcoin; see "Controlled Supply," Bitcoin Wiki, last modified Feb. 11, 2020, https://en.bitcoin.it/wiki/Controlled_supply#Projected_Bitcoins_Long_Term. Another complication is that some (fractions of) bitcoins will be "lost" over the decades as people die or forget their private keys, and so on. Therefore, even though these (fractions of) bitcoins will have been mined, they will forever be inaccessible in transactions, making them effectively removed from the quantity of bitcoins available to the public. They will be economically equivalent to gold coins that went down with a ship and are sitting at the bottom of the ocean.

6. For a thorough explanation of the cryptography behind Bitcoin transactions, see Barta and Murphy, *Understanding Bitcoin,* in particular pp. 14–35.

7. The confusion may come from the fact that both encryption and authentication are topics

Let us return to our fictitious world of Bill and Sally, where the money is based on publicly recognized "ownership" of the 21 million integers. Our story above had one glaring problem we need to address: How do the accountants verify the identity of the people who try to buy things with numbers? In our example, Bill wanted to sell his public claim on the numbers **3** and **12** to Sally for her car. Now, in our story, we assumed that Bill really was the owner of the numbers **3** and **12**; he can afford Sally's car, because she's asking "two numbers" for it. The accountants will verify, if asked, that Bill is the owner of those numbers; under the "3" column and the "12" column in all of their ledgers, it says "Bill" in the last row that has an entry in it.

But here's the problem: When the nearby accountants see Bill trying to buy the car from Sally, how do they know that that particular human being actually IS the "Bill" listed in their ledgers? There needs to be some way that the real Bill can demonstrate to all of the accountants that he is in fact the same guy referred to in their ledgers. To prevent fraudulent spending of one's currency by an unauthorized party, this mechanism must be such that only the real Bill will be able to convince the accountants that he's the guy.

In the real world, solving this problem is where all of the complicated public-/private-key cryptography comes in. To reiterate, in the Bitcoin guide cited in the footnotes, we go over all of this material in a thorough yet intuitive way, but for our purposes here, we want to provide a basic understanding of how the Bitcoin protocol works without wading into technical details.

Unfortunately, at this point our story of Bill and Sally gets a little silly, but it's the best the present author could come up with. So, without further ado, suppose the following is how the people in our fictitious world deal with the problem of matching the names in the accountants' Excel ledgers with real-world human beings: each time one of the numbers is transferred in a sale, the new owner has to invent a riddle that only he or she can solve. You see, the people in the community are clever enough to recognize the correct answer to the riddle when they hear it, but they are not nearly creative enough to discover the answer on their own.

For example, when Bill himself received the numbers 3 and 12 from his employer—suppose he gets paid "two numbers" every month in salary—the accountants said to him:

OK, Bill, to protect your ownership of these two numbers, we need you to invent a riddle that we will associate with them. We will embed the riddle inside the same cell in

within the field of cryptography. They are also "dual" to each other in that in public key systems the operation of signing a message is the same as decrypting one, and the operation of verifying a signature is the same as encrypting a message. But to repeat, strictly speaking, Bitcoin doesn't rely on encryption, even though many people often say that it does.

our ledger as the name "Bill," in the columns under **3** *and* **12***. Then, when you want to spend these two numbers, you tell us the answer to your riddle. We will only release these numbers to a new owner if the person claiming to be "Bill" can answer the riddle. Keep in mind, Bill, that you might be on the other side of town, surrounded by accountants you have never seen before, when you want to spend these numbers. That's why our seeing you right now isn't good enough. We need to put down a riddle in our ledgers, which will also be copied thousands of times as the information pertaining to this sale reverberates throughout the community, so that every accountant will eventually have "Bill" and your riddle embedded in the correct cell in his or her ledger.*

Bill thinks for a moment and comes up with an ingenious riddle. He tells the accountants, "When is a door not a door?" They dutifully write down the riddle, which then gets propagated throughout the community, along with the fact that "Bill" is the new owner of **3** and **12**.

A few days later, some villain tries to impersonate Bill. He wants to buy a necklace that has a price tag of "one number." So the villain says to the accountants in earshot, "I'm Bill. I am the owner of **12**, as everyone can see; these spreadsheets are public information. So I hereby transfer my ownership of **12** to this jeweler, in exchange for the necklace."

The accountants say, "OK, Bill, just verify your identity. What is the solution to your riddle? Tell us, 'When is a door not a door?'"

The villain thinks and thinks but can't come up with anything. He says, "When the door isn't a door!" The accountants look at each other, scratch their heads, and agree, "No, that's a dumb answer. That didn't solve the riddle." So they deny the sale; the villain is not given the necklace.

Now, a few weeks later, we are up to the point at which our story originally began, at the beginning of this chapter. The *real* Bill wants to buy Sally's car

for "two numbers." He announces to the nearby accountants, "I am the owner of **3** and **12**. I verify this by solving my riddle: a door is not a door when *it's ajar*." The accountants all beam with delight! Aha! *That* is a good answer to the riddle. They agree that this must be the real Bill and allow the sale to go through. They write down "Sally" in the next-available rows in columns **3** and **12**, and then ask Sally to give them a new riddle, to which only Sally would know the answer.

Thus ends our analogy to explain the basics of what Bitcoin is and how it works. In the real world, of course, rather than generating and solving verbal riddles, there are complex math problems that only the legitimate owners of the bitcoins can quickly solve (using their *private keys*). But we have hopefully given enough of a sketch of Bitcoin so that we can now analyze it in terms of the economic framework that we developed way back in chapter 1 of the present book.

Is Bitcoin a Type of Money?

Recall our discussion of the theory of money in chapter 1. We first pointed out the limits of direct exchange—remember the farmer who needed his shoes repaired and had eggs to offer, but the cobbler wanted bacon? We saw in that story how *indirect exchange* could solve the problem. Specifically, when the farmer traded his eggs to the butcher in exchange for bacon, the bacon became a *medium of exchange*. The farmer accepted the bacon not because he wanted to use it directly, but because he intended to trade it away in the future for something else.

After we explained what a medium of exchange was, we went on to provide this formal definition: ***money** is a medium of exchange that is universally accepted in a given community.* This means there are two criteria that must be satisfied for a good to be classified as money: First, the good must be something that people are willing to accept, not because they plan on using it directly, but because they plan on trading it away again in the future. (This makes it a medium of exchange.) Second, (just about) everyone in the community must be willing to do so; if only a fraction of the public accepts a particular good in this way, then it is still a medium of exchange, but it's not *money*.

After reviewing this standard terminology, we can apply it to Bitcoin. At this point in its history, Bitcoin is no doubt a medium of exchange; there are thousands of people around the globe, who trade away valuable goods and services in exchange for receiving public acknowledgement—codified in the blockchain—that they control certain (fractions of) bitcoins. The *reason* these sellers accept bitcoins, of course, isn't because they intend on eating them or using them to produce mousetraps. Rather, people accept bitcoins in trade because they expect them to have purchasing power in the future; they want the ability to trade the bitcoins away for other goods and services, down the road.

However, even though bitcoins clearly count as media of exchange for some people, we are currently nowhere near the point at which they are *universally accepted* in any economically relevant community (unless we cheat by defining the relevant community as "those people who are happy to receive bitcoins in trade"). Thus far, then, Bitcoin doesn't count as money, though in principle Bitcoin—or some other cryptocurrency that surpasses it in popularity—could achieve this status in the future.

Relating Bitcoin to the Work of Mises

In closing, we should address a controversy regarding Bitcoin and the monetary work of the famous Austrian economist Ludwig von Mises. In his masterful 1912 book, translated as *The Theory of Money and Credit*, Mises took the new theory of subjective value—pioneered in the early 1870s by economists including Carl Menger, founder of the Austrian school—and applied it to the valuation of money itself.[8]

Previous economists had thought this approach wouldn't work, because it seemed to involve a circular argument. It made sense to use Menger's framework for explaining, say, the value of potatoes or wine; people subjectively valued the satisfactions that these goods delivered, and that was the starting point for understanding their exchange value in the marketplace.

But when it came to explaining the market value—or *purchasing power*—of money itself, Menger's subjective value theory seemed like a dead end, because the only *reason* you value money is that it allows you to buy things in the market. Thus it seemed as if the economist had to argue that people value money because people value money. This was a circular argument, and that's why most economists used Menger's subjective value theory to explain the market value of all goods and services *except* money.

Yet in his 1912 work Mises showed the way out of this logjam. The solution was to introduce the *time* element. Specifically, when people accept money in trade right now, it's because they expect the money to have purchasing power *in the future.* And their expectations of this purchasing power are based on their observations of money's ability to fetch goods and services *in the immediate past.* To put it succinctly: people value money *today* because they expect money to have a certain value *tomorrow*, and this in turn is based on their memory of its value *yesterday*.

So far, so good: Mises had eluded the apparently circular argument by introducing the time element. But now he faced a different objection: If the

8. For a more detailed treatment of this topic, see Robert P. Murphy, "The Origin of Money and Its Value," *Mises Daily*, Sept. 29, 2003, https://mises.org/library/origin-money-and-its-value.

economist using subjective value theory ends up explaining the purchasing power of money *today* based on observations of its purchasing power *yesterday*, then how do we explain its purchasing power yesterday? Why, we have to go back to the day *before* yesterday, and so on. The critics then asked, Hasn't Mises merely replaced a circular argument with an argument suffering from an infinite regress? It still seemed as if applying Menger's new value theory to money itself wasn't going to work.

Yet Mises solved this problem too. He pointed out that we *don't* need to trace back the purchasing power of money for an infinite distance into the past. Rather, we just have to trace it back to the point at which the monetary good was a regular commodity, *before* it was valued in its role as a medium of exchange.

For example, in our story involving the farmer, we have no problem using Menger's subjective value theory to explain why people in the community would value bacon directly, for its ability to satisfy hunger in a tasty way. Then, we could add the complication of how bacon's market value would be *augmented* once the farmer accepted it in trade not because he wanted to eat it, but because he wanted to trade it to the cobbler. Notice that there is no infinite regress in this procedure.

This technique is what came to be known as Mises's *regression theorem*. By explaining the market value of money with reference to a historical chain going back to the emergence of regular commodities out of a world of direct exchange, Mises was able to solve the problems that had prevented other economists from applying "modern" (i.e., post-1871) subjective value theory to money itself.

Because Mises had to cite the emergence of money from a state of direct exchange in order to satisfactorily explain its current market value, he made some pretty definitive statements about the type of past that money necessarily had to have. Here are two examples from Mises's classic work, *Human Action*:

> *[N]o good can be employed for the function of a medium of exchange which at the very beginning of its use for this purpose did not have exchange value on account of other employments.* (Mises 1998, p. 407)

and

> *A medium of exchange without a past is unthinkable. Nothing can enter into the function of a medium of exchange which was not already previously an economic good and to which people assigned exchange value already before it was demanded as such a medium.* (Mises 1998, p. 423)

In light of Mises's sweeping claims, we can quickly see why so many fans of the Austrian school have a major problem with Bitcoin: Since Bitcoin was *born* to be a currency—rather than first serving as a regular commodity—doesn't that mean it *can't* be money? Or, going the other way, if Bitcoin ever *did* become money, wouldn't that mean that Mises must have been wrong?

At the risk of being evasive, we are not here going to explore the fascinating question of whether the case of Bitcoin violates the regression theorem, or whether its unorthodox features can be made compatible with Mises's monetary framework (which he obviously conceived with tangible goods in mind). Other economists familiar with the Austrian school and Bitcoin have weighed in on this intriguing issue.[9]

Rather, here we are going to make a much more modest claim: whether Bitcoin violates or is compatible with the regression theorem is *not* an empirical question at this point. As the quotes from Mises above indicate, the regression theorem actually doesn't refer to a good becoming *money*, but rather a good becoming a medium of *exchange*.

And as we've already argued, Bitcoin has clearly *already become* a medium of exchange (though it is not money under any reasonable standard). So it must already be the case one way or the other: either the emergence of Bitcoin as a medium of exchange violated the regression theorem, or it didn't. (Reasonable cases can be made for both options.) There is no *further* hurdle that the regression theorem imposes that would hinder Bitcoin's adoption by the community at large and hence its becoming not just a medium of exchange, but money.

To sum up: whether Bitcoin becomes a *bona fide* money is still an open empirical question, but at this point—since Bitcoin is already a medium of exchange—Mises's regression theorem doesn't have any bearing on the outcome.

9. See, for example, Laura Davidson and Walter Block, "Bitcoin, the Regression Theorem, and the Emergence of a New Medium of Exchange," *Quarterly Journal of Austrian Economics* 18, no. 3 (Fall 2015): 311–38, available at https://cdn.mises.org/Bitcoin%20the%20Regression%20Theorem%20and%20the%20Emergence%20of%20a%20New%20Medium%20of%20Exchange.pdf.

Chapter 17

An Austrian Reaction to Modern Monetary Theory (MMT)[1]

The Deficit Myth: Modern Monetary Theory and the Birth of the People's Economy
by Stephanie Kelton
New York: PublicAffairs, 2020, 336 pp.

I've got good news and bad news. The good news is that Stephanie Kelton—economics professor at Stony Brook and advisor to the 2016 Bernie Sanders campaign—has written a book on Modern Monetary Theory that is very readable, and will strike many readers as persuasive and clever. The bad news is that Stephanie Kelton has written a book on MMT that is very readable and will strike many readers as persuasive and clever.

To illustrate the flavor of the book, we can review Kelton's reminiscences of serving as chief economist for the Democratic staff on the US Senate Budget Committee. When she was first selected, journalists reported that Senator Sanders had hired a "deficit owl"—a new term Kelton had coined. Unlike a deficit *hawk* or a deficit *dove*, Kelton's deficit *owl* was "a good mascot for MMT because people associate owls with wisdom and also because owls' ability to rotate their heads nearly 360 degrees would allow them to look at deficits from a different perspective" (p. 76).

Soon after joining the Budget Committee, Kelton the deficit owl played a game with the staffers. She would first ask if they would wave a magic wand that had the power to eliminate the national debt. They all said yes. *Then* Kelton

1. Reprinted from the *Quarterly Journal of Austrian Economics* 23, no. 2 (Summer 2020): 232–51.

would ask, "Suppose that wand had the power to rid the world of US Treasuries. Would you wave it?" This question—even though it was equivalent to asking to wipe out the national debt—"drew puzzled looks, furrowed brows, and pensive expressions. Eventually, everyone would decide against waving the wand" (p. 77).

Such is the spirit of Kelton's book, *The Deficit Myth*. She takes the reader down trains of thought that turn conventional wisdom about federal budget deficits on its head. Kelton makes absurd claims that the reader will think surely *can't* be true...but then she seems to justify them by appealing to accounting tautologies. And because she uses apt analogies and relevant anecdotes, Kelton is able to keep the book moving, despite its dry subject matter. She promises the reader that MMT opens up grand new possibilities for the federal government to help the unemployed, the uninsured, and even the planet itself...if we would only open our minds to a paradigm shift.

So why is this bad news? Because Kelton's concrete policy proposals would be an absolute disaster. Her message can be boiled down into two sentences (and these are my words, not an exact quotation): *Because the Federal Reserve has the legal ability to print an unlimited number of dollars, we should stop worrying about how the government will "pay for" the various spending programs the public desires. If they print too much money, we will experience high inflation, but Uncle Sam doesn't need to worry about "finding the money" the same way a household or business does.*

This is an incredibly dangerous message to be injecting into the American discourse. If it were *mere* inflationism, we could hope that enough of the public and the policy wonks would rely on their common sense to reject it. Yet because Kelton dresses up her message with equations and thought experiments, she may end up convincing an alarming number of readers that MMT really *can* turn unaffordable government boondoggles into sensible investments, just by changing the way we think about them.

Precisely because Kelton's book is so unexpectedly impressive, I would urge longstanding critics of MMT to resist the urge to dismiss it with ridicule. Although it's fun to lambaste "*Magical* Monetary Theory" on social media and to ask, "Why don't you move to Zimbabwe?", such moves will only serve to enhance the credibility of MMT in the eyes of those who are receptive to it. Consequently, in this review I will craft a lengthy critique that takes Kelton quite seriously, in order to show the readers just how *wrong* her message actually is, despite its apparent sophistication and even charm.

Monetary Sovereignty

In her introductory chapter, Kelton lures the reader with the promise of MMT, and also sheds light on her book title:

> [W]hat if the federal budget is fundamentally different than your household budget? **What if I showed you that the deficit bogeyman isn't real?** What if I could convince you that we can have an economy that puts people and planet first? That finding the money to do this is not the problem? (p. 2, bold added)

The first chapter of the book makes the fundamental distinction for MMT, between currency issuers and currency users. Our political discourse is plagued, according to Kelton, with the fallacy of treating *currency issuers* like Uncle Sam as if they were mere *currency users*, like you, me, and Walmart.

We mere currency users have to worry about financing our spending; we need to come up with the money—and this includes borrowing from others—before we can buy something. In complete contrast, a currency *issuer* has no such constraints, and needn't worry about revenue when deciding which projects to fund.

Actually, the situation is a bit more nuanced. To *truly* reap the advantages unlocked by MMT, a government must enjoy *monetary sovereignty*. For this, being a currency issuer is a necessary but insufficient condition. There are two other conditions as well, as Kelton explains:

> To take full advantage of the special powers that accrue to the currency issuer, **countries need to do more than just grant themselves the exclusive right to issue the currency. It's also important that they don't promise to convert their currency into something they could run out of (e.g. gold or some other country's currency). And they need to refrain from borrowing...in a currency that isn't their own.** When a country issues its own nonconvertible (fiat) currency and only borrows in its own currency, that country has attained monetary sovereignty. **Countries with monetary sovereignty, then, don't have to manage their budgets as a household would.** They can use their currency-issuing capacity to pursue policies aimed a maintaining a full employment economy. (pp. 18–19, bold added)

Countries with a "high degree of monetary sovereignty" include "the US, Japan, the UK, Australia, Canada, and many more" (p. 19) (And notice that even these countries weren't "sovereign" back in the days of the gold standard, because they had to be careful in issuing currency lest they run out of gold.) In contrast, countries today like Greece and France are *not* monetarily sovereign, because they no longer issue the drachma and franc, but instead adopted the euro as their currency.

The insistence on issuing debt in their own currency helps to explain away awkward cases such as Venezuela, which is suffering from hyperinflation and yet has the ability to issue its own currency. The answer (from an MMT perspective) is that Venezuela had a large proportion of its foreign-held debt denominated in US dollars, rather than the bolivar, and hence the Venezuelan government couldn't simply print its way out of the hole.[1] In contrast, so goes the MMT argument, the US government owes its debts *in US dollars*, and so never need worry about a fiscal crisis.

Yes, Kelton Knows About Inflation

At this stage of the argument, the obvious retort for any post-pubescent reader will be, "But what about inflation?!" And here's where the critic of MMT needs to be careful. Kelton repeatedly stresses throughout her book—and I've seen her do it in interviews and even on Twitter—that printing money is *not* a source of unlimited real wealth. She (and Warren Mosler too, as he explained when I interviewed him on my podcast[2]) understands and warns her readers that if the federal government prints too many dollars in a vain attempt to fund too many programs, then the economy will hit its genuine resource constraint, resulting in rapidly rising prices. As Kelton puts it:

> Can we just print our way to prosperity? Absolutely not! **MMT is not a free lunch. There are very real limits, and failing to identify—and respect—those limits could bring great harm.** MMT is about distinguishing the real limits from the self-imposed constraints that we have the power to change. (p. 37, bold added)

In other words, when someone like Alexandria Ocasio-Cortez proposes a Green New Deal, from an MMT perspective the relevant questions are *not*, "Can the Congress afford such an expensive project? Will it drown us in red ink? Are we saddling our grandchildren with a huge credit card bill?" Rather, the relevant questions are, "Is there enough slack in the economy to implement a Green New Deal without reducing other types of output? If we approve this spending, will the new demand largely absorb workers from the ranks of the unemployed? Or will it siphon workers away from existing jobs by bidding up wages?"

The Fundamental Problem with MMT

Now that we've set the table, we can succinctly state the fundamental problem with Kelton's vision: Regardless of what happens to the "price level," monetary

1. See, e.g., Ellen Brown, "The Venezuela Myth Keeping Us from Transforming Our Economy." *Truthdig* blog post, Feb. 7, 2019. https://www.truthdig.com/articles/the-venezuela-myth-keeping-us-from-revolutionizing-our-economy/. (2019).

2. See Robert P. Murphy, "Episode 18: Warren Mosler Defends the Essential Insights of Modern Monetary Theory (MMT)." *The Bob Murphy Show*, Feb. 22 (2019). https://www.bobmurphyshow.com/episodes/ep-18-warren-mosler-defends-the-essential-insights/. (2019b).

inflation transfers real resources away from the private sector and into the hands of political officials. If a government project is deemed unaffordable according to conventional accounting, then it should also be denied funding via the printing press.

What makes MMT "cool" is that it's (allegedly) based on a fresh insight showing how all of the mainstream economists and bean counters are locked in old habits of thought. Why, these fuddy-duddies keep treating Uncle Sam like a giant corporation, where he has to make ends meet and always satisfy the bottom line. In contrast, the MMTers understand that the feds can print as many dollars as they want. It's not revenue but (price) inflation that limits the government's spending capacity.

I hate to break it to Kelton and the other MMT gurus, but economists—particularly those in the free-market tradition—have been teaching this for decades (and perhaps centuries). For example, here's Murray Rothbard in his 1962 treatise, *Man, Economy, and State*:

> At this time, let us emphasize the important point that government cannot be in any way a fountain of resources; all that it spends, all that it distributes in largesse, it must first acquire in revenue, i.e., it must first extract from the "private sector." **The great bulk of the revenues of government, the very nub of its power and its essence, is taxation, to which we turn in the next section. Another method is inflation**, the creation of new money, which we shall discuss further below. A third method is borrowing from the public.... (Rothbard 1962, 913–14, bold added)

To repeat, this is standard fare in the lore of free-market economics. After explaining that government spending programs merely return resources to the private sector that had previously been taken from it, the economist will inform the public that there are three methods by which this taking occurs: taxation, borrowing, and inflation. The economist will often add that government borrowing can be considered merely *deferred* taxation, while inflation is merely *hidden* taxation.

And it's not merely that inflation is equivalent to taxation. No, because it's harder for the public to understand what's happening when government money-printing makes them poorer, there is a definite sense in which standard taxation is "honest" whereas inflation is insidious. This is why Ludwig von Mises considered inflationary finance to be "essentially antidemocratic"[3]: the printing press allows the government to get away with spending that the public would never agree to explicitly pay for, through straightforward tax hikes.

3. Ludwig von Mises, *Omnipotent Government* (New Haven, CT: Yale University Press. [1944] 2010), p. 252

Kelton and other MMT theorists argue that inflation isn't a problem right now in the US and other advanced economies, and so we don't need to be shy about cranking up the printing press. But whether or not the Consumer Price Index is rising at an "unacceptably" high rate, it is a simple fact that when the government prints an extra $1 million to finance spending, then prices (quoted in US dollars) are higher than they otherwise would have been, and people holding dollar-denominated assets are poorer than they otherwise would have been. Suppose that prices would have *fallen* in the absence of government money-printing. Then in this case, everybody holding dollar assets would have seen their real wealth go *up* because of the price deflation. If the government merely prints enough new dollars to keep prices stable, it is still the case that those original dollar-holders end up poorer relative to what otherwise would have happened.

Now to be sure, Kelton and other MMT theorists would object at this point in my argument. They claim that if there is still some "slack" in the economy, in the sense of unemployed workers and factories operating below capacity, then a burst of monetary inflation can put those idle resources to work. Even though the rising prices lead to redistribution, if *total* output is higher, then per capita output must be higher too. So on average, the people still benefit from the inflation, right?

On this score, we simply have a disagreement about how the economy works, and in this dispute I think the Austrians are right while the MMTers are wrong. According to Mises's theory of the business cycle,[4] the existence of "idle capacity" in the economy doesn't just fall out of the sky, but is instead the result of the malinvestments made during the preceding boom. So if we follow Kelton's advice and crank up the printing press in an attempt to put those unemployed resources back to work, it will simply set in motion another unsustainable boom/bust cycle. In any event, in the real world, government projects financed by inflation will not merely draw on resources that are currently idle, but will also siphon at least *some* workers and raw materials out of other, private-sector outlets, as I elaborate elsewhere.[5]

In summary, the fundamental "insight" of MMT—namely, that governments issuing fiat currencies need only fear price inflation, not insolvency—is something that other economists have acknowledged for decades. Where the MMTers *do* say something different is when they claim that printing money

4. See Robert P. Murphy, "Ludwig von Mises's 'Circulation Credit' Theory of the Trade Cycle." *Mises Wire*, May 14 (2020). https://mises.org/wire/ludwig-von-misess-circulation-credit-theory-trade-cycle. (2020b).

5. See Robert P. Murphy, "Episode 18: Warren Mosler Defends the Essential Insights of Modern Monetary Theory (MMT)," *The Bob Murphy Show*, Feb. 22 (2019). https://www.bobmurphyshow.com/episodes/ep-18-warren-mosler-defends-the-essential-insights/.

only carries an opportunity cost when the economy is at full employment. But on this point, the MMTers—like their more orthodox cousins, the Keynesians—are simply wrong.[6]

Tough Questions for MMT

A standard rhetorical move is for proponents to claim that MMT is not ideological, but merely describes how a financial system based on fiat money actually works. (For example, this was the lead argument Mike Norman used when he and I were dueling with YouTube videos.[7]) Yet since so much hinges on whether a government has "monetary sovereignty," it's amazing that the MMTers never seem to ask why some governments enjoy this status while others don't.

For her part, Kelton criticizes certain non-monetarily-sovereign governments for particular actions, such as joining a currency union (p. 145), but she doesn't ask the basic question: Once an MMT economist explains its benefits, why doesn't every government on earth follow the criteria for becoming a monetary sovereign? Indeed, why don't all of us as *individuals* issue our own paper notes—in my case, I'd print RPMs, which has a nice ring to it—and furthermore only borrow from lenders in our own personal currencies? That way, if you fell behind in your mortgage payments, you could simply print up more of your own personal notes to get current with the bank.

Posed in this way, these questions have obvious answers. The reason Greece adopted the euro, and Venezuela borrows so much in US-dollar-denominated debt, and the reason I use dollars rather than conducting transactions in RPMS, is that the rest of the financial community is very leery of the Greek drachma, the Venezuelan bolivar, or the Murphyian RPM note. Consequently, the Greek and Venezuelan governments, as well as me personally, all subordinated our technical freedom to be "monetary sovereigns" and violated one or more of Kelton's criteria.

In short, the reason most governments (including *state* governments in the US) in the world aren't "monetary sovereigns" is that members of the financial community are worried that they would abuse a printing press. The Greek government knew its economy would receive more investment, and it would be able to borrow on cheaper terms, if it abandoned the drachma and adopted the euro. The Venezuelan government knew it could obtain much larger "real" loans if they were denominated in a relatively hard currency like the USD, rather

6. "Does 'Depression Economics' Change the Rules?" *Mises Daily,* Jan. 12, (2009). https://mises.org/library/does-depression-economics-change-rules.

7. See, e.g., Robert P. Murphy, "It's Like Mike Norman Never Showed Up to This Video." YouTube. Oct. 1 (2013). https://www.youtube.com/watch?v=ETPhXVME5Gs&feature=youtu.be.

than the Venezuelan currency which could so readily be debased (as history has shown). And I personally can't interest *anybody* in financial transactions involving my authentic RPM notes, and so reluctantly I have to join the dollar-zone.

Now that we've covered this basic terrain, I have a follow-up question for the MMT camp: What would it take for a government to *lose* its monetary sovereignty? In other words, of those governments that are currently monetary sovereigns, what would have to happen in order for the governments to start borrowing on foreign currencies, or tie their own currency to a redemption pledge, or even to abandon their own currency and embrace one issued by a foreign entity?

Here again the answer is clear: A government that engaged too recklessly in monetary inflation—thus leading investors to shun that particular "sovereign" currency—would be forced to pursue one or more of these concessions in order to remain part of the global financial community. Ironically, current monetary sovereigns would run the risk of forfeiting their coveted status if they actually followed Stephanie Kelton's policy advice.

MMT Is Actually Wrong About Money

For a framework that prides itself on neutrally describing the actual operation of money and banking since the world abandoned the gold standard, it's awkward that MMT is simply *wrong* about money. In this section I will summarize three of the main errors Kelton makes about money.

Money Mistake #1
The Treasury Needs Revenue Before It Can Spend

A bedrock claim of the MMT camp is that unlike individuals and Walmart, the US Treasury doesn't need to have money before spending it. Here's an example of Kelton laying out the MMT description of government financing:

> Take military spending. In 2019, the House and Senate passed legislation that increased the military budget, approving $716 billion.... There was no debate about how to pay for the spending.... Instead, Congress committed to spending money it did not have. It can do that because of its special power over the US dollar. Once Congress authorizes the spending, agencies like the Department of Defense are given permission to enter into contracts with companies like Boeing, Lockheed Martin, and so on. **To provision itself with F-35 fighters, the US Treasury instructs its bank, the Federal Reserve, to carry out the payment on its behalf. The Fed does this by marking up the numbers in Lockheed's bank account. Congress doesn't need to "find the money" to spend it. It needs to find the votes! Once it has the votes, it can authorize the spending. The rest is just accounting. As the checks go out, the Federal Reserve clears the payments by crediting the sellers' account with the appropriate number of**

> **digital dollars**, known as bank reserves. That's why MMT sometimes describes the Fed as the scorekeeper for the dollar. The scorekeeper can't run out of points. (Kelton, p. 29, bold added)

For a more rigorous, technical treatment, the advanced readers can consult Kelton's peer-reviewed journal article from the late 1990s on the same issues.[8] Yet whether we rely on Kelton's pop book or her technical article, the problem for the MMTers is still there: Nothing in their description is unique to the US Treasury.

For example, when I write a personal check for $100 to Jim Smith who also uses my bank, we could explain what happens like this: "Murphy *instructed* Bank of America to simply add 100 digital dollars to the account of Jim Smith." Notice that this description is exactly the same thing that Kelton said about the Treasury buying military hardware in the block quotation above.

Now of course, I can't spend an *unlimited* amount of dollars, since I am a currency user, not a monetary sovereign. In particular, if I "instruct" Bank of America to mark up Jim Smith's checking account balance by more dollars than I have in my *own* checking account, the bank may ignore my instructions. Or, if my overdraft isn't too large, the bank might go ahead and honor the transaction, but then show I have a negative balance (and charge me an Insufficient Funds fee on top of it).

The only difference between my situation and the US Treasury's is that I actually have overdrawn my checking account, whereas the US Treasury hasn't had the legal option of doing so since 1981—and even before then, the Treasury only exercised the option rarely, and out of convenience not necessity.[9] Indeed, Kelton's own journal article[10] shows that the Treasury consistently maintained (as of the time of her research) a checking account balance around $5 billion, and that the daily closing amount never dipped much below this level.

Indeed, the Treasury itself sure acts as if it needs revenue before it can spend. That's why the Treasury Secretary engages in all sorts of fancy maneuvers[11]—

---

8. Stephanie Bell, "Do Taxes and Bonds Finance Government Spending?" *Journal of Economic Issues* 34, no. 3 (2000): 603–20, is the published journal article, but future references to this work will refer to Bell "Can Taxes and Bonds Finance Government Spending?" Levy Economics Institute Working Paper Collection 244, Annandale-on-Hudson, N.Y.: Levy Economics Institute (1998), an earlier draft which is not behind a paywall.

9. For the history of the Treasury's overdraft privileges see: George Selgin, "On Empty Purses and MMT Rhetoric, Alt-M, Mar. 5, 2019, https://www.alt-m.org/2019/03/05/on-empty-purses-and-mmt-rhetoric/.

10. Bell, "Can Taxes and Bonds Finance Government Spending?" p. 11, figure 4.

11. See Erika Gudmundson, "Secretary Geithner Sends Debt Limit Letter to Congress," *Treasury Notes*, 2011, Washington, D.C.: Department of the Treasury. https://www.treasury.gov/connect/blog/Pages/letter-to-congress.aspx.

such as postponing contributions to government employees' retirement plans—whenever there's a debt ceiling standoff and Uncle Sam hits a cash crunch.

The MMTers take it for granted that if the Treasury ever actually tried to spend more than it contained in its Fed checking account balance, that the Fed would honor the request. Maybe it would, and maybe it wouldn't; CNBC's John Carney (who moderated the debate at Columbia University between MMT godfather Warren Mosler and me [Modern Money Network 2013]) thinks it's an open question in terms of the actual legal requirements, though Carney believes in practice the Fed would go ahead and cash the check.

Yet, to reiterate, at least going back to 1981 the Treasury hasn't spent money that it didn't already have sitting in its checking account. The MMT camp would have us believe that there is something special occurring day in and day out when it comes to Treasury spending, but they are simply mistaken: so far at least, the Treasury has never dared the Fed by overdrawing its account.

Indeed, Kelton herself in her technical article from the late 1990s implicitly gives away the game when she defends the MMT worldview in this fashion:

> [S]ince the government's balance sheet can be considered on a *consolidated* basis, given by the sum of the Treasury's and Federal Reserve's balance sheets with offsetting assets and liabilities simply canceling one another out...the sale of bonds by the Treasury to the Fed is simply an internal accounting operation, providing the government with a self-constructed spendable balance. Although *self-imposed* constraints may prevent the Treasury from creating *all* of its deposits in this way, there is no real limit on its *ability* to do so. (Kelton 1998, 16, italics in original)

What Kelton writes here is true, but by the same token, we can consider the Federal Reserve and Goldman Sachs balance sheets on a consolidated basis. If we do that, then Goldman Sachs can now spend an infinite amount of money. Sure, its accountants might still construct profit and loss statements and warn about bad investments, but these are *self-imposed* constraints; so long as the Fed in practice will honor any check Goldman Sachs writes, then all overdrafts are automatically covered by an internal loan from the Fed to the investment bank. The only reason this *wouldn't* work is if the Fed actually stood up to Goldman and said "No." But that's exactly what the situation is with respect to the Treasury too.

Whenever I argue the merits of MMT, I debate whether or not to bring up this particular quibble. In practice, it would be very naïve to think the Fed actually enjoys "independence" from the federal government that grants the central bank its power. And I for one think that the various rounds of quantitative easing (QE) were not *merely* driven by a desire to minimize the output gap, but instead were necessary to help monetize the boatload of debt incurred during the Obama years. (Of course Trump and Powell are doing a similar dance.)

Even so, I think it is important for the public to realize that the heroes of MMT are misleading them when they claim there is something unique to Uncle Sam in the way he interacts with his banker. So far, this is technically not the case. Even when the Fed has clearly been monetizing new debt issuance—such as during the world wars—all of the players involved technically went through the motions of having the Treasury *first* float bonds in order to fill its coffers with borrowed funds, and only *then* spending the money. The innocent reader wouldn't know this if he or she relied on the standard MMT accounts of how the world works.

Money Mistake #2
Taxes Don't Prop Up Currencies

Another central mistake in the MMT approach is its theory of the origin and value of money.[12] To set the stage, here is Kelton explaining how Warren Mosler stumbled upon the worldview that would eventually be dubbed Modern Monetary Theory:

> Mosler is considered the father of MMT because he brought these ideas to a handful of us in the 1990s. He says...it just struck him after his years of experience working in financial markets. He was used to thinking in terms of debits and credits because he had been trading financial instruments and watching funds transfer between bank accounts. One day, he started to think about where all those dollars must have originally come from. It occurred to him that before the government could subtract (debit) any dollars away from us, it must first add (credit) them. He reasoned that spending must have come first, otherwise where would anyone have gotten the dollars they needed to pay the tax? (Kelton, p. 24)

This MMT understanding ties in with its view of the origin and money, and how *taxes* give money its value. Kelton explains by continuing to summarize what she learned from Mosler:

> [A] currency-issuing government wants something real, not something monetary. It's not our tax money the government wants. It's our time. To get us to produce things for the state, the government invents taxes...This isn't the explanation you'll find in most economics textbooks, where a superficial story about money being invented to overcome the inefficiencies associated with bartering...is preferred. In that story, money is just a convenient device that sprang up organically as a way to make trade more efficient. Although students

12. If you want to see the Austrian view, see Robert P. Murphy, "The Origin of Money and Its Value," *Mises Daily*, Sept. 29 (2003), https://mises.org/library/origin-money-and-its-value, on the contributions of Menger and Mises.

> are taught that barter was once omnipresent, a sort of natural state of being, scholars of the ancient world have found little evidence that societies were ever organized around barter exchange.
>
> MMT rejects the ahistorical barter narrative, drawing instead on an extensive body of scholarship known as chartalism, which shows that taxes were the vehicle that allowed ancient rulers and early nation-states to introduce their own currencies, which only later circulated as a medium of exchange among private individuals. From inception, the tax liability creates people looking for paid work...in the government's currency. The government...then spends its currency into existence, giving people access to the tokens they need to settle their obligations to the state. **Obviously, no one can pay the tax until the government first supplies its tokens. As a simple point of logic, Mosler explained that most of us had the sequencing wrong. Taxpayers weren't funding the government; the government was funding the taxpayers.** (Kelton, pp. 26–27, **bold added**)

I have included these lengthy quotations to be sure the reader understands the superficial appeal of MMT. Isn't that intriguing—Mosler argues that the *government* funds the *taxpayers*! And when you think through his simple point about debits and credits, it seems that he isn't just probably correct, but that he *must* be correct.

Again, it's a tidy little demonstration; the only problem is that it's demonstrably false. It is simply not true that dollars were invented when some autocratic ruler out of the blue imposed taxes on a subject population, payable only in this new unit called "dollar." The MMT explanation of where money comes from doesn't apply to the dollar, the euro, the yen, the pound...Come to think of it, I don't believe the MMT explanation applies even to a single currency issued by a monetary sovereign. All of the countries that currently enjoy monetary sovereignty have built their economic strength and goodwill with investors by relying on a history of *hard money*.

In a review of Kelton's book, I'm not going to delve into the problems with the alleged anthropological evidence that purportedly shows ancient civilizations used money that was invented by political fiat, rather than money that emerged spontaneously from trade in commodities. For *that* topic, I refer the interested reader to my review of David Graeber's book.[13]

Yet let me mention before leaving this subsection that the MMT story *at best* only explains why a currency has a nonzero value; it does not explain the actual amount of its purchasing power. For example, if the IRS declares that

---

13. Robert P. Murphy, "Origin of the Specie," *American Conservative*, April 11, (2012). https://www.theamericanconservative.com/articles/origin-of-the-specie/.

every US citizen must pay $1,000 in a poll tax each year, then it's true, US citizens will need to obtain the requisite number of dollars. But they could do so whether the average wage rate is $10 per hour or $10,000 per hour, and whether a loaf of bread costs $1 or $1,000.

Furthermore, other things equal, if the government lowers tax rates, then it *strengthens* the currency. That's surely part of the reason that the US dollar rose some 50 percent against other currencies after the tax rate reductions in the early Reagan years.[14] So the MMT claim that taxes are necessary, *not* to raise revenue (we have a printing press for *that*), but to prop up the value of the currency, is at best seriously misleading.

Money Mistake #3
Debt Isn't Money

Amazingly, even though their system claims to explain how money works, the MMTers apparently don't know the simple difference between *money* and *debt*. Here's Kelton trying to defuse hysteria over the national debt:

> The truth is, we're fine. The debt clock on West 43rd Street simply displays a historical record of how many dollars the federal government has added to people's pockets without subtracting (taxing) them away. Those dollars are being saved in the form of US Treasuries. If you're lucky enough to own some, congratulations! They're part of your wealth. While others may refer to it as a *debt* clock, it's really a US dollar *savings clock*. (Kelton, pp. 78–79.)

To drive home the equivalence of US Treasuries and dollars, shortly afterward Kelton says, "Heck, I don't even think we should be referring to the sale of US Treasuries as borrowing or labeling the securities themselves as the national debt. It just confuses the issue and causes unnecessary grief" (p. 81).

For an even starker illustration of the MMT confusion between debt and money, consider Kelton's approving quotations of a thought experiment from Eric Lonergan, who asked, "What if Japan monetized 100% of outstanding JGBs [Japanese government bonds]?" That is, what if the Bank of Japan issued new money in order to buy up every last Japanese government bond on earth? Lonergan argues "nothing would change" because the private sector's *wealth* would be the same; the BOJ would have engaged in a mere asset swap. In fact, because their interest income would now be lower while their wealth would be the same, people in the private sector would spend *less* after the total debt monetization, according to Lonergan.

In response to these observations, I make two simple points: First, one can't

---

14. See FRED, "Trade-Weighted U.S. Dollar Index: Major Currencies, Goods" (DTWEXM): https://fred.stlouisfed.org/series/DTWEXM.

spend Treasury securities or Japanese government bonds in the grocery store. That's why money and debt are different things.

Second, if Kelton were right and the US national debt were a tally of how many dollars on net the government has "spent into existence," then when Andrew Jackson *paid off* the national debt, the American people would have had no money—the last dollar would have been destroyed. And yet even Kelton doesn't claim that dollars were temporarily banished from planet Earth. She merely claims that Jackson's policy caused a depression.[15]

Do Government Deficits Equal Private Savings?

In Chapter 4, Kelton lays out the MMT case that government deficits, far from "crowding out" private sector saving, actually are the sole *source* of net private assets. Using simple accounting tautologies, Kelton seems to demonstrate that the only way the nongovernment sector can run a fiscal surplus, is if the government sector runs a fiscal deficit.

Going the other way, when the government is "responsible" by running a budget surplus and starts paying down its debt, by sheer accounting we see that this must be reducing net financial assets held by the private sector. (This is why it should come as no surprise, Kelton argues, that every major government surplus led to a bad recession. [p. 96])

In the present review, I won't carefully review and critique this particular argument, as I've done so earlier.[16] Suffice it to say, one could replace "government" in the MMT argument with any other entity and achieve the same outcome. For example, if Google borrows $10 million by issuing corporate bonds and then it spends the money, then the net financial assets held by The-World-Except-Google go up by precisely $10 million. (Or rather, the way one would define terms in order to make these claims true, is the same way Kelton gets the MMT claims about Uncle Sam to go through.) So did I just prove something really important about Google's finances?

Obviously something is screwy here. Using standard definitions, people in the private sector can save, and even accumulate net financial wealth, without considering the government sector at all. (This is all spelled out in my 2020 article.[17]) For example, Robinson Crusoe on his deserted island can "save" out of his coconut income in order to finance his investment of future labor hours

15. For the Austrian take on this historical episode, see Dan Sanchez, "The 19th-Century Bernanke," *Mises Daily*, Sept. 1 (2009), https://mises.org/library/19th-century-bernanke-0.

16. Robert P. Murphy, "The Upside-Down World of MMT," *Mises Daily*, Jan. 23 (2019). https://mises.org/library/upside-down-world-mmt.

17. Robert P. Murphy, "Keynesian Fallacies Are Not Just Wrong, but Dangerous," *Mises Wire*, May 1 (2020). https://mises.org/wire/keynesian-fallacies-are-not-just-wrong-dangerous.

into a boat and net. Even if we insist on a modern financial context, individuals can issue shares of equity in new corporations, thus acquiring assets that don't correspond to a "debit" of anyone else.

It is a contrived and seriously misleading use of terminology when MMT proponents argue that government deficits are a source of financial wealth for the private sector. Forget the accounting and look at the big picture: Even if the central bank creates a new $1 million and hands it to Jim Smith, it hasn't made the community $1 million richer except in the sense that we could all be millionaires with this practice. There aren't any more houses or cars or acres of arable farmland available. Printing new money doesn't make the community richer—at best it's a wash with redistribution—and in fact in practice it makes the community poorer by distorting the ability of prices to guide economic decisions.

The MMT Job Guarantee

The last item I wish to discuss is the MMT job guarantee. Strictly speaking, this proposal is distinct from the general MMT framework, but in practice I believe every major MMT theorist endorses some version of it.

Under Kelton's proposal, the federal government would have a standing offer to employ any worker at $15 per hour (p. 68). This would set a floor against all other jobs; Kelton likens it to the Federal Reserve setting the federal funds rate, which then becomes the base rate for every other interest rate in the economy.

Kelton argues that her proposal would eliminate the unnecessary slack in our economic system, where millions of workers languish in involuntary unemployment. Furthermore, she claims her job guarantee would raise the long-term productivity of the workforce and even help people find better *private sector* job placement. This is because currently, "Employers just don't want to take a chance on hiring someone who has no recent employment record" (p. 68).

There are several problems with this proposal. First of all, why does Kelton assume it would only draw workers out of the ranks of the unemployed? For example, suppose Kelton set the pay at $100 per hour. Surely even she could see the problem here, right? Workers would be siphoned out of productive, private sector employment and into the government realm, providing dubious service at best at the direction of political officials.

Second, why would employers be keen on hiring someone who has spent, say, the last three years working in the guaranteed job sector? This would be, by design, the cushiest jobs in America. Kelton admits this when she says the base wage rate would be the *floor* for all other jobs.

Looking at it another way, it's not really a job *guarantee* if it's difficult to maintain the position. In other words, if the people running the federal jobs program are allowed to fire employees who show up drunk or who are simply awful workers, then it's no longer a guarantee.

Conclusion

Stephanie Kelton's new book *The Deficit Myth* does a very good job explaining MMT to new readers. I must admit that I was pleasantly surprised at how many different topics Kelton could discuss from a new view, in a manner that was simultaneously absurd and yet apparently compelling.

The problem is that Kelton's fun book is utterly wrong. The boring suits with their standard accounting are correct: It actually costs something when the government spends money. The fact that since 1971 we have had an unfettered printing press doesn't give us more options. It merely gives the Fed greater license to cause boom/bust cycles and redistribute wealth to politically connected insiders.

Index

(Index by Sven Thommesen)

The Mises Institute, founded in 1982, is a teaching and research center for the study of Austrian economics, libertarian and classical liberal political theory, and peaceful international relations. In support of the school of thought represented by Ludwig von Mises, Murray N. Rothbard, Henry Hazlitt, and F.A. Hayek, we publish books and journals, sponsor student and professional conferences, and provide online education. Mises.org is a vast resource of free material for anyone in the world interested in these ideas. For we seek a radical shift in the intellectual climate, away from statism and toward a private property order.

For more information, see mises.org, write us at contact@mises.org, or phone us at 1.800.OF.MISES.

To become a Member, visit mises.org/membership

Mises Institute
518 West Magnolia Avenue
Auburn, Alabama 36832
mises.org

Made in the USA
Monee, IL
22 April 2023

72f9870f-4c5f-4c47-8dc3-6538e3c2d9e3R03